FROM ENEMY TO ALLY

SINO-AMERICAN RELATIONS, 1952-1979

WASHINGTON RECOGNIZES "RED CHINA"

JOSEPH F. HARRINGTON

Available for purchase on Amazon.com
http://createspace.com/ 5259685

ISBN-10: 1507579136
ISBN-13: 9781507579138
LCCN: 2015900816
CreateSpace Independent Publishing Platform, North Charleston, SC 29406

TABLE OF CONTENTS

Thanks to my wife Brenda, whose love and encouragement gave me the time to write, to our daughter Megan Harrington Booth, our son Christopher Joseph Harrington, and my very good friend Matthew Carlo Romano, for their support. I accept full responsibility for errors and omissions.

PREFACE

At the close of World War II, Sino-American relations were between Washington and the Nationalist Government of Chiang Kai-shek in Beijing. In 1949, relations between the two continued, except the site was Taipei on the island of Taiwan. This situation would prove problematic for the White House for 30 years. While Truman initially wanted to recognize the new Beijing government, opposition forces gathered and formed a "China Lobby" led by a number of editors, senior military, businessmen and conservative Republican congressmen who attacked the White House as being "soft" on Communism. The administration was accused of "selling out" China, in spite of it publishing a White Paper defending its position. But the lengthy document, did not tell the whole story, and only produced more criticism of the White House. Truman failed to act in 1949, much due to anti-Communist pressure and then would be unable to act with the outbreak of the Korean conflict with Beijing's support of Pyongyang. But the conflict would prove to have value. It provided the first opportunity for America to reach out to Beijing for the release of several pilots forced down over China during combat. Initially, the talks were indirect through British go-betweens, but the 1954 Geneva Conference called to discuss the Korean cease fire and provide a graceful way for the French to leave Indochina, provided an opportunity for direct talks. Sino-American negotiations focused on the repatriation of detained American nationals, as well as the return of Chinese students held in the United States. While little would be resolved, the talks implied some sort of American recognition of Beijing, and this gave new ammunition to the China Lobby.

Mao Xedong was riding a wave of success. He had overthrown the Nationalist Government and fought the United States to a draw in Korea. Aiming to capitalize on the moment, he attacked islands off the coast of Taiwan and made threats against the island itself. The China Lobby, along with support from President Eisenhower, enabled Congress to approve a Mutual Defense Treaty with Taiwan, followed by the president's Formosa Doctrine promising American protection for Taiwan and the nearby Pescadore Islands.

The talks in Geneva would continue and struggle forward through Warsaw, to New York, to Beijing, to Shanghai, and to Washington. Due to the Vietnam War, the public turned away from the Democratic Party and voted for Richard Nixon as president. Little did they know that Nixon's vision of America's foreign policy called for multiple centers of power including Beijing. With Kissinger doing the grunt work, and Nixon providing the direction, the president and China's Premier Zhou Enlai worked out the details of the Shanghai Communique on February 28, 1972 which promised the restoration of diplomatic relations between Beijing and Washington. This of course left Taiwan out in the cold, but not without supporters. The China Lobby re-emerged and used the media and conservative, anti-Communist congressmen to delay any implementation of Beijing's recognition.

This is the story of the gradual change in Sino-American relations from enemies to friends, from antagonists to partners, from non-recognition to diplomatic relations. The change was much due to a common goal of preventing the "Polar Bear" in the north from achieving global hegemony. Threats of Soviet expansion proved to be the link joining Washington and Beijing. Many historians have ignored the twenty years preceding the Shanghai Communiqué, since there appeared to be little progress until Richard Nixon's election. And historians have generally minimized the years immediately following Nixon's defeat, since Sino-American relations lost their glamour. The common excuses for the delay were the years of confusion following Nixon's resignation, the deaths of Mao Xedong and Zhou Enlai, the fall and rise of Deng Xiaoping, Kissinger's departure, the conflict between Secretary of State Cyrus Vance and National Security Advisor Zbigniew Brzezinski, and Jimmy Carter's

2

instructions "not to 'kiss-ass'" the Chinese.[1] This conclusion ignores the ongoing talks between Beijing and Washington which expanded trade, developed mutual trust, identified common interests, shared goals albeit approached by different paths, and created an atmosphere making President Carter's decision to award Beijing diplomatic recognition a very quick process. He needed only eight months, in contrast to the six years between the Shanghai Communique and recognition on January 1, 1979.

This work is based heavily upon documents in the United States Foreign Relations Series, especially the recently released two China volumes covering the period from 1973 until 1980. These, coupled with an abundance of memoirs of the principle American players, provide the bricks to fill in the seemingly "missing" holes from the earliest talks in 1952 until recognition in 1979. Years of Washington's entreaties came to fruition, and China finally crossed a threshold opening herself to products and ideas from America and the world.

CHAPTER I

FIRST STEPS: LONDON AND GENEVA, 1952-1956

The road to normalizing relations began during the Korean War. Soon after World War II, the Truman Administration adopted George Kennan's "containment" policy designed to stop the spread of Communism. The outbreak of hostilities in Korea, with North Korean forces crossing into South Korea threatening American occupation troops brought Washington into the conflict. In 1952, Americans elected Dwight D. Eisenhower as president and he soon appointed John Foster Dulles as his Secretary of State. Dulles was firmly committed to containment, and wanted to have nothing to do with Beijing. However, the plight of several American nationals held prisoners by Beijing would provide an opportunity for talks to begin concerning their release.

Communication with Beijing began through Lionel Lamb, the British Charge d'affaires in Beijing. Due to London's support of America during the Korean War, the PRC had detained several British, Canadian, and Australian nationals and Lamb had been negotiating for their release. He agreed to include America nationals as well and on April 21, 1952 he sent a list of 20 American nationals reportedly under house arrest. The note requested the nature of the charges against the detainees, any sentences imposed, their whereabouts and health and welfare.[1] London also reached out to India, and asked the Indian Ambassador to Beijing for help, but without success. The conclusion was that little to nothing would be done as long as the Korean War continued.[2]

Since Lamb had failed in his initial efforts, Washington sent notes directly to her Ambassador in India, Chester Bowles, requesting the new Indian Ambassador to Beijing, Nedyan Raghavan, to approach the Chinese government on humanitarian grounds for the release of American nationals, citing the approaching harsh winter conditions and the deaths of three Americans who had already died during their imprisonment.[3] However, Raghavan was reluctant to begin his new appointment with this request, and refused to become involved. Lamb pursued the issue directly to the PRC in December, but without success.[4] However, during the armistice talks leading to a Korean cease-fire, Beijing released over 400 Americans, mostly soldiers captured during the war, but that did not include civilians. Rather than raise the civilian issue, which might compromise the further release of prisoners-of-war, Washington chose to remain silent until after the cease-fire.[5]

In September, 1953 the State Department resumed its efforts especially to secure the release of Christian missionaries, including six of eight American priests arrested and imprisoned in Shanghai in June. Washington appealed for help to the Soviet representative to the United Nations (UN), Andrew Vyshinsky. Relations between the two countries had significantly improved following the death of Stalin the previous March. Vyshinsky told the department that it ought to use their present representative at the cease fire talks in Panmunjom to speak directly to the PRC rather than going through intermediaries.[6] While the State Department did not follow through on the suggestion, it did reach out to Humphrey Trevelyan, Lamb's replacement as the British Charge d'affaires in Beijing. On December 3, he reported that in spite of his efforts, "there is little chance of missionaries being released in the future." However, much to his surprise, and for no apparent reason, Beijing released several priests from prison in mid-January, 1954.[7]

Meanwhile, French pride prevented her from accepting the fact that she was losing Indochina. By the time of the Korean armistice in 1953, the United States was already committed to defending the French against the aggressive Viet Minh Communist forces. In early 1954, the French army was encamped at Dien Bien Phu, a heavily fortified base located deep in a valley. By mid-March, it was clear that the French were struggling under a Viet Minh siege and that only outside intervention could save them. Though President Eisenhower was determined to prevent a Communist victory in Vietnam, the U.S. Congress and officials in the administration were equally determined not to intervene unless they were part of a larger force. Britain and other members of NATO declined to participate in what they saw as a lost cause. Dien Bien Phu fell in May, and the French retreated from Vietnam. In the wake of the French defeat, the great powers agreed to meet in Geneva to bring peace to Vietnam.

The conference met from April 26, 1954 through July 20 and produced two agreements, one a cease fire and a division of the country at the 17th parallel, while the other, called for general elections in 1956 to unite the country. Realizing that Ho Chi Minh, the heroic leader of the Vietminh, would bring the Communists to power, Washington refused to sign the second agreement. Instead she would support a South Vietnamese government which would begin America's embarrassing involvement in Southeast Asia until 1973. However, during the conference American and PRC delegates needed to negotiate and this provided an opportunity for Washington and Beijing to begin direct communication, for the first time.

The end of the Korean conflict and the war in Vietnam enabled the PRC to focus on her economic problems and in 1954 she began her first Five Year Plan, which required having a peaceful and stable international environment. She also needed time to prepare for her invasion of Taiwan, a task postponed by the Korean War. Beijing realized that there was little value in maintaining her isolation from the West, including the US. Mao Xedong and Zhou Enlai had both reached that conclusion, and in early May, Zhou indicated that he would be willing to deal directly with American representatives through their Geneva delegation.[8] For her part, America, while not wanting to recognize Red China, knew that world order was dependent on her dealing with Beijing and its 600 million people. The lesson of Korea showed that the failure of communication was a direct

6

cause of Beijing's entrance into the war. To not repeat the past, Washington agreed to enter direct communications with a representative of the PRC.

On May 4, Humphrey Trevelyan, the British Charge d'affaires in Beijing, agreed to raise the issue of UN Command personnel detained in China. The International Red Cross (IRC) took a similar approach. Washington hoped to piggy back on Trevelyan and the IRC efforts, but without much success. On May 4, Huang Hua, a member of the PRC Geneva delegation, explained that the Americans being held in China were "being held hostage for the fifty Chinese students that the US would not allow to return to China." As for the IRC, it refused to become involved with America's problem, while Trevelyan said that while he was willing to help, his main focus was on the return of British nationals.[9]

On May 17, Trevelyan reported that he had made some progress concerning the return of some British nationals. More importantly to Washington, Trevelyan reported that Huang acknowledged that the PRC had retained America airmen who had violated PRC airspace. In light of this progress, he changed his mind and felt that he could serve as an intermediary for America's interests in Beijing.[10] In his discussions with Huan Hsiang of the PRC Geneva delegation on May 27, he reported that Beijing was willing to deal directly with an American representative or through an introduction by Trevelyan. The State Department saw the overture as a means to facilitate the release of detained Americans, but suspected that China's real goal was to begin a process of having Washington grant Beijing diplomatic recognition.

Trevelyan wanted to bring the two sides together, without compromising his principle task of releasing British citizens detained in China. He was willing to set up a meeting, but that would end his involvement. Dulles was not really on board. However, he had no other ideas as to how to bring home America servicemen, missionaries and nationals still in the PRC. On May 30, Beijing wanted to know the rank of the American representative, since "equal footing" was an obsession with the Chinese. While Walter Robertson had been involved early on with Trevelyan, Dulles decided that the Assistant Secretary of State for Far Eastern Affairs, was too high ranking an official. Instead Dulles appointed Alexis Johnson, the US Coordinator for the Geneva Conference, to represent Washington.[11] On June 3, Zhou Enlai cabled Mao that arrangements were underway for direct contact, and that the PRC approach would be to inform the Americans that nationals who were guilty of crimes against the PRC would be treated differently than other Americans in China.[12]

On June 5, Johnson along with Edwin Martin, Deputy Director of Chinese Affairs, and Trevelyan met with Wang Bingnan, the head of the Chinese delegation at Geneva along with Huan Hsiang and interpreters. Johnson made it clear that the main purpose of the meeting was the release of Americans detained in China. During the next several meetings, each side exchanged lists of nationals supposedly being illegally held by each country. Johnson presented a list of 18 Air Force and 11 Navy and Coast Guard personnel while Wang countered with a list of 120 Chinese. Wang did agree to permit relatives of imprisoned Americans to send them packages through the National Red Cross Society of China.

The checking of lists would postpone rapid advancement in the negotiations. Further, the Chinese were in no hurry to complete the talks in the hope that the delay would help postpone ongoing talks in Washington concerning a defense treaty with Taiwan.[13] As the Geneva conference wound down, the two sides looked for a new site to continue negotiations. The Chinese suggested a third country having diplomatic relations with Washington and Beijing, but the White House was not interested.[14] Instead, it suggested that Trevelyan be the go-between for future talks. Since there was no agreement on a new site for negotiations both sides agreed to stay in Geneva at the Beau-Rivage Hotel.

On July 22, the Chinese delegation announced that they had freed six American nationals, who were not involved in any criminal activity. While this appeared to be gracious move, from the Chinese view it required an American response since Beijing insisted upon "equality and reciprocity." Washington shared the same view, and similar to Beijing, would only release Chinese nationals, usually students, at the same slow pace set by China. On July 29, at the first consular meeting, the American representatives showed they understood the *quid pro quo* and gave the Chinese Consul Hsiah Fei a list of seven Chinese students that Washington had approved for departure. The meeting was brief, over in 40 minutes, but it was a start at a new level of negotiations.[15]

However, the talks would be postponed in light of the ROC's decision to reinforce two island groups they had seized following their flight from China in 1948-1949. Chiang Kai-shek sent 60,000 troops to the Quemoy islands located just two miles off the coast of mainland China, blocking the port of Amoy. He also sent 15,000 troops to the Matsu islands which were ten miles away from the mainland, blocking the port of Foochow. While the islands could serve as a base for a later attack on Beijing, the principal reason for the reinforcements was the fear that if the islands fell to the Chinese Communists, the nearby Pescadore islands and Taiwan would be next.

The assessment was correct for on the mainland Mao had begun to make plans to attack Taiwan. He had stabilized the economy after nearly two decades of warfare, and began his First Five Year Plan designed to bring about a transition to socialism. He no longer feared the West. He had fought the UN and the US to a draw in Korea, and had enabled the North Vietnamese to defeat the French. Further, he believed that Washington had lost interest in Asia. In September, Beijing began shelling the islands of Quemoy and Matsu.

While the bombing did not end the consular talks, meetings were less frequent. Two months went by before negotiations resumed and only for a day, September 29. Consul Hsiah announced the release of three Americans who had been captured in March, 1953 while sailing on a yacht. Two weeks later, on October 18, the American consular negotiator, John Shillock, noted the departure of six Chinese students from the US, and that arrangements had been approved for five others to leave.[16]

In November, Beijing began to shell the Tachen Islands, a non-strategic group of islands north of Taiwan. In Washington the Joint Chiefs of Staff urged the president to use nuclear weapons against the mainland. Eisenhower refused. He would not attack mainland China because that would bring the Soviet Union into the conflict, and the little islands off Taiwan were not worth the risk of a nuclear war. He also would not commit American ground troops to defend these islands. However, when word was received in Washington that thirteen American airmen, who had been shot down during the Korean war, were imprisoned for espionage under terms that ranged from four years to life, Congress sprang into action.[17] Senator Knowland of California called for a blockade of the Chinese coast. Eisenhower refused but needed to do something to show support for Chiang Kai-shek. The solution was the 1954 treaty between the US and the ROC, including the Pescadore islands. If either country were attacked, the other would come to its aid. In turn, Chiang agreed not to attack mainland China without Washington's approval.[18]

As for the convicted airmen, Secretary of State Dulles looked to Great Britain, Canada and New Zealand for help in the UN General Assembly to free the servicemen. Washington's position was that the UN General Assembly should force the release of the American airmen since the US had entered Korea to implement UN Resolution 84.[19] Washington needed to keep the issue out of the Security Council since Moscow would undoubtedly cast a veto in support of her Communist neighbor. On December 10, the General Assembly adopted Resolution 906 which requested the Secretary General, Dag

Hammarskjold, to seek the release of the eleven imprisoned Americans.[20]

The defense treaty angered Mao, and on December 14, Zhou Enlai gave the order that when opportune the military should attack the island of Yijiangshan, eight miles from the Tachens. On January 10, Communist planes raided the Tachen Islands and captured Yijiangshan by week's end, killing about 1,000 Nationalist troops. Eisenhower needed to draw a line in the sand, but the Tachens would not be the line. They had no strategic value, so he ordered Taipei to begin their evacuation on February 10. The Chinese did not interfere with the withdrawal, and four days later captured the islands. While the Tachens were not worth saving, their loss did provide an impetus for Eisenhower to make a statement. On January 19, he met with Dulles to discuss a congressional resolution. The result was the famous Formosa Doctrine which authorized the president to use military force to protect Formosa (aka Taiwan) and the Pescadores against armed attack. While deliberately not including Matsu and the Quemoy islands group, the doctrine did include language which gave the president a "blank check" which permitted him to protect them if needed. Both houses of Congress passed the resolution with near unanimous consent. Two weeks later, Eisenhower signed the Mutual Defense Treaty. While the treaty and the doctrine did not immediately stop the exchange of gunfire, Eisenhower's conversation with Vyachleslav Molotov, a member of the Soviet Politburo, did. Moscow pressured Beijing to reduce tension, and two months later the crisis passed.[21]

Meanwhile, Hammarskjold had met with Zhou Enlai in early January and told him that "he should release the prisoners." Zhou appeared to consider the request, but he could not do so in a manner in which he "would lose face in Asia."[22] Continued talks did not change the situation and gradually Dulles began to question using the UN Secretary-General as a conduit. In turn, Hammarskjold was disturbed by statements coming from the State Department that the whole

11

airmen issue was simply a vehicle for propaganda, and that he was part of the plan. Further, he believed that he had not been kept informed of Dulles' plans for the airmen's release, and he believed that by being blind-sided he was unable to be as successful as anticipated.[23]

During the next several months, Hammarskjold tried to trade the release of the fifteen servicemen with the release of seven Chinese fishermen rescued from a reef in May, 1954. Added to the list were seventy-four Chinese students who had been originally cleared for their return to China, but in light of the imprisonment of the American airmen, had their return temporarily postponed. While not mentioned in so many words, the Chinese appeared to make a connection between American civilians in China, and Chinese students in the US, but not between Chinese students and American airmen.[24]

April would be a sea change in Sino-American relations. In December 1954, representatives from Burma, India, Indonesia, Pakistan and Sri Lanka met and organized an Afro-Asian conference which opened on April 18 in Bandung, Indonesia. The twenty-nine participating countries gathered to discuss peace and the role of the Third World in the Cold War, economic development, and decolonization. The delegates had built their agenda on the Five Principles of Peaceful Coexistence agreed to by China and India in April 1954. Among the principles were the mutual respect for each other's territorial integrity and sovereignty, mutual non-aggression, and peaceful co-existence. The day before the conference ended Zhou Enlai, having narrowly escaping an assassination attempt, presented a moderate and conciliatory attitude to reassure that China had no aggressive intentions. He declared "the Chinese people and the American people had always been on friendly terms. The Chinese people do not want to fight a war against the US. The Chinese government is willing to sit down and enter into negotiations with the government of the US to discuss how to ease the tensions in the Far East, especially the tension in the Taiwan region."[25] Later, Zhou gave a report to the Communist hierarchy in Beijing. In it, he emphasized that China did not want to have a war with America. The Chinese people were friendly toward America, and wanted the two countries to meet, perhaps as part of an international conference. But Nationalist China could not be part of the meeting because the people living in Taiwan were Chinese, and any liberation of Taiwan was a domestic issue of the PRC not a topic for an international forum.[26]

While America's European allies, as well as the United Kingdom, viewed Zhou's remarks as sincere and ground breaking, Dulles remained extremely cautious. After initially downgrading the speech, the State Department welcomed it as Washington would any speech supporting world peace. But added, that as evidence of Beijing's sincerity, she could agree to an immediate cease-fire in the Taiwan area, and she could release the imprisoned American airmen. On the 27th, Washington took a step forward and in a press conference the president announced that he would talk with "Red China about a Formosa cease-fire and anything else not affecting Nationalist China's own affairs."[27] Having made this offer, the White House decided that the ball was in Beijing's court.

In the event the Chinese Communists accepted the president's offer, the State Department began to search for appropriate meeting places. While Geneva could continue, the department believed that either Wang Bingnan, the Chinese Ambassador at Warsaw, or Huan Hsiang, the Chinese Charge d'affaires in London could be the conduits. Bingnan had been Alexis Johnson's counterpart earlier at Geneva concerning the return of American prisoners.

Meanwhile events moved quickly. Dag Hammarskjold had returned to the prisoner negotiations and on May 24 reported that Zhou would announce his decision concerning the American airmen by month's end.[28] Six days later Beijing announced that four airmen, who had been imprisoned for violating Beijing's airspace, and a Catholic missionary, Bishop Donaghy, detained since 1951, were deported and flown to San Francisco. While Washington would thank

13

Beijing, it also sent an updated list of the remaining eleven airmen still held in detention. But to not appear rude, the State Department noted that all Chinese students except for two, who did not want to leave the US, were free to depart.[29] Progress on the remaining airmen would be slow as Washington prepared for the 10th anniversary of the UN in San Francisco in June, a Four Power Geneva Conference in July, and negotiations with Beijing to reduce tensions over Taiwan and her adjacent islands.

By July 1, the negotiations concerning Chinese students and American prisoners appeared to have reached an impasse. Beijing and Washington were far more concerned about the propaganda value of the issue, rather than an immediate exchange of eligible identified people. Simply put, each side used its exchangeable bodies for political gain. And there had been political gain, by Beijing. Zhou's speech had resonated well among NATO countries, who saw that a breakthrough had been made. Yet, America seemed slow to respond irritating her allies, especially London. One of the problems for Washington was that there was no direct communication with the leadership in Beijing, since America did not recognize the PRC. Consequently, the use of intermediaries, including Britain, India, Burma, Russia, and the UN often led to misunderstandings. In a final effort to bring Americans in Red China home, Dulles suggested on July 11 raising the talks to an ambassadorial level, which would place the two countries in direct contact with their governments, without third party involvement. However, the suggestion did not indicate diplomatic recognition of the Beijing government. The secretary of state suggested that the agenda begin with the return of civilians to their respective countries, following which there could be additional talks on "certain other practical matters now at issue between the two of us." Dulles's note also suggested that "there should be no publicity until mutual agreement…had been reached."[30]

Zhou quickly responded, accepting the terms and offering July 21 as the first meeting in Geneva. Dulles was not prepared for a

14

quick response, and suggested August 1, which Zhou accepted. Alexis Johnson, the current American ambassador to Czechoslovakia, would represent the US and his old Geneva counterpart, Wang Bingnan, would be Beijing's ambassador. Johnson's instructions suggested that once the issue of student and servicemen exchanges were successful, he should move forward on the return of POWs as prescribed by the terms of the Korean War Armistice. He should also anticipate that Bingnan might bring up the issue of the use of force towards Taiwan, since Beijing viewed the island as part of China and therefore a domestic issue. Dulles suggested he counter with the situation in Germany, Korea and Vietnam, all divided countries, whose reunifications were viewed as domestic issues, and had been easily resolved.[31]

On July 31, as promised earlier, Beijing released the eleven airmen as a sign of good will.[32] On the following day negotiations began and in spite of initial optimism, negotiations progressed neither quickly nor smoothly. The first problem, which had been an ongoing issue, was identifying each country's detained nationals. And then there was Dulles, who initially refused to reach any agreements until Wang agreed to release all Americans detained in China. Wang refused to be pressured into such an agreement. Instead, he raised the issue of Americans in China who were involved in civil and criminal cases and until these were resolved, they could not be repatriated.[33]Taking the initiative, Johnson offered an alternative to the "all or nothing" Dulles approach. He suggested a two part return of American nationals and servicemen, some now and some within a two to three month time period. Wang was amenable and both agreed that the remaining Americans would be returned "expeditiously" within a determined time period.[34]

While precise wording would take an additional two weeks, on September 10, 1955 both sides acknowledged the right of Americans in China and Chinese in the US to return freely and "expeditiously" to their countries of origin. It further permitted

15

anyone who believed his or her return was being prevented to seek assistance from a designated third party.[35] Later Zhou Enlai would say that had the negotiations only resulted in the release of Qian Xuesen, which it had, they would have been successful. Xuesen would be known as the Father of China's Space Program, and under his leadership and direction, Beijing would launch her first missiles, and in 1970 her first satellite.[36]

While the agreement appeared to resolve the return of civilians and servicemen, the time frame was amorphous. "Expeditiously" had no time line, and this would continue to be a stumbling block for the State Department. Believing that the repatriation issue was solved, Wang wanted to move forward on the US economic blockade and embargo on China, as well as to make preparations for higher level discussions at the foreign ministry level to eliminate tensions over Taiwan. Following Dulles' instructions, Johnson announced that the return of the identified Americans in China was the *sine qua non* for discussion on any other topic. In private, Dulles told Johnson that when appropriate he could raise the issues of the repatriation of unaccounted Korean War servicemen as well as a renunciation of force agreement concerning Taiwan. Dulles's intransigence was designed to keep talks going, and thereby reduce the tension over the Taiwan area.[37]

After two weeks of no progress, Dulles authorized Johnson to focus on the reciprocal renunciation of force agreement as a means to solve problems.[38] While the agreement would apply to all conflicting policies, the focus was on Taiwan. The ROC was especially concerned and nervous about any renunciation of force agreement between Beijing and Washington. Chiang Kai-shek's government was convinced that were Beijing to sign such an agreement it would be worthless, since China would take advantage of world developments and make its move against Taiwan. However, Taipei's objections did not affect the ongoing Geneva talks.

By the end of October, 1955 negotiations became less frequent. The block remained the same: complete the return of detained Americans or else no renunciation of force agreement. China was interested in this agreement since she did not want to be at war with the US. She was ill prepared, and needed to spend time and effort in transforming China into a socialist country. However, she had no intention of surrendering her interest in Taiwan, an island she viewed as part of China and could be dealt with accordingly. From Chiang's viewpoint, any renunciation of force agreement with Beijing was a waste of paper. When convenient, China would make its move against Taiwan.

The new year did not bring any progress. On January 12, 1956 Johnson again presented his force renunciation proposal, with minor changes, and it was met with rejection. For his part, Wang tried to work into any agreement a proviso implying diplomatic recognition to the PRC. The most obvious being to raise the level of negotiations to a foreign ministers' meeting. To further impede progress, Beijing still held thirteen Americans in prison in spite of the September, 1955 agreement.[39] From October, 1955 through July, 1956, Wang and Johnson met 35 times, without any real progress.

Dulles's stubbornness was to show Congress and the American public that the return of American nationals and servicemen took precedence over any other issue involving Beijing. Further, prolonged talks would counter the growing belief that America was pro-Taiwan and excessively anti-Communist. Further, by continuing to focus on the status of detained airmen and nationals, Washington would appear to be the aggrieved party.[40] What Washington did not know was that Mao shared a similar view, he was in no hurry to complete negotiations. On January 27, 1957 he told his colleagues at a US-Chinese Relations Conference in Beijing that it was "better to establish diplomatic relations with the US several years later than sooner." He wanted to wait until he had completed the Third Five Year Plan in the mid-1960s, before considering forming diplomatic relations with Washington. He did not mind if America did not grant recognition for one hundred years, but he did not believe that it would continue to refuse in the one hundred and first year.[41] With this combined thinking in Beijing and Washington, the lack of progress in negotiations was not surprising. Progress would be measured in halting steps through 1967.

CHAPTER II

FROM GENEVA TO WARSAW, 1957-1969

On June 28, 1957 Dulles made a nationally televised speech outlining America's China policy. His audience was America, and those Americans who believed that the White House should reach out to Beijing, and work to reduce tensions between the two. Without dwelling on America's normal critique of Communism, Dulles simply stated the reasons why Washington had not extended diplomatic relations to Communist China, had continued to oppose Beijing's admission to the UN, and had not traded or encouraged cultural interchanges with her. The principal reason for Washington's attitude was that recognition was not a "right," it was "a privilege," which gave the recipient international prestige and influence. America did not view recognition as inevitable, and would await until the Communist regime ended its monopoly of power in China, and granted freedom to its people.[1] Naturally Dulles ignored the fact that the KMT had a monopoly of power in Taiwan, and restricted peoples' freedoms.

The speech had little impact on Beijing. Rather, Mao was focused on changing relations with the Soviet Union. Nikita Khrushchev's 1956 speech at the 20th Party Congress of the Soviet Union criticizing Stalin, and the accompanying uprisings in Hungary and Poland, concerned Mao. The death of Stalin had made him the senior leader in the world Communist movement, and his Second Five Year Plan indicated that he was going to end his "lean to one side" policy toward Moscow. His Great Leap Forward Program called for significant expansion of agricultural collectivization, and a "backyard furnace program" designed to increase China's steel production to ultimately rival the West. The secretary of state's speech made no impact on Mao.

Dulles' speech and developments within the world Communist movement, resulted in less attention being paid to talks in Geneva. By November, the White House decided to change strategies. America's representative would be downgraded, below the rank of ambassador, and the venue could change from Geneva to Warsaw. Dulles told Johnson to inform Wang of the change, explaining that he was being reassigned to Prague. His replacement would be Edwin Martin, a seasoned State Department official, and would represent the US with whomever Beijing wished to appoint. The logic behind the move, was to show that while Washington was willing to continue talks, she was disappointed in Beijing's refusal to release all of the detained Americans. On December 12, Johnson informed Wang of his reassignment, Martin as his replacement, and left the date of the next meeting up to Wang.[2] Beijing responded by refusing to set a date for the meeting indicating that she did not want to deal with any American representative in lower rank than an ambassador.

On June 27, Washington indicated that in light of Beijing's release of two Catholic priests, that talks could resume in Warsaw. But before any formal announcement would be made,[3] Beijing began shelling the islands of Quemoy and Matsu on August 23. While the attack was a surprise, military plans for the defense of Taiwan had been on the table since early August.[4] The objective was political, not military. Mao wanted to have Washington become more involved in the Taiwan area, a move designed to have the American people question Washington's motives in being involved with two insignificant islands over one hundred miles from the Taiwan coast.

The shelling would also create a problem between Beijing and Moscow. Relations had begun to deteriorate following the successful flight of Sputnik in October 1957. China saw this as a victory for Communism, and announced that the "East wind prevails over the West." Mao wanted Moscow to become more confrontational with Washington, using its space success as a lever to gain greater influence in the White House. What Mao failed to understand was that the new leader of the Soviet Union, Nikita Khrushchev, wanted to use Sputnik as a means to improve relations with the West. Relations with Beijing began to deteriorate, with Mao calling America a "paper tiger," a phrase that did not concur with Khrushchev's desire to establish an early form of "détente" with Washington. The shelling of Quemoy and Matsu came as a complete surprise to Moscow, and only added fuel to the fire of a diminishing relationship with Beijing, one which would terminate in 1960 when the Soviet Union pulled her nuclear engineers out of China and ended supplying her with nuclear technology. This would also end America's view of a homogeneous Communist Bloc.

On September 4 Dulles publically committed America to defending the offshore islands.[5] The US sent a large task force to the Taiwan Strait area, and assigned ships to escort supplies to the endangered areas. The suddenness of the attack, prompted Washington to call for a resumption of the Geneva talks, but at a new venue. Beijing agreed provided they were at an ambassadorial level. Washington conceded and appointed the American Ambassador to Poland, Jacob Beam, to resume talks on September 15 in Warsaw. Beijing sent Wang Bingnan back to the negotiating table. The talks would focus on the Taiwan area, no longer on the repatriation of detained nationals.

From the outset, Washington had little hope for any real progress in the discussions. But the talks had value for both sides, since each wanted to show the world that she was the aggrieved party. The State Department wanted the talks to end tension in the area, and bring a quick end to hostilities. Since the Chinese had no interest in ending the talks, they had no interest in compromising. Time after time, Wang would make proposals which basically called for America to withdraw her support from Taiwan and the offshore islands, and remove her troops from the area as well. Since this was totally unacceptable to Washington, the talks reminded one of a dialogue of the deaf.[6]

The continued naval protection for supplies to reach Quemoy and Matsu succeeded on September 29, Chairman of the Joint Chiefs of Staff General Twining announced that the supply crisis was "broken" in the offshore islands, and was no longer an issue. President Eisenhower, who had never really wanted to get involved in the offshore islands issue, was pleased since "he did not want to fight a war on the ground of someone else's choosing." He urged the general to find some way to have Chiang Kai-shek agree to leave the offshore islands.[7] The degree of Eisenhower's concern was reinforced in a dispatch from Dulles to the American Ambassador in Taipei, emphasizing that "we are being dragged into a world war by Chiang, that we have put the destinies of the American people at his disposal, and that we have no flexibility in our position because Chiang is stubborn and will not agree because he feels that his only real hope is to precipitate world war."[8]

On October 6, Beijing announced a cease-fire through October 13. Washington saw this as a victory of sorts enabling Taipei to resupply her troops on Quemoy and Matsu. However, the ROC's government saw the cease-fire as a Trojan horse. It was a psychological ploy to soften American public opinion and make it less supportive of further American support of Taiwan.[9]. On October 13, Beijing announced that it would extend the cease-fire for an additional two weeks. Washington viewed this as the beginning of the end of the Taiwan crisis. Beijing understood State Department threats that if a solution were not quickly found, the US would bring the entire issue to the floor of the UN and present the notes of the Geneva talks beginning in 1955 as evidence of Beijing's unwillingness to negotiate. Mao was not willing to have this as the end game.

On October 17, Mao distributed an internal party circular which analyzed the Taiwan situation. In the conclusion, he noted that the liberation of Taiwan and the offshore islands "is an arduous task." He was willing to leave Chiang's troops in Quemoy and Matsu, since they later could be used as a cause for conflict. In the meantime, Mao could use a lengthy cease fire to implement his Second Five Year Plan. He concluded that "sooner or later there will be changes inside the Chiang Kai-shek clique. We can then take advantage of the situation....We shall totally discredit the US and create favorable conditions to liberate Taiwan, the Pescadore Islands, Quemoy and Matsu all together." On October 26, he told Lin Ke, his Secretary for International Affairs, that "now our principle is to aid Chiang to resist the US and strongly oppose the idea of 'two Chinas.'"[10]

As for the talks in Warsaw, they became far less frequent, and continued to make no progress between 1958 and May 1962. But they did serve a purpose and in 1961 Washington finally decided to set up a Mainland China desk calling it the Office of Asian Communist Affairs. If nothing else, the State Department bureaucracy had given Beijing recognition.[11] The PRC was concerned about developments in Taipei and feared that Chiang was eager to attack the mainland. Zhou Enlai sent Wang to Warsaw to meet with the new American Ambassador, John Cabot. On June 23, the two had tea and Wang shared Beijing's concern emphasizing that any such attack on the mainland had to have the support of Washington. Cabot assured him that America's role in Taiwan was defensive, not offensive. Cabot's remarks curbed Beijing's fears of an eminent attack.[12]

That was the only meeting of substance until April 1964. In the interim, France became the first European country to recognize Beijing, Lyndon B. Johnson had become president of the United States, the Sino-Soviet rift had expanded, America had taken a more active role in the Vietnam conflict, and Wang would be replaced after 120 meetings. On April 8, he gave his final presentation which continued to blame Washington for the continued failure of the talks to reach any conclusions. Both sides still had detained nationals, and there was no change in America's continued support to Taiwan preventing Beijing from securing what she saw as rightfully hers.[13]

In late July, Cabot met with the new Chinese negotiator, Ambassador Wang Kuo-chuan. The talks began on a positive note when both sides agreed to release the detained nationals. While this was real progress, negotiations soon broke down over Taiwan. However, the talks became more of a side show than before. In October, China detonated her first atomic bomb, and Khrushchev fell from power, ending the rule of the person Mao believed to be responsible for the Sino-Soviet split. Beijing's entry into the nuclear club provided a new topic for the Warsaw talks, but this did not bring about any progress. Rather, the talks fell apart, not due to the negotiators, but to America's increased involvement in the Vietnam War, and to the internal disruptions in Beijing due to Mao's efforts to return to power via a Cultural Revolution. In total, there were five meetings in Warsaw in 1964, and only fifteen between 1964 and 1968.[14]

At the 128th meeting, on December 16, 1965 Ambassador John Gronouski replaced John Cabot as America's new negotiator. In his first meeting with Wang Kuo-chuan, he was impressed by the "inflexibility of the Chinese position and their refusal to give any indication of willingness to resolve the Viet-Nam crisis or anything else on any terms other than their own." He was also amazed by Wang's belief that America had hostile intentions against China.[15] Gronouski's surprise was because he knew that Washington was reconsidering her relationship with Beijing, and this became known on March 16, 1966 when Secretary of State Rusk addressed the House Committee on Foreign Affairs. "We expect China to become someday a great world power...In the ordinary course of events, a peaceful China would be expected to have close relations-political, cultural, and economic-with the countries around its borders and with the US." He called for the continuance of the Warsaw talks, if for no other reason, than to be a conduit to exchange information and attitudes in "times of crisis."[16]

The secretary's remarks served as a prelude to President Johnson's nationally televised speech on July 12 concerning "US Foreign Policy in Asia." An essential development for peace was "reconciliation between nations that now call themselves enemies." As a symbol of a growing reconciliation, Johnson announced that Washington had cleared a passport for a leading business man to meet with Beijing representatives. While this might not appear to be a great accomplishment, a meeting between American specialists and their Chinese counterparts had been consistently rejected by Beijing.[17] According to Wang, as a result of these remarks, Gronouski referred to Beijing as the "People's Republic of China," the first time the phrase was used. In his memoir published in 1995, Wang noted that "we lost a favorable opportunity to give Sino-American relations a timely push. It must be a regretful thing in the history of diplomacy."[18]

On August 18, 1966 Mao began his Great Proletarian Cultural Revolution, which produced massive chaos throughout China to the point that by 1968, nearly every province had formed its own government. At the outset, the White House was confused as to why Mao had challenged the existing order. But the State Department saw that the chaos could provide a means to reach out to Beijing. Rusk wanted to open doors for cooperative enterprises between the two countries. Congress was considering relaxing travel and trade sanctions against Beijing. However, the Vietnam War had begun to take its toll on the American public. The new videos coming from the front lines showing wounded and dead servicemen prompted some viewers to question why America was involved in any war in Southeast Asia.

The Warsaw meetings continued and were contentious throughout 1967. While talks about the few remaining detained nationals were still in play, the real focus was on the Vietnam War. The arguments were vitriolic as could be anticipated, with no real progress. The Cultural Revolution placed Wang in an awkward position not knowing what was the "correct" direction to pursue, in light of the continually changing political landscape in Beijing. As a result, meetings occurred at four to five month intervals throughout year.[19] And the first meeting in 1968 on January 8, showed no progress. But Grounouski noted a change in tone, the Chinese negotiator was much less belligerent.[20] However, the May scheduled talks made no progress and the next round was indefinitely postponed.

However, throughout 1968, independent of Warsaw, there were subtle changes in Beijing-Washington relations. In early August, the Republican Party Convention nominated Richard Nixon as its standard bearer. This was the man who had written a little read, but later frequently referenced, article in *Foreign Affairs* magazine in October 1967. In his "Asia After Viet Nam," he suggested that "taking the long view, we simply cannot afford to leave China forever outside the family of nations...There is no place on this small planet for a billion of its potentially most able people to live in angry isolation...The world cannot be safe until China changes. Thus our aim, to the extent that we can influence events, should be to induce change."[21] He told the National Convention delegates on August 8 that "after an era of confrontation, the time has come for an era of negotiation. Where the world's super powers are concerned, there is no acceptable alternative to peaceful negotiations." "We believe this should be an era of peaceful competition...We extend the hand of friendship to all people, to the Russian people, to the Chinese people, to all people in the world."[22]

Beijing heard the message, and ten days later events gave it greater importance. Soviet troops had marched into Prague, Czechoslovakia, and ended the "Prague Spring." Leonid Brezhnev, the Secretary General of the Soviet Union, justified the invasion as Moscow's responsibility as leader of the world socialist movement, to protect socialist states from the threat of capitalism. To Beijing, the threat of Soviet invasion was ominous. Moscow had already made veiled threats of a possible attack on China's nuclear installations. Nearly a million Soviet troops were stationed along the Chinese border, and border clashes became more frequent.[23] While Beijing saw both Washington and Moscow as enemies, Mao began to view the Soviet Union as a far greater threat.

Mao instructed Zhou Enlai to reopen the Warsaw talks in November, suspended since the previous May. However, two days before the talks were to begin on November 25, a Chinese diplomat defected, which postponed the meeting.[24]

The defection did not necessarily require postponing the Warsaw talks. A better reason could have been to give the new president, Richard Nixon, time to organize his administration's strategies. However, the defection also gave ammunition to those opposed to Mao's willingness to reach out to Washington. Mao's inability to reign in the Cultural Revolution forced him to look to the military to restore order. The army responded, and crushed the Red Guard, students who had supported Mao's revolution. As leader of the military, Lin Biao grew in importance, and began to challenge Mao looking to share power with the Chairman. Lin was opposed to any negotiations with Washington, and he was able to capitalize on his success in ending the chaos. The postponement of the November talks was only the beginning. Scheduled talks for February 20, 1969 too would fail to materialize.

CHAPTER III

NIXON REACHES OUT TO BEIJING

By the time Nixon entered the White House, American public opinion toward Beijing was changing. The "Brezhnev Doctrine" justifying Moscow's actions in Prague, along with a decline in the congressional "China Lobby" rhetoric, and the fatigue felt by many Americans over the forever long Vietnam War, produced an environment which could tolerate a change in Washington's view of Beijing. And Richard Nixon, later supported by his new NSC advisor, Henry Kissinger, would *carpe diem* and move toward forming a new relationship with the PRC. As president-elect he had encouraged Johnson to accept Zhou Enlai's offer to resume the Warsaw talks, and while the November meeting failed to materialize, Nixon would continue to reach out to Beijing. However, since Lin Biao and his supporters, including the infamous Gang of Four, were sharing power with Mao, nothing of substance through Warsaw would develop in 1969; but not for a lack of effort. As a lead into Nixon's inaugural address, Secretary of State-designate William Rogers testified before the Senate Foreign Relations Committee on January 1. In response to a question, answered "I think it is important to develop channels of communication with Red China...The Red Chinese have proposed a meeting in Warsaw in February sometime and we obviously will pursue that initiative." Five days later Nixon used his Inaugural Address to send a message to both Moscow and Beijing. He said: "After a period of confrontation we are entering an era of negotiation. Let all nations know that during this administration our lines of communication will be open. We seek an open world."[1] On January 27, he told reporters that he was not ready to admit Beijing to the UN, but was eager to listen to the Chinese Communists in Warsaw. The immediate response from Beijing was quite positive. She published

Nixon's Inaugural Address, emphasizing Nixon's willingness to improve relations with *all* countries in the world.[2] On February 1, Nixon told Kissinger that he should privately, and without any connection to the White House, seek avenues in Poland that might lead to the possibility of a rapprochement with Beijing.[3]

Two weeks later on February 16, Mao held a meeting and asked Zhou Enlai to meet with four marshals: Chen Yi, Ye Jianying, Nie Rongzhen and Xu Xiangquian, all of whom had undergone re-education programs following their failure to understand the Cultural Revolution. Now brought back to work, Mao asked them to "study international strategic studies."[4] While the marshals deliberated, sporadic fighting broke out on the Sino-Soviet contested island of Zhenbao, or Damansky as Moscow preferred. The six week conflict resulted in a Soviet withdrawal, but not before leaving the island "looking like the surface of the moon."[5] More important the clash provided Mao with a rallying point to counter the growing criticism of his Cultural Revolution. As for the marshals' report, it suggested that China should end her isolation, and discourage American or Soviet "adventurism." But as for anything specific, the marshals gave no advice.[6]

Mao wanted more information. In April, the Chinese Communist Party (CCP) held its Ninth National Congress, and Lin Biao gave the main address indicating that his star was continuing to rise. Several weeks later, Mao asked the marshals to view the international scene without traditional guidelines. Unlike Lin, who saw Moscow and Washington as predators, Mao saw the need to end China's isolation, and decided that America would be a better vehicle; Washington was much further away and did not share a border with China. As a result he sent the marshals back for further recommendations.

In Washington, the Central Intelligence Agency (CIA) and the National Security Council (NSC) along with members of the State and Defense Departments had prepared a Special National Intelligence

Estimate, or SNIE, on March 6, 1969. The report concluded that "as long as Mao is the dominant figure, major changes in China's international posture do not appear likely." This would prove to be one of many intelligence estimates that would prove faulty.[7] In contrast, with Republicans in control of Congress, Washington could more easily pursue a conciliatory policy toward China since they were not viewed as liberal or as left leaning as the Democrats. Outside organizations including the League of Women Voters, the National Committee on US-China Relations, as well as the editorial pages of *The New York Times* and *New Republic* called for change, including the admission of China to the UN. Nixon was not ready in the summer of 1969 to adopt any such change. But he was willing to make gestures, including relaxing the existing trade embargo for Americans returning from China permitting them to bring home up to $100 worth of goods. Further, passports for students, teachers, scientists, doctors, journalists and other professionals would be automatically validated.[8]

But unknown to the public, Nixon was willing to reach out further to China. Following a request by the president, Charles de Gaulle agreed in March to send a message to China and did so in early May stating that America was willing to open talks "at the highest level."[9] This was Nixon's first effort to directly reach Beijing, and it would not be the last. When Nixon came into the White House he did so with a new view toward relations with Moscow and Beijing. Past administrations had maintained a bipolar world, America and the Communist Bloc. This thinking produced a tit-for-tat foreign policy, one of action and reaction with the goal of maintaining the *status quo*. Nixon wanted to move forward and to do so he introduced two new strategies, multipolarity and linkage. Multipolarity broadened the field of diplomacy. The president saw five world regions. While Moscow and Washington would continue to be the principal players at the outset, he wanted to include Beijing, Tokyo and Western Europe. By expanding the roster of players, he could use one against the other to effect change, sometimes against a third player. Linkage meant linking together apparently disparate elements to force countries to trade items, not normally linked, but viewed as equally important by each side. Multipolarity and linkage, coupled with secrecy, would be the currency of world diplomacy during the Nixon-Kissinger years, and thereafter.

China was part of Nixon's multipolarity approach, as evidenced in Secretary of State Rogers address to the Associated Press annual luncheon in New York City on April 21. "One cannot speak of a future Pacific community without reference to China...We know that by virtue of its size, population, and the talents of its people, mainland China is bound to play an important role in East Asian and Pacific affairs...We shall take initiatives to reestablish normal relations with Communist China."[10] As evidence of Nixon's continued outreach, when Rogers visited Pakistan on May 24, President Yahya Khan agreed to be a conduit for messages to Beijing.[11]

However, Beijing would rebuff these early overtures. In a telegram from Romania's Ambassador to Beijing, Aurel Duma reported that China did not see any changes in America's foreign policy since it continued "to occupy Taiwan and lead a two-China policy. The US persists in its hostile position towards the PRC."[12] However, this assessment did not take into account the private thoughts of Mao. According to his physician, Li Zhisui, Mao was open to talks with Washington. Mao described China as being surrounded by possible enemies, the Soviet Union to the north and west, India to the south, and Japan to the east. If all were to attack, what should China do? And his answer was "Beyond Japan is the US. Didn't our ancestors counsel negotiating with faraway countries while fighting with those that are near?" He further explained that unlike the Soviet Union, "The US never occupied Chinese territory. America's new president, Richard Nixon, is a longtime rightist, a leader of the anti-Communists there. I like to deal with rightists. They say what they really think—not like the leftists, who say one thing and mean another."[13]

On July 20, 1969 the world saw Apollo 11 land on the moon and astronaut Neil Armstrong be the first person ever to step out onto the surface of the moon. As he said, "one small step for man, one giant leap for mankind." Four days later, Nixon watched the splashdown of the space module in the Pacific, and on the 25th he visited Guam. Surrounded by reporters, the president agreed to an informal press conference at which he enunciated what became known as the "Nixon Doctrine." While the US would continue to honor her commitments to her friends and allies, America would look to the threatened nation to assume the primary responsibility for providing manpower for its own defense. America would no longer shoulder the entire responsibility for the defense of the free world and place large numbers of combat troops in harm's way.[14]

Continuing his tour, Nixon arrived in Pakistan on August 1 and met with President Yahya Khan. He said he had passed on Nixon's note to Zhou Enlai who told him that "it was all right to go ahead and open negotiations on his behalf." [15]On the following day, the president arrived in Romania. This was his only stop in a Communist country and he did so, according to Romania's Ambassador to the US, Corneliu Bogdan, to "tweak the nose of the Russians." Bucharest had been a maverick member of the Warsaw Pact, and had been a supporter of Beijing's independence from Moscow.[16] The president received an overwhelming reception. Hundreds of thousands of people greeted him at the airport, fondly recalling his 1967 visit, when he was simply a private citizen. In discussions with Nicolae Ceausescu, Nixon said "I can't change our China policy now, but in the long view…China is a reality and no real peace is possible without China's playing a role in stabilizing Asia and the world."[17] Before he left, Ceausescu agreed to act as a mediator between Washington and Beijing.

Both the Pakistan and Romanian mediation efforts as well as those through de Gaulle were held in great secrecy by Kissinger and Nixon. The president had deliberately left his Secretary of State William Rogers out of the loop because he saw the State Department as the Department of Leaks, a sieve which leaked confidential information. This decision would frequently prove embarrassing, as seen within a week following Nixon's visit to Bucharest. On August 8, Rogers announced, without any knowledge of the White House, that "Communist China obviously has long been too isolated from world affairs. This is one reason why we have been seeking to open up channels of communication...We would welcome a renewal of talks with Communist China."[18]So much for secrecy, and in the future Rogers would be kept out of the Kissinger-Nixon China strategy.

There are always rumors especially in diplomacy, and secret negotiations often become a prime target. Having heard that Nixon had met with the presidents of Pakistan and Romania, Taiwan feared that the meetings concerned a change in Washington's policy toward Beijing and therefore Taipei. On August 6, Kissinger told the Taiwan Ambassador, Zhou Shu-kai, that there had been no such discussion with either Khan or Ceausescu. "He reiterated that there had been no change in the US position regarding Beijing and we were not talking with it anywhere."[19] This policy of misleading Taiwan would be the norm for Washington throughout the 1960s and most of the 1970s.

The March Sino-Soviet battles over Damansky Island, proved to be just an opening salvo between Beijing and Moscow. There were numerous clashes between the two countries along the border between Chinese Xinjiang province and Soviet Kazakhstan which intensified in May and June.[20] On August 13, an entire Chinese brigade was killed by Soviet troops at Damansky. The outbreak produced an interesting discussion in Washington. In a special meeting with the Cabinet, according to Kissinger, Nixon "startled" them by mentioning that "it was against our interests to let China be 'smashed' in a Sino-Soviet war." Kissinger added that "It was a major event in American foreign policy when a president declared that we had a strategic interest in the survival of a major Communist country, long an enemy, and with which we had no contact."[21] Washington gave no indication of any interest in the Sino-Soviet conflict even though by mid-August, Moscow had massed nearly 285,000 troops along the border. Mao prepared for war. He "laid out a strategy of digging the cave deeply, accumulating grain extensively, and preparing for war or famine."[22] By month's end, he had mobilized the army and the citizenry. He also sent a strong signal to Moscow when he tested at least two hydrogen bombs over the desert, and the radioactive fallout drifted into Kazakhstan and Mongolia. The message was clear, Mao was willing to raise the ante to nuclear war. On October 20, Sino-Soviet boundary negotiations began which ended the threat of war.

The boundary clashes encouraged the White House to capitalize on the situation. China felt threatened by Moscow, which forced Beijing to consider Washington's overtures more seriously. On September 9, Nixon told Ambassador Stoessel to return to Warsaw and approach the Chinese Charge at some convenient time and indicate that the president was "seriously interested in concrete discussions with China."[23] At the same time, Ion Maurer, effectively the Romanian Prime Minister, met with Zhou Enlai in Beijing and told him that Nixon was interested in normalizing relations with China. Maurer was quite convinced that Nixon was genuine in his interest and wanted to establish a dialogue at the top level of leadership.[24]

No response emanated from Beijing, but it was not because Mao opposed the idea of a rapprochement, it was just too soon in light of the Sino-Soviet issues. The White House continued its outreach to Mao, and Nixon ordered that the two destroyers which patrolled the Taiwan Straits be withdrawn.[25] Meanwhile, on September 17, the four marshals submitted their second report. Among the conclusions was that "the U.S. imperialists have suggested in resuming the Sino-American ambassadorial talks, to which we should respond positively

34

when the timing is proper." Chen Yi, the senior marshal spoke out strongly in support of renewed talks, and to avoid the issue of Taiwan, which had been a fourteen year stumbling block. "The Taiwan question can be gradually resolved by talks at higher levels."[26]

Stoessel finally met with the Chinese Charge, but his request for a resumption of talks was rejected. Having heard little response through Bucharest or Islamabad, Nixon told Stoessel to approach a Chinese diplomat and raise the issue directly. Following a fashion show at the Yugoslavian Embassy on December 3, Stoessel approached a Chinese diplomat. He fled, Stoessel gave chase, caught up with him and told him that he had an important message for the Chinese embassy.[27] According to Mao's physician, Dr. Li Zhisui, the Chairman showed him the letter and said "we have been talking without saying anything for over eleven years. Now we can start over again and talk seriously. Nixon must be sincere when he sends word that he is interested in talking with us."[28] As a show of good faith, on December 7, China released two American citizens whose yacht had strayed into Chinese territorial waters.

Three days later, Stoessel received an invitation to come to the Chinese embassy on December 11. The first meeting was cordial, with the intent for the second to address more serious issues.[29]

CHAPTER IV

1970: FROM WARSAW TO BEIJING AND WASHINGTON

1970 opened auspiciously, with a Warsaw meeting on January 8 between Ambassador Stoessel and the Chinese Charge Lei Yang at the American Embassy. The informal exchange promised subsequent meetings alternating between each nation's embassy. On January 20 at the 135th meeting, which proved to be the last of the Warsaw meetings, Stoessel suggested that it was time to raise the talks to a higher level, suggesting that Washington send a representative to Beijing, or China send a similar high ranking representative to Washington. Stoessel reported that the Charge's "language is unquestionably the most forthcoming of any we have heard in the history of the Warsaw talks, except for one brief period in 1955." A couple of weeks later, Nixon sent his first Foreign Policy Report to Congress. In it, he described "the Chinese are great and vital people who should not remain isolated from the international community…it is certainly in our interests…that we take what steps we can toward improved practical relations with Beijing."[1] On February 20, Lei announced that Beijing would welcome a high-ranking American official.[2] As to the value of the Warsaw talks, they had permitted an exchange of views on Vietnam, and assured Beijing that Washington did not want the Vietnam War to extend into China. Kissinger would later say that the talks were "sterile," and that the only breakthroughs would occur once he and Nixon became directly involved in negotiations. Of course this was typical Henry.[3]

Unaware that the Warsaw talks would soon end, Nixon decided to expedite matters and sent a message through Pakistan stating that "we are prepared to open a direct channel of communication from the White House to Beijing. If Beijing agrees [to

36

establish such a channel], its existence will not be known by anyone outside the White House." Zhou Enlai received the message on March 21, recalling that it was the same process Washington employed in the American-Vietnamese negotiations.[4] Nixon wanted to make sure that the State Department did not become involved in the talks, a view strongly supported by Kissinger. Independent of the fact that the NSC advisor wanted to be the only person to implement the president's foreign policy, Rogers did not understand Nixon's approach to Beijing. While Rogers was concerned about talks with Beijing undermining Washington's relations with Taiwan, the president and Kissinger had their focus on Red China, not the ROC.[5]

The progress made at the February 20th meeting came to an abrupt halt in March. Several events combined to postpone further talks. Cambodia's Prince Norodom Sihanouk, while on an annual vacation, fled to Beijing for protection following a coup led by the pro-American General Lon Nol. Then, without consulting Lon Nol, American and South Vietnamese soldiers invaded Cambodia. When word leaked out about the invasion, massive protests broke out in the US. While student protests had occurred since 1967, none were as strong as those following the invasion, and the subsequent killing of six Kent State University students by National Guard troops trying to restore order. While Nixon would withdraw the troops from Cambodia, American planes would continue to bomb the country until August, 1973. The purpose being to prevent Cambodia from becoming a North Vietnamese satellite, a view secretly supported by Mao.

On May 18, 1970 Beijing announced the postponement of further talks in Warsaw, and two days later, in front of hundreds of thousands of protesters in Tienanmen Square, Mao lashed out at the US. "U.S. imperialism, which looks like a huge monster, is in essence a paper tiger, now in the throes of its death-bed struggle...People of the world, unite and defeat the U.S. aggressors and all their running dogs!"[6] While the rhetoric was hostile, Beijing did not want to cut off all contact with Washington. Much of what he said was for home consumption. Mao's heir, Lin Biao, had begun to assert himself at the Chairman's expense. He believed that in using the military to restore order during the Revolution that he deserved to be recognized as equal to Mao; the gun had saved the party. However, he forgot, that one of Mao's classic statements was "the party should control the gun." Mao needed to regroup and his May 18th outburst was to show the military that he was in charge. As a sign that his speech was not directed at Washington, on July 10 Beijing quietly released Bishop James Walsh, an American citizen imprisoned since 1958 on espionage charges.[7]

The power struggle continued between Lin and Mao and soon rose to a higher level. The military leader was totally opposed to any reconciliation with Washington, advocating instead a hard line toward both superpowers, or a compromise with Moscow.[8] The showdown came at the Central Committee plenary session held from August 23 to September 6, where Mao gained the support of the committee members. Throughout this struggle, Mao had found little time to deal with Washington. However, in the fall, Mao invited his long time author friend, Edgar Snow, to visit China. Snow's relationship with Mao began during the Long March, and he gained Mao's confidence following the publication of *Red Star Over China,* a firsthand account of Mao's revolution from the 1920s through the mid-1930s. On October 1, 1970 Snow stood beside Mao at Tienanmen Square to review the National Day parade in Beijing. Pictures showing Mao and Snow together on front pages of Chinese newspapers were meant to be a signal to the Chinese people and to Nixon that change was in the air. And while this was unprecedented, no American had ever being so honored, Kissinger admitted that "we had missed the point when it mattered. Excessive subtlety had produced a failure of communication."[9]

On October 25, many heads of state came to New York City to participate in the 25th anniversary of the United Nations. Nixon used this opportunity to meet with the leaders of Pakistan and Romania. He met with Yahya Khan in the Oval Office and asked him

38

to tell China that America had no interest in joining a condominium against China, and that he was willing to send a high level representative, including Kissinger as a secret envoy to Beijing. On the following day, Nixon repeated the message to Ceausescu before honoring him at a state dinner. In his toast to Ceausescu, he spoke of Romania's ability to maintain relations with all the superpowers including the US, the Soviet Union and the People's Republic of China, the first time he had publicly used the phrase to identify the Beijing regime.[10]

In mid-November, Zhou told both Pakistani and Romanian ambassadors that a high level American representative was most welcome provided they wanted to discuss Taiwan. Neither message reached the White House until December 8, when Agha Hilaly, the Pakistani Ambassador to the US, sent word that Mao, Lin Biao and Zhou Enlai were all interested in meeting with Nixon's representative to talk about Taiwan and the Strait of Taiwan.[11] On December 18, Edgar Snow interviewed Mao who praised the president saying "I like the Republican Party better (than Democrats). We prefer the Nixon administration because he is more honest." Adding that if Nixon "wishes to visit Beijing, tell him to come secretly and not make it open." The interview did not appear in *Life* magazine until three months later per request of Mao.[12]

In January, 1971 Kissinger received a new message from Beijing through Ambassador Bogdan. While similar to the Pakistani note, it added that "since President Nixon had visited Bucharest and Belgrade, he would also be welcome in Beijing." The references to the two capitals was because they were the most independent of Moscow, indicating China's growing estrangement from Moscow. The Romanian note was a step up by inviting Nixon by name to visit Beijing.[13] While excited by the response, Nixon wanted to be cautious. He did not want to "appear too eager," and told Kissinger "Lets cool it." Mao too was cautious, but with greater reason. He was angry with Washington for expanding the Vietnam War into Laos.[14]

39

The bombings were to cut off supplies coming from Hanoi to North Vietnam troops fighting in South Vietnam along what was called the Ho Chi Minh Trail. Further, Mao had read the anti-war demonstrations, which grew in size and number, as a sign that Nixon's government could collapse.[15] As a result, progress was put on hold until spring, 1971.

The event, which would result in the resumption of talks, could not have been anticipated: a ping-pong match. The Chinese table tennis team, considered one of the best in the world, had not been able to play in the world championships in 1967 and 1969 due to the Cultural Revolution. Japan was scheduled to host the 1971 championship and early in the year invited the Chinese to participate at the games in Nagoya scheduled to begin in March. Initially Mao and Zhou showed little interest in China's participation, since they viewed it as a political issue. However, by 1971 there was a changed atmosphere. On March 14, Zhou arranged a meeting with the state Physical Culture Commission and the Chinese table tennis team. The outcome recommended that the team not participate for fear that the numerous threats made against China's athletes might materialize. Serendipitously, on the following day, Washington lifted its last remaining passport restrictions on Americans travelling to the PRC.[16] And nine days later, the last American and South Vietnamese troops withdrew from Cambodia. On April 4, Zhou urged Mao to approve the team's participation. At the same time, in Nagoya, Chinese and American students had made contacts. Glenn Cowen, a nineteen year-old American player accidentally boarded a bus carrying Chinese players. There was a sudden quiet until Zhuang Zedong, the three time world champion, approached him giving him a scarf as a present. Cowan reciprocated on the following day by giving Zhuang a Beatles' T-shirt, with the slogan "Let It Be." Two days later, Mao agreed to have the team participate, and more importantly, to make plans for receiving the American team in China.[17]

"Ping Pong Diplomacy" entered the world's lexicon as a symbol for a new beginning in Sino-American relations. On April 14, Zhou Enlai officially welcomed the American team to China in the Great Hall, along with several other invited teams. World newspapers carried news of the visit, as did most television stations showing the American team visiting the Summer Palace and the Great Wall. In Washington, the White House was thrilled. Kissinger credited the president with having been sufficiently stubborn to force China to open her doors to America.[18] Further, the new relationship would begin Triangular Diplomacy. Sino-American relations could help Washington deal with Moscow. To show his immediate appreciation of the Chinese invitation, on the day of the team's arrival in Beijing, Nixon announced a further relaxation of trade and travel restrictions.[19]

Nixon wanted to move quickly to capitalize on the euphoria created by the table tennis team's visit. Zhou Enlai had called the visit a move towards "people's diplomacy" and the president wanted labeled it the People-to-People program. The initial State Department response was caution. The department saw Beijing's welcoming a means to enhance her image to the American people, anticipating that they might be able to pressure Washington to change her views on Taiwan. For the same reason, the department anticipated that Beijing would be open to more visitors from America and Europe, but did not anticipate any significant change in trade.[20] In turn, the publicity given to the visit through the Chinese media served Mao well in preparing the Chinese people for the impending transformation in Sino-American relations.

Several days after the team returned home, Nixon received a letter from Zhou Enlai through Yahya Khan. This April 21 note recognized the importance of the tennis team's visit as the vehicle to renew relations between the two countries. There were important questions that needed attention, and Zhou offered to "receive publicly in Beijing a special envoy of the president such as Mr. Kissinger, or the Secretary of State or even the president himself for direct meetings

41

and discussions." Zhou added that if this was not an appropriate time for such high level discussions, they could be deferred to a later date.[21] On the 27th, Nixon received another note from Zhou through the Pakistani channel which reaffirmed the original invitation. The president was delighted and according to his memoir, he and Kissinger spent several days trying to decide who to send to Beijing. Through clever maneuvering, Kissinger managed to eliminate the opposition, especially Rogers, and finally Nixon said "Henry, I think you will have to do it."[22] Although he was presumed to be the architect of Washington's foreign policy, Rogers was completely in the dark about the change in Sino-American relations. So much so, that he told the press that China's offer to receive the president was "not a serious invitation."[23]

Roger's remarks sent shivers through Beijing questioning the seriousness of Nixon's outreach. To counter this, Nixon used his news conference on April 29 to give a hint that a change was coming in Sino-American relations. "At the end of my reply to a general question about our China policy, I said 'I would finally suggest—I know this question may come up if I don't answer it now—I hope, and, as a matter of fact, I expect to visit mainland China sometime in some capacity—I don't know in what capacity. But that indicates what I hope for the long term.'" Beijing understood the message, and it was reinforced by the near simultaneous publication of *Life* magazine's issue carrying Snow's December interview with Mao, noting that Mao would welcome Nixon visiting him in Beijing.[24]

Per usual, Nixon was fixated on privacy, and wanted as few people as possible to know about Kissinger's impending visit to China. While the Pakistani channel through Ambassador Hilaly would continue, Nixon wanted an American on the ground in Pakistan involved with Kissinger's visit. With that thought in mind, Kissinger notified Joseph Farland, Washington's Ambassador to Pakistan, to arrange a secret round trip flight to Palm Springs California to meet him. The purpose of the May 7 meeting was to bring Farland up to speed on Kissinger's impending visit to China, and for him to make all the necessary arrangements. The NSC Advisor planned to leave Washington on an "information" trip taking him to Saigon, Bangkok, Delhi, Islamabad, and Paris. There would be no newsmen on board the plane, and he intended to simply provide the local media with an overview of his visit. Farland needed to secure the help of Yahya Khan, who could invite Kissinger to spend a weekend in some suitable retreat. Kissinger intended to leave his plane in a conspicuous place at the airport, and then fly to China in another plane prepositioned in Pakistan. The final destination would be determined later. He would return to Islamabad within thirty-six hours and fly on to Paris as though nothing had happened. Farland believed that all of this was manageable.[25] With that, Kissinger and Nixon sent their reply to Zhou on May 9, via Pakistan. The president proposed a secret meeting after June 15 between Kissinger and Zhou, or another appropriate high ranking Chinese official. The meeting would be in China, somewhere close to Pakistan, since Kissinger was only scheduled for a thirty-six hour disappearance from Islamabad. The note concluded that "the visit of President Nixon to Beijing could be announced within a short time" after Kissinger's meeting.[26]

As part of Nixon's multipolarity and linkage strategies, he had continued to maintain relations with Moscow. The Soviets wanted an arms agreement limiting the deployment of anti-ballistic missile systems (ABM's). Moscow had used most of the 1960s to catch up with America's missile arsenals, shown to be far superior during the Kennedy era. By 1969, the Soviets believed they had reached parity with Washington and wanted to solidify that status via a treaty. Nixon wanted to link arms to Moscow's help in ending the Vietnam War. Moscow refused, and that ended the ABM talks. However, they were far from secret, and in anticipation of the new relationship with China, Nixon notified Beijing on May 20, that while there were Soviet-American arms talks, he would conclude no agreement which could be directed against the PRC.

In analyzing China's reasons for agreeing to have a meeting of heads of state, the National Security Council concluded, that Beijing wanted to use the talks as a lever against the Soviet Union and to undermine the ROC's international position. Beijing was also motivated by her interest in joining the UN on her own terms, meaning the expulsion of Taiwan. The "People-to-People" tact increased Beijing's chances of gaining support for her position, and a Beijing-Washington summit could give support to her agenda and encourage other nations to deal more meaningfully with the Middle Kingdom. She also wanted to show the world that the moderates were now in control of China, not the radical elements of the Red Guard, and Gang of Four.

The National Security Administration's (NSA) analysis of America's interest in a Chinese summit was clear, but focused on the negative, seeing Taiwan as a reason that nothing promising could be forthcoming. But this attitude was not new. It was the mantra of conservative congressmen, as well as the State Department, which were not fully aware of the Nixon-Kissinger playbook. In taking steps to improve relations with Beijing, the US had to avoid their being misinterpreted by America's allies as well as by China, Taiwan and the Soviet Union.

Two days before the NSA report, Zhou Enlai called a meeting of the core group of the Foreign Ministry to discuss the various messages received through Pakistan, Romania and via an old friend of Kissinger's, Jean Paul Sainteny. He was the former French Delegate General in Hanoi, who had acted as a messenger between Washington and North Vietnam as early as 1968, and was willing to provide the same service for Kissinger.[27] Following the meeting Zhou sent Mao a report which contained new policy guidelines. While it maintained Beijing's constant refrain that American forces needed to be removed from Taiwan, "it did not persist in the precondition that the US must end all ties with Taiwan." While repeating that the issue with Taiwan was a domestic issue for Beijing, it emphasized the solution would be

44

done through peaceful means. And for the first time, the report "accepted the idea of establishing liaison offices in Washington and Beijing."[28] Warsaw would no longer be the meeting place much to the delight of Kissinger, who since January 29, 1971 had said that the site was a "very public place," meaning that secrecy was easily compromised.[29]

On May 29, Zhou sent a message to Nixon through Hilaly. Mao had agreed to meet with Nixon in Beijing in a "direct conversation" in which each side would be free to raise principle issues of concern. Zhou welcomed Kissinger as the advance man arriving between June 15-20, and expected the meetings would last three to four days. Secrecy would be key, and Yahya Khan had guaranteed that by permitting Kissinger to fly to Beijing from Islamabad.[30] When Hilaly delivered the message on June 2, Kissinger was "ecstatic." According to Dallek, he left the West Wing and "arrived 'out of breath' and 'beaming' at the White House to tell Nixon.[31] The president was hosting a dinner for President Anastasio Somoza of Nicaragua. Kissinger had him called out of the State Dining Room, and "trembling" told him of the invitation. Kissinger recalls that "Buoyantly, he took me to the Lincoln Sitting Room, found some brandy and two glasses, and proposed a toast…to generations to come who may have a better chance to live in peace because of what we have done."[32]

On June 4, the White House notified Beijing that due to prior commitments, Kissinger would be unavailable until the first week in July. The president suggested July 9 as a date for the visit and two days later Zhou agreed to make all necessary arrangements for the July 9 visit.[33]

CHAPTER V

KISSINGER IN CHINA: OVERWHELMED IN MEETING ZHOU ENLAI

During the next several weeks, the White House was agog with preparations for Kissinger's visit as well as for the impending wedding of Nixon's daughter Tricia to Edward Cox on June 12. On June 10, the president, with congressional approval, announced a further relaxation in trade restrictions with China, including an end to a requirement that 50% of all food shipments to Communist countries had to go on American vessels.[1] On the day after the wedding the president watched the public's reaction to *The New York Times* publication of the *Pentagon Papers*. While the latter described prior administrations' conduct of the Vietnam War, and did not include Nixon's first term, the outcry reassured Nixon that secrecy was of utmost importance.

And secrecy was essential in Kissinger's visit to Beijing. Code named Polo, after Marco Polo, Kissinger's visit would later be remembered by some for the famous "stomachache maneuver." Kissinger would embark on an Asian tour, stopping in Vietnam for consultations, two days in India, with no real agenda except to give greater credence to his need to stay in Pakistan for three days. Shortly thereafter the NSC advisor would land in Islamabad for talks with Yahya Khan. The talks would be interrupted because Kissinger was suffering from a severe stomachache, and was moved to a mountain retreat to recuperate for a few days.[2] During the "recuperation period" Kissinger flew off to Beijing. Afterwards, he would return to Islamabad, be visible to reporters, and return to Washington. While secrecy was the byword, the president had all he could do not to tell America about Kissinger's meeting. The closest hint that he gave was during a July 6 speech in Kansas City. He declared that there were

46

five great power centers in the world, and "Mainland China" was one of these.[3]

Throughout all of these developments, the secretary of state was kept pretty much in the dark. Finally, on July 8, with Kissinger preparing to fly to Beijing, the president brought Rogers up to speed. In order to mollify the secretary, he told him that the Beijing talks would probably be a prelude to a presidential invitation to visit Beijing, a visit which would include Rogers. According to Haldeman, "Rogers took it all extremely well."[4] Realizing that Kissinger would be unable to send any details on his meetings, the president was eager to learn if his China trip were approved. He decided that if Beijing approved his visit, Kissinger would send a cable with one word "Eureka."[5]

There is little reason to go into a detailed report on Kissinger's visit to Beijing since it has been well documented and frequently reported and analyzed. In his memoir, he allocates 51 pages to his two day meetings with Zhou Enlai. Briefly, when he arrived, he quickly realized that the Chinese "had designed an almost improbable leisurely schedule." Before he met with Zhou, he had a four hour visit to the Forbidden City, and then had to wait until 4:30 P.M. to meet the premier. In total, Kissinger would have seven hours of formal meetings with Zhou on July 9 and six on July 10.

Kissinger was overwhelmed by his meetings with Zhou. He described him as "one of the two or three most impressive men I have ever met."[6] He was "short, elegant, with an expressive face, framing luminous eyes, he dominated by exceptional intelligence and capacity to intuit the intangibles of the psychology of his opposite number." "He had made himself indispensable as the crucial mediator between Mao and the people...translating Mao's sweeping visions into concrete programs. While Mao was always in charge, even when not present, Zhou was able to curb the Chairman's excesses...Mao was eager to accelerate history; Zhou was content to exploit its currents".

A saying he often repeated was "the helmsman (Mao) must ride with the waves."[7]

Taiwan was Zhou's first item on the July 9 agenda. Kissinger acknowledged that America was "not advocating a 'two China' solution or a 'one China, one Taiwan' solution." He believed that the political evolution of the problem would "be in the direction" which Zhou proposed, i.e. one China. But, this solution could not be immediately done.[8] America first had to establish a cease-fire in Vietnam and then bring the war to a close. Zhou hoped that this would be the beginning of America withdrawing all of her troops out of Asia including those in Japan, the Philippines, Thailand and South Korea. But this was said for effect, and wishful thinking. Of equal importance, was Kissinger's early remarks in which he addressed the ongoing talks with Moscow. He reassured Zhou that America would "never collude with other countries against the PRC, either with our allies, or with some of our opponents...To make these thoughts concrete, President Nixon has authorized me to tell you that the US will not take any major steps affecting your interests without discussing them with you and taking your views into account."[9]

Following a visit to the Imperial Palace, talks began in the morning of the second day. Zhou took a more aggressive stance knowing that Kissinger's main mission was to get an invitation for Nixon to visit Beijing. He reiterated his position on Taiwan that it would be absorbed into mainland China. He again raised the issue of America's troop presence throughout the Pacific Rim, viewing it as a threat to China. Zhou also feared a possible Moscow-Tokyo-Washington war on China, with the mainland divided between the three countries. All in all a very negative and confrontational approach to America within an international context. As a counter, the NSC advisor reassured Zhou that Nixon did not support a two China solution, and would make that clear after the upcoming presidential election in 1972. Washington had to be silent on several issues, especially normalization of relations, but these could be resolved shortly after Nixon's reelection.[10]

After lunch, the talks resumed and Kissinger worked to have Zhou offer an invitation to the president. He told the premier that the only president who could visit China was Nixon. "Other political leaders might use more honey-eyed words, but would be destroyed by what is called the 'China Lobby' in the US." Since Nixon's support came from the center and center-right he could be attacked by the conservative right, but would never be attacked by the liberal Democratic left. Zhou understood and said that after Chairman Mao "heard of the direction set by your president, he particularly wanted to meet with him because he could be able to talk about anything with him."[11] That settled the issue of an invitation, but the timing had to be addressed. Zhou wanted Nixon to visit after May 1, 1972. Kissinger had already set up a meeting in Moscow for August and he wanted to keep the two apart. He really preferred a meeting before May, so that he could use the Beijing meeting as pressure for his arms talks with Moscow. Zhou agreed to a pre-May meeting, with time to be determined. He also told Kissinger that he or another representative should come back to Beijing to work out the specifics of the president's visit. During the early hours of July 11, the two sides worked on the language which would be jointly announced on July 15. At that point, Kissinger sent a cable to the president, "Eureka."

Following his return to California, Kissinger gave Nixon a lengthy narrative of the meetings, and a two page conclusion, which described what he believed was important about a revived Sino-American relationship. "I am frank to say that this visit was a very moving experience. The historic aspects of the occasion the heroic stature of Zhou Enlai, and the intensity and sweep of our talks combined to make an indelible impression on me and my colleagues...We have laid the groundwork for you and Mao to turn a page in history." In promoting his accomplishment, Kissinger continued. "Furthermore, the process we have now started will send enormous shock waves around the world. It may panic the Soviet Union into sharp hostility. It could shake Japan loose from its heavily American moorings. It will cause a violent upheaval in Taiwan. It will have major impact on our other Asian allies, such as Korea and Thailand. It will increase the already substantial hostility in India. Some quarters may seek to sabotage the summit over the coming months...Our dealings, both with the Chinese and others, will require reliability, precision, finesse. If we can master this process, we will have made a revolution." Interesting to note, that the NSC advisor implies that the "we," refers to Kissinger and Nixon, not as in "we" the US.[12]

Nixon was ecstatic, but wanted to make sure that neither Kissinger nor Rogers eclipsed him in winning credit for the China initiative. He was especially concerned about Henry, who thoroughly enjoyed media coverage. "The magazines will want him for a cover. He is not to cooperate." As for the State Department, there would be considerable speculation, but it would be left in the dark for the time being. Later, Rogers could be brought up to speed.[13] On July 15, in a nationally televised address, Nixon spoke to the American nation in a speech that would "shake the world." "I talked for only three and a half minutes, but my words produced one of the greatest diplomatic surprises of the century." He told the world that he had been invited to China at a date before May 1972, and the purpose was to "seek the normalization of relations between the two countries and also to exchange views on questions of concern to the two sides."[14]

Soon the hard-line anti-Communists challenged the president including William F. Buckley, Arizona Senator Barry Goldwater and California Governor Ronald Reagan. However, the White House was prepared. It countered with the ongoing ABM talks with Moscow which would curb Moscow's drive for missile superiority. In Vietnam, the administration assured Nixon's detractors, that America would not abandon Thieu's government. Washington was also still committed to supporting Chiang Kai-shek's regime in Taiwan.

While these points took some of the sting out of Nixon's opponents, it did little to assuage Japan. Tokyo was very concerned about the talks. She thought she was America's anchor in the Pacific, and as such she should have been notified ahead of time of the Chinese talks. She would receive another surprise a few weeks later when Washington unilaterally imposed a 10% surcharge on imports, thereby effecting Japan's export trade. The tax stemmed from Nixon's August 15 decision to take America off the Gold Standard, a mechanism to regulate world currency which in 1944 valued gold at $35.00 per ounce. This 1944 Bretton Woods agreement lasted until 1971, when the price of gold was substantially higher, and America could no longer exchange $35.00 for one ounce of gold. Again, Japan was not given any foreknowledge and similar to other countries, had to quickly reevaluate her currency.[15]

Not unlike Japan, Congress had been left in the dark. Nixon met with bipartisan congressional leaders emphasizing that the meeting could never have taken place without secrecy. He met with his cabinet and told them that the "summit will not be a 'goodwill trip, it's not cosmetics, it's not to see China, it's to see the men, and build a new relationship." Rogers warned all branches of government that there was no "secret agreement" between Beijing and Washington, and reassured them that America stood by Taiwan via her mutual defense treaty. He cautioned that anyone who misspoke, would "be in deep trouble." But in true Nixon-Kissinger fashion, no one told Congress or anyone else, that the handwriting was on the wall, i.e. China would replace Taiwan in the UN, since there could only be one China seat.[16]

Direct communications with Beijing were still problematic. China had never experienced a presidential visit, with its accompaniment of White House staffers, advisors, and a brigade of reporters and media personnel. Since the president would only fly on Air Force One, political and technical problems arose since no American plane had flown into China since 1949. There was also the issue of China and the UN. Kissinger had told Zhou in his secret meeting that Washington was going to submit a resolution permitting both China and Taiwan to have seats in the UN. Zhou said that "dual representation in any form would not be accepted by Beijing; on the other hand China had existed for a long time without membership in the UN, and could wait a while longer." On August 16, Kissinger met with Beijing's French Ambassador Huang Zhen in Paris and suggested that his pre-presidential visit begin between October 18-20, because he was due back in Washington for a meeting with Tito, the Yugoslavian leader.[17]

In September, Kissinger noted, "we suddenly became aware that all of China's leaders had disappeared from public view for five days; all Chinese planes had been grounded for the same time. As the month wore on, it became clear that several leaders had been removed from office...foremost among the missing was Lin Biao, Minister of Defense...and... the heir and successor to Chairman Mao Xedong."[18] Soon the White House would learn that on September 12, Lin Biao and his family had died in an airplane crash over Mongolia. Later evidence suggested there was no crash, since there were no airplane parts or body parts found in the area where the supposed crash occurred. Rather, Mao had finally positioned himself to reassert his earlier claims, that the party controls the gun, unlike Lin who believed that his efforts in suppressing the violence prompted by the Cultural Revolution gave him equal status with the Chairman. Beijing would later cancel the annual parade on October 1 in honor of the Chinese Revolution.

In the interim, Kissinger had met with Huang Zhen in Paris, and the two agreed that his visit should begin on October 20. The ambassador wanted to make the announcement on October 14, instead of Washington's suggestion of September 21 or 22. Kissinger explained that he wanted to make the announcement before the arrival of Soviet Foreign Minister Andrei Gromyko to New York for his annual visit to the United Nations. He did not want the China announcement to look like a reaction to Gromyko's visit. Kissinger explained that he needed to check with Nixon as to the date for the announcement.[19]

On September 22, Washington lost a crucial vote in the UN. While it was a procedural question, it was important. The General Assembly decided to place an Albanian resolution granting Beijing full membership in the UN replacing Taiwan as the China representative. This resolution would be voted upon before the American resolution calling for a two country solution. The handwriting was on the wall. By September 30, Kissinger and Nixon knew that they had lost the vote, and that the timing of Kissinger's October visit would have no bearing on the outcome, while postponement would not change the results. During the UN debates, the Chinese representative notified Washington that the announcement of Nixon's visit could be made jointly on October 5.

Throughout all of this, Kissinger and Nixon had to fight Rogers. He strenuously objected to being left out of the October visit, arguing that it would interfere with our strategy on Chinese representation at the UN. According to Kissinger, Rogers was correct "in principle: presidents should not send emissaries who are independent of the Secretary of State."[20] However, Kissinger was not one known for standing on principles. His Metternichian approach to diplomacy and life, meant that principles were only important if they helped promote your own position.

On October 16, Kissinger set off on Marco Polo II, landing first in Hawaii and then in Guam, giving the advance party time to arrive in Beijing. Upon his arrival in the capital on October 20, he was greeted by signs such as "Overthrow the American imperialists and their running dogs." There were similar bulletins left in Kissinger's hotel rooms. Rather than dealing with ideology, he simply collected the pamphlets and handed them to a Chinese protocol officer, who received them without comment.[21]

From the first formal meeting on October 21, the principle topic was Taiwan, and China's right to assume control over the island. However, Zhou understood that this was not going to happen soon, but that did not end his discussion of the issue. One of the reasons for the meeting was to prepare China for Nixon's arrival. Considering that the president's and Mrs. Nixon's visit would be between five and seven days, Kissinger wanted to build a temporary installation at the airport, connected to a satellite, which would handle all television, radio and direct communication with the White House. He assured Zhou that his people would have total access to the installation, and could be in it at all times. Kissinger said that about 275 reporters would join the president in addition to a number of advisors as well as "several battalions" of technicians. There was also the question of the American Secret Service, dedicated to protecting the president wherever he went. While willing to accept members of the Service in China, Zhou insisted that the Chinese security service would provide the bulk of the protection, and would "liaise with the Secret Service." Discussion also included the return of four men detained in China, two CIA agents and two pilots who had violated Chinese airspace during the Vietnam War. Zhou said he would look into the CIA agents' situation. Richard Fecteau would be released on December 13, while John Downey's life sentence was reduced to five years. The pilots would remain in prison.[22]

On the evening of October 22, Kissinger went to the Great Hall of the People to see a "revolutionary" Beijing opera. He described the performance as "an art form of truly stupefying boredom in which villains were the incarnation of evil and wore black, good guys wore red, and as far as I could make out the girl fell in love with a tractor." On the following day, Kissinger visited the Great Wall and the Ming Tombs. In addition to visits, Kissinger and Zhou discussed Taiwan *ad infinitum*, and exchanged views on other international developments especially in Asia and in Moscow. Finally, the two agreed to the details of Nixon's upcoming trip. The date was set for February 21, 1972. The two and their staffs spent fifteen hours drafting a final communiqué, which would be made public at the close of the Nixon visit. The communiqué produced very strong reactions as each side tried to bully the other into accepting language that seriously challenged and conflicted with their announced positions. Taiwan was the most difficult issue. The two sides argued and fought throughout the day and night on October 25, the date Kissinger had to leave. Talks continued into the next morning. At 8:10 a.m. on October 26, both sides reached agreement on Taiwan. Kissinger had adapted a phrase from a State Department planning document for negotiations which had aborted in the 1950s. Zhou and Kissinger agreed that "the US acknowledge that all Chinese on either side of the Taiwan Straits maintain there is but one China. The US does not challenge that position." While there were still loose ends, Kissinger and Zhou were certain that they could be resolved in February. While other issues were included in the communiqué, the Taiwan piece was what the meeting had been all about.[23]

During the meetings, Nixon told Kissinger to postpone his return to Washington by a day. The White House correctly anticipated the UN vote and preferred that Kissinger was not in town during the defeat of the American resolution, principally to save face. As expected on October 25, the UN General Assembly voted to replace Taipei with Beijing as the official representative of China. The American delegate, having failed to secure support for a dual membership, did not cast a ballot. The vote forced Taiwan out of the Security Council and the General Assembly and left her outside the international organization. She would annually request admission to return through 2009, but each time Beijing vetoed her request, as Taipei had vetoed China's request since 1949. Kissinger's plane was rerouted to Anchorage, Alaska "for repairs" and arrived in Washington on the twenty-sixth in time for him to have dinner with Nixon that evening.[24] On November 29, Washington and Beijing announced that the president and Mrs. Nixon would arrive in Beijing on February 21 for a seven day visit, with one night spent in Hangzhou, to accommodate a request by the First Lady.

Following his return, Kissinger met with the ROC's Ambassador Shen to reassure him that the UN vote did not affect America's commitment to the defense treaty. He shared very little information with Shen even to the date of the president's visit. Shen was very concerned and asked Kissinger "what did the US want them, the ROC, to do? Mr. Kissinger responded emphatically that we wanted them to stay alive, and to maintain their integrity and their identity. We would do what we could to support them, and to keep them in as many international organizations as possible." Kissinger assured Shen that the impact from the UN vote and any results from the president's visit would not be felt until 1973. Shen quoted rumors from Hong Kong that Taipei wanted to reach out to Beijing. Kissinger thought that this was "very ill-advised." If they did so, the White House would not participate; it would be their doing and their problem.[25]

In addition to making preparations for the Nixon visit, the White House was involved in bringing the final touches to the ABM treaty, the terms of which had been agreed to in May, but were put on hold by Moscow to resolve some issues concerning Berlin. There was also the Strategic Arms Limitation Talks (SALT) which needed closure before the Moscow summit the following May, as well as the ongoing Vietnam peace talks in Paris.[26] While all of the above took time, according to Kissinger the India-Pakistan war of 1971 was "perhaps the most complex issue of Nixon's first term" and it played out in Washington throughout the fall and into the first half of December. It would be especially memorable for the fierce division between the State Department and the White House, the former supporting Pakistan, and the latter India. The Rogers-Kissinger December meetings revealed not only philosophical differences, but "personality clashes that did neither of us any credit."

The origin of the war stemmed from a 1947 decision by Britain, the latest conquering power, to grant independence to India and Pakistan, dividing the latter into two parts along religious lines resulting in two countries, East and West Pakistan. The West was dominated by the Punjab, and the East, by Bengali, and the two were separated by about 1,000 miles of India. The primary common ground between the East and West was their Muslim religion, in contrast to India's Hinduism. Pakistan "looked on its larger neighbor with fear, with resentment, and occasionally with hatred."[27] To complicate matters a bit more, there was Kashmir, a disputed state occupied by China, India and Pakistan.

India's democracy attracted support in Congress, while Nixon had been well treated by Pakistan when he was out of office, and he did not forget his cordial reception. Historically, Pakistan had been unable to maintain a stable government, with each one being the result of a coup, either civilian or military. In 1970, Yahya Kahn was in charge, and had close ties to Nixon, especially as a channel for Nixon to reach Beijing in preparation for his visit to the Middle Kingdom. Kahn had approved elections to form a constitutional government for East and West Pakistan. He anticipated that his role would be to arbitrate, since he envisioned that the two parts would be constantly arguing and threatening each other. On November 12-13, a devastating cyclone struck East Pakistan killing upwards of 200,000 people. Millions of refugees fled to India. Recovery efforts were slow and ineffective, and soon the people blamed the Yahya Kahn government. In December, the scheduled elections took place, and the East Pakistan results called for independence from West Pakistan. Islamabad quickly responded arresting leaders of the independence movement and imposed martial law in March, 1971. During the next several months, the military brutally suppressed thousands of civilian demonstrators.

Washington stayed out of the fray, since Pakistan was America's best conduit to China. In secret, Kissinger called a meeting of the Washington Special Action Group, or WSAG. It was an NSC committee for contingency planning and crisis management to consider the impact of an independent East Pakistan, to be called Bangladesh. Of concern, were the possible actions of Moscow and Beijing. The Soviet Union was a long time ally of India, and had supplied her with war materials. On August 9, the two countries signed a Treaty of Peace, Friendship and Cooperation, as their way of balancing the growing link between Washington and Beijing. If nothing else, the treaty reaffirmed China's view of India as an enemy. One which could threaten her, especially in her rather injured state following the Cultural Revolution. At the WSAG meetings, there was little progress since Rogers maintained the State Department's long time support of India, and Kissinger threw his weight behind Pakistan. In the meantime, India continued to support East Pakistan's demands for independence, and helped to train, equip and encourage guerillas to infiltrate East Pakistan to maintain the unstable conditions in Dhaka, the capital city. Efforts to bring the UN into play consistently failed, due to the Soviet veto.

On November 4, Indira Gandhi, the Prime Minister of India visited the Oval Office. She assured the president that "India has never wished for the destruction of Pakistan or its permanent crippling...We want to eliminate chaos at all costs." A month later, the Indian army attacked East Pakistan at the same time that fighting erupted along the West Pakistan border. Gandhi had lied to Nixon. East Pakistan had no chance to protect herself from the Indian invasion. The White House wanted to make sure that Moscow did not get involved, and Nixon sent a letter to Brezhnev implying that if Moscow and Washington did not work together to solve the subcontinent issue, there might not be a May summit. The president knew that Brezhnev really wanted the meeting, especially for its arms control agreements. Intelligence reports indicated that Mrs. Gandhi planned to turn her attention to West Pakistan since the East Pakistan government was crumbling. She also announced that not only would

India "liberate" East Pakistan but it would do the same in the Pakistani controlled area of Kashmir.[28]

Nixon decided that if there were to be a war, Pakistan should go on the offensive first and attack India. The president looked to get some help from Beijing, even if they simply moved some troops toward the Indian border. China said no, knowing that she had nothing to gain. As the old expression goes, "she did not have a dog in the fight." Nixon turned again to Brezhnev for help to restore order to the area, and to make his point more clearly, on December 10 he sent the nuclear aircraft carrier *Enterprise* and nine accompanying warships to the Bay of Bengal.[29]

On the same day, the Pakistani commander in East Pakistan offered a cease fire. Immediately, the White House feared that India could quickly move her troops from East Pakistan to West Pakistan and crush the invading West Pakistani forces. On December 11, Kissinger sent Moscow an ultimatum, that Washington needed assurances that India would not move against West Pakistan. The following day, Moscow assured the president that "India had no aggressive designs in the West." On December 16, the Pakistani commander in East Pakistan surrendered, and on the following day Pakistan and India agreed to an unconditional cease fire in the West. There would be no attack on either West Pakistan or Kashmir.[30]

The Indo-Pakistani War, albeit relatively short-lived, had numerous repercussions. Moscow was able to strengthen her ties to India while Delhi's actions made her the significant player in South Asia. She had removed a thorn in her side by replacing East Pakistan with a friendly Bangladesh. China had shown that she was not strong enough to become involved, since the involvement could include Moscow, and Beijing was in no position following the Cultural Revolution and the disappearance of Lin Biao to take any military action. She rebuffed Washington's request to move her troops closer to the Indian border, fearing that Moscow would move her troops closer to China. Beijing had nothing to gain by threatening India. She was more concerned about aiding Pakistan. The US had preferred staying out of the fray rather than risk her multipolarity approach of improving relations with Moscow and Beijing, by playing one off against the other. America's movement of her navy into Bay of Bengal, was the highpoint of Washington's involvement, but it was only designed to be a show of force. America stayed on the sidelines and with support from Moscow helped bring an end to the war leaving intact a West Pakistan and a status quo in Kashmir. Delhi-Washington relations deteriorated. Nixon's encounter with Indira Gandhi, whom he called a "bitch," and "that goddamn woman...suckering us" concerning her intentions toward East Pakistan, set a tone of distrust which would have repercussions for the next several administrations.[31] During the affair, Secretary of State Rogers, who as usual was left out of the Kissinger-Nixon strategies, became confrontational. This resulted in nothing but acrimony between the State Department and the White House, to the point that secrecy trumped progress in Washington's dealing with the war. Ultimately, Rogers would lose when Kissinger replaced him as secretary of state. As for West Pakistan, soon to be called Pakistan, she was left naked and more dependent on America and China for survival.

CHAPTER VI

NIXON GOES TO CHINA

In preparation for his visit to the Middle Kingdom, the president sent Kissinger's deputy General Alexander Haig to meet with Zhou Enlai on January 3, 1972. Nixon was paranoid about the visit, wanting it to be so successful as to undermine congressional opposition. Haig explained this problem to the Chinese. There "is a strange merger of forces within the US—all dedicated to either preventing the president's visit to Beijing or to contributing to its failure. The forces which have converged are composed of "the American Left which is essentially pro-Soviet...the Left has been joined in a strange wedding with those conservative elements who are strong supporters of Taiwan. A third area of difficulty for us...is a degree of bureaucratic haggling concerning the wisdom of the initiative to visit Beijing (read Rogers versus Kissinger)." To help counter the opposition, Haig asked Zhou Enlai if China would "reconsider very carefully the language in the Joint Communiqué that pertains to Taiwan, and hopefully agree to a formulation that is somewhat less truthful and somewhat less precise than the language which Dr. Kissinger carried away with him" following his October visit.[1]

To give the president as much support as possible, Haig wanted to prevent any "public embarrassment to the president as a result of his visit to Beijing. It is in our mutual interest that the visit reinforce President Nixon's image as a world leader." And to facilitate this, Haig made sure that the media accompanying the president were television people. Since most Americans did not read, television was the best medium to reach the electorate. China offered the convenience of a country thirteen hours ahead of the US meaning that morning events in China could be watched during the evening, and evening events in China would be on American television sets in the morning. The key to success was Beijing's cooperation. As Kissinger wrote, "fortunately for us, the Chinese had time-honored ways of withstanding barbarian invaders. Once they understood what the advance men had in mind, the veterans of the Long March immediately grasped the benefit of being introduced on American television by an American President and thus becoming immediately acceptable."[2] As a good will gesture three days before his departure, Nixon announced a serious reduction of trade sanctions against China. All commodities available for sale in the Soviet Union and Eastern Europe would be available to the PRC.

The China visit has been covered in detail by numerous historians and journalists. In addition to the *Foreign Relations of the United States* documents, there are numerous day-by-day accounts of serious conversations and site seeing ventures. One of the best for daily coverage is Margaret Macmillan's *Nixon and Mao: The Week That Changed the World* .Rather than replicate her work, and that of many others, the following will only detail the major developments during the president's eight day visit to the Middle Kingdom.

Nixon left Andrews Air Force Base on February 16 in *Air Force One* which the president renamed the *Spirit of '76* and flew to Beijing via Hawaii, Guam and Shanghai. Kissinger reminded him the Chinese were "fanatic and pragmatic." While they may disagree with Washington's world vision, they are aware that they need America because of the Soviet threat, a resurgent Japan and Taiwan. He reminded the president, that while he was concerned about the outcomes of his visit, so too were Mao and Zhou. They were in their seventies, and they wanted to provide China with security before they died. They had taken a gamble, considering the fallout from the Cultural Revolution and the death of Lin Biao, the heir apparent. "They will need to show some immediate results for their domestic audience."[3]

Upon his arrival in Beijing on the 21st, Nixon left the plane alone, leaving Kissinger, Rogers and the rest of the White House retinue behind. He wanted this to be his show and no one was to leave the plane until he had reached out and shaken hands with Zhou Enlai. This was to undo the insult by John Foster Dulles who refused to shake hands with Zhou in Geneva in 1954. The hand shake was well choreographed and televised worldwide. After a quick motorcade ride through nearly empty streets in Beijing, which appeared to be an anomaly, the president arrived at the guest house in the center of town. Within hours of their arrival, Zhou suddenly announced that Mao was ready to meet the president and Dr. Kissinger. If anyone thought of bringing the secretary of state along for the meeting, no one mentioned it.

Throughout the seven days of talks, Zhou and Mao usually placed topics within an historical context. In reviewing the past, China normally portrayed herself as being the victim of Western aggression, and poorly treated. A principle objective of this summit was to show that the past, was in the past. There was a new China, and Mao and Zhou made sure that the results of the meetings would project an image that Beijing was at least equal to the US. The 2:30 p.m. meeting was a type of get-to-know-you gathering. Kissinger was overwhelmed being in the presence of Mao. "This was the colossus into whose presence we were now being ushered." "Mao just stood there surrounded by books, tall and powerfully built for a Chinese…I have met no one, with the possible exception of Charles de Gaulle, who so distilled raw, concentrated will power…he dominated the room…by exuding in almost tangible form the overwhelming drive to prevail."[4]
During their discussions, Mao acknowledged Kissinger's ability to keep his first trip to Beijing a secret. Nixon added that while he did not look like "a secret agent. He is the only man in captivity who could go to Paris (for Vietnam negotiations) twelve times and Beijing once, and no one knew it—except possibly a couple of pretty girls." The conversations ran the gamut of concern about Moscow's world

ambitions, and issues in Asia, but not Taiwan. The chairman described the island "as not an important" topic. "Rather the small issue is Taiwan, the big issue is the world." Each day's meetings concluded with a dinner banquet accented by multiple glasses of Mao Tai followed by toasts. Nixon gave the first toast and said "let us, in these next five days, start a long march together, not in lock-step but on different roads leading to the same goal...The world watches. The world listens. The world waits to see what we will do.... Seize the day, seize the hour. For this is the hour, this is the day for our two peoples to rise to the heights of greatness which can build a new and better world."[5]

On the 22rd, Nixon wanted Zhou to know what his position was on Taiwan. He referred to Kissinger's five principles announced earlier and reiterated them as his own. The first was that "there is one China, and Taiwan is part of China." Second, America will not support any Taiwan independence movement. Washington would use its influence to insure that Japan did not play a large role in Taiwan, and would not support any Taiwan efforts to return to the mainland. Finally, "we seek the normalization of relations with the PRC," while recognizing that Taiwan is an issue needing resolution before normalization can occur. He restated some of Kissinger's earlier concerns about congressional reaction, and to reduce the tension language needed to be found to prevent those opposed to closer Beijing-Washington relations saying that "the American President went to Beijing and sold Taiwan down the river."[6]

The conversation moved to other topics including India where Washington and Beijing shared different views, with the former viewing her as a potential enemy and a threat to China's ally Pakistan. Beijing viewed Japan as long time opponent and feared Tokyo's increased presence in Taiwan and Korea. Zhou urged Nixon to rapidly withdraw American troops out of Indochina, including Vietnam, Cambodia and Laos. Nixon noted that since he came into office, he had withdrawn 400,000 of the original 500,000 present when he entered the White House and while he intended to continue the withdrawals, America could not completely abandon Saigon. He could not "remove the government of South Vietnam and in effect turn over the government to the North Vietnamese."[7] After the meeting, Kissinger talked with Qiao Guanhua, the Deputy Foreign Minister, and gave him a rundown of Soviet forces along the Sino-Soviet border, including troops, aircraft and missiles. He promised that he would continue to provide this intelligence and would do so until 1975 when Sino-American relations soured.[8] Following a banquet, Nixon, Mao and their staff watched a ballet, "The Red Detachment of Women," a wonderful mix of propaganda and skilled performers.

Nixon, Zhou and Kissinger met on the afternoon of February 23 amidst a snow storm. And for the first time, Rogers participated in talks, albeit in a different building, with the Chinese Foreign Minister, Chi P'eng-fei. The secretary of state was not satisfied with this situation, although his title was commiserate with that of a foreign minister. Rogers would continue to complain through Haldeman that by virtue of his position, he should be involved in the Mao-Nixon talks. Kissinger showed no interest in including him in the discussions; Henry wanted to make sure that he, and he alone, would share the spotlight in Beijing.[9] Talks on the 23rd concerned international issues including more of the history of India-Chinese relations, Beijing's concern about Japan, and the background to the Sino-Soviet split resulting in rather testy relations between Beijing and Moscow. The evening banquet was hosted by the president and the Chinese kitchen cooked up a "delicious American dinner" with fish, steak, vegetables, ice cream and pastries, followed by an athletic exhibition in the gymnasium.[10]

After the snow stopped on the following day, Nixon and his entourage visited the Great Wall and the Ming tombs, returning for a rather lengthy meeting from 5-8 p.m. The communiqué which would be jointly announced was the purpose of the discussions. Zhou wanted the Five Principles of Peaceful Coexistence included, of which the most important to Nixon was an agreement to normalize relations, while Zhou focused on language calling for non-interference in the domestic affairs of one another which included Taiwan.[11] Nixon had known that this would be the issue that would make or break the communiqué and possibly the normalization of relations. The communiqué could be written so that it gave his opponents the opportunity to say that he had come "16,000 miles in order to repudiate a commitment to the government on Taiwan, this could poison our relationship in the months ahead." He needed "running room" within the language of the communiqué, it could not be rigid, but at the same time it had to meet the needs of Beijing as well. He told Zhou that he did not see a permanent American military presence on the island, and was willing to work for the gradual withdrawal of all troops following a resolution of the Vietnam War. He envisioned the total withdrawal to take about four years, half way into his expected second administration. He also reiterated that he would not support a Taiwan Independence Movement.[12] In light of the growing importance of the communiqué and the little time remaining, Nixon assigned Kissinger to work with Qiao Guanhua, the Vice Minister of Foreign Affairs, to find language that would meet the needs of both parties. In the time remaining, Zhou again showed his concern about an aggressive Japan. He reminded Nixon that "a state of war actually still exists today between China and Japan because the so-called peace treaty with Chiang Kai-shek cannot count; even Chang Kai-shek admits that."[13] Nixon reassured Zhou that America's defense commitment with Japan would safeguard China's interests. The day ended with a Peking Duck banquet for the official party in the Great Hall of the People, with more Mai Tais and toasts.

Throughout the visit, television crews were permitted to show footage of the Nixon party visiting tourist sites and enjoying the evening banquets. Without question, the visit reinforced and expanded the positive image established by the ping-pong team's visit the prior

66

April. However, the number of tourist attractions that were scheduled during the visit began to strain Nixon's nerves. "He was bored." He had trouble sleeping, was tired and grumpy.[14] And the agenda for February 25 did little to sooth his feelings. It began with another television opportunity showing the president's visit to the Forbidden City. During the afternoon meeting, Zhou spent considerable time reviewing Sino-Soviet relations, noting that there were numerous differences especially concerning the geographic border between the two, and different ideologies. He was quite concerned that Beijing not be sacrificed on the altar of a Soviet-American rapprochement at their upcoming summit scheduled for May. He was especially concerned since Moscow and Washington each were far better militarily prepared for a conflict than Beijing. She was vulnerable, and needed to make sure that Moscow and Washington did not broker a deal effecting China. The meeting also highlighted the need for Kissinger and Qiao Guanhua to speed up their work on the final communiqué, since on the following day the Nixon's were going to visit Hangzhou as their first stop on their return to the US.

Prior to departing for Hangzhou, there was a brief gathering of the principals on the 26th including the first inclusion of Secretary of State Rogers and his Chinese counterpart. The two quickly described their work including improved visa regulations to facilitate Chinese visits to America, agreements on cultural exchanges as well as more people-to-people contacts including members of the scientific, medical and educational communities. Throughout this meeting, no one mentioned the communiqué, and Rogers continued to be left in the dark.[15]

Nixon's mood had not improved since the last evening's banquet. The pressure of not having the communiqué written, along with mixed reactions around the world concerning the visit, left the president sullen, and angry. He assumed that his visit would be seen by most as a signature move toward world peace, but he was unsure. The degree of Nixon's angst is well documented by Margaret

Macmillan. While they were sitting in the airport awaiting their flight, Zhou tried to lighten the moment noting various pictures of China on the walls. "Nixon tried to ignore him, but was eventually forced to look. His smile grew strained, then disappeared. 'What the hell are you talking about?' he snapped." If Zhou understood, he remained silent.[16]

Hangzhou is a beautiful summer resort replete with lakes and gardens. Even though it was cloudy, the Nixons enjoyed seeing the "mountains rise mistily in the background, and the lakes…full of lotus flowers. The pagoda-like guesthouse…was set in the middle of a lake." The two remembered their stay in Hangzhou as "the most delightful interlude of the trip."[17]

On the morning of the 27th, the American and Chinese teams flew to Shanghai on Zhou's plane. Upon arrival, the Shanghai Revolutionary Committee provided a tour for Pat Nixon to a school, and the president to an industrial exhibition. At the same time, Kissinger was working out the final details of the communiqué, and at 5:30 p.m. he gave the assembled journalists a sketch of the main points. The final document was unique. It was the first time ever in a communiqué that both sides included areas where they could not find accommodation, as well as areas of agreement.

Washington's Preface included its support of individual freedom and social progress for all people, free of outside intervention. She would withdraw forces from Indochina, continue to support South Korea, maintain close relations with Japan, and support the India-Pakistan cease fire. Beijing's opening statement was more ideological emphasizing the right of rebellion against oppression, safeguarding a nation's independence, and the withdrawal of all foreign troops to their home nations. Both sides accepted the Five Principles of Peaceful Coexistence first enunciated in 1954. In conformity with these principles, both sides agreed that "progress toward the normalization of relations between China and the US is in the interests of all countries." Both agreed not to seek hegemony in

68

the Asia-Pacific region and to oppose efforts by any other nation to do so. Finally, both agreed that major countries ought not divide up the world in spheres of interest. As for Taiwan, both sides saw her as the main obstacle to normalization, but both agreed that in the final analysis, Taiwan was a domestic issue for Beijing. Nixon also agreed to the gradual withdrawal of troops and military installations from the island. The original version had called for the "final withdrawal" but the president had "final" removed; he needed running room to keep his congressional opponents at bay. Both sides agreed to strengthen their connections in science, technology, culture, journalism and people-to-people exchanges as well as an increase in trade.[18]

No sooner had the draft been approved by Nixon and the Chinese Politburo, a casualty of secrecy soon appeared. When Rogers and his staff member Marshall Green, a State Department China expert, saw the communiqué they saw a major error, one of omission. Among the countries enumerated that America would support from Japan to New Zealand, Taiwan was not mentioned. This was reminiscent of Dulles' famous Press Club remarks in January, 1950 when in describing America's Asian commitments omitted Korea. Rogers wanted the communiqué changed and finally managed to see Nixon. According to Haldeman, the "P hit Bill [Rogers] hard,' and told him to "stay behind us 100 per cent," which Rogers did.[19] The omission was deliberate to accommodate Beijing. In his book, *On China*, Kissinger ignores the Taiwan omission, and in his memoir he labeled Rogers' concerns as nit-picking and trivial.

With everything settled, Beijing and Washington simultaneously announced their Shanghai Communiqué on February 27. At the final banquet, Nixon declared that the communiqué provided a foundation "in the years ahead to build a bridge across 16,000 miles and twenty-two years of hostility which has divided us in the past." He raised his glass in the final toast saying "we have been here a week. This was the week that changed the world."[20]

On the morning after, Nixon had one last meeting with Zhou assuring the Communist leader that the record of their discussions would remain secret, even from the American government. They both agreed not to attack each other unnecessarily, and that Taiwan was still a sticking point between the two governments. But Zhou saw the issue in a different light. "We, being so big, have already let the Taiwan issue remain for twenty—two years, and can still afford to let it wait there for a time."[21] At the close of their last talks, the two men knew that they had built a bridge for future generations to cross. The Nixon entourage and accompanying journalists left Shanghai and flew back to Washington via Anchorage, Alaska.

So what was the effect of the China visit and the Shanghai Communiqué? Two sets of responses are required: immediate and within an historical context. Initially, the Asian nations felt themselves vulnerable. South Korea was not convinced that China wanted stability in the peninsula, Taiwan believed that she had been sold down the river, the Japanese, who had never been given an early warning about the Sino-American summit, were convinced that the two countries had made agreements to the detriment of Tokyo, and in South Vietnam, Laos and Cambodia, whose governments were totally dependent on Washington, little was said, but each feared that the summit may have jeopardized their future.

As for the American press, which had been ignored throughout the negotiations due to the Kissinger-Nixon-Zhou decision to maintain total secrecy, the journalists decided to get even. According to Kissinger, they "fell upon the Shanghai Communiqué like tigers on raw meat thrown into their cage." *The Washington Post* carried a story on February 28 that "President Nixon has acceded to Chinese Communist demands by pledging, for the first time, to withdraw all American forces and military installations from Taiwan." The *Detroit Free Press* observed "They got Taiwan, we got egg rolls," and *The Boston Globe* headline read: "Nixon makes concessions on Taiwan, Pledges Pullout." But within days, the firestorm ended especially after Nixon arrived in Washington and explained that America had not reduced its defense treaty with Taipei. The *Christian Science Monitor* best summarized the president position, "what President Nixon agreed to was what he was going to do anyway." On the 29[th,] *The Washington Post* backed off its prior day's bombast and in an editorial defended Nixon against a "sell out" of Taiwan. Upon his arrival at Andrews Air Force Base, a bipartisan contingent of congressmen and the vice president gave him a triumphal welcome. On the following day, he met with the bipartisan leadership of both houses of Congress and received strong support. And as weeks went by, America viewed the trip as a great success.[22]

As for the long term impact of the Shanghai Communiqué, Nixon and Kissinger deserved nothing but plaudits. Nixon was able to compartmentalize Taiwan and Vietnam, enabling him to deal with Mao and Zhou on the larger picture of politics in greater Asia. The summit resulted in a significant change in international relations, there were now three superpowers, giving Washington the ability to play one off against the other for America's interests. The inclusion of anti-hegemonic clauses in the communiqué initially focused on Asia, but within the year it would be common language among the great powers. This would soon be seen in the Moscow summit in May in which both sides agreed to work toward a détente and promote "peaceful coexistence." And as evidence, the two would soon sign the ABM and SALT I treaties, each of which aimed to limit nuclear weapons. And of all the principles agreed to in the Shanghai Communiqué, the most important and far reaching was an agreement to "progress toward the normalization of relations between China and the US." Work would begin on this shortly after Nixon's return to establish liaison offices in each country, but in the interim communication would continue in Paris through Arthur Watson, the American Ambassador to France and his Chinese counterpart, Huang Zhen. Issues requiring direct correspondence between Nixon and Zhou, would be done via a secret channel in New York, through

Huang Hua, recently reassigned to be China's Ambassador to the United Nations. Concerned that secrecy could be violated by the State Department, Nixon sent Rogers a note. "There will be no further public commentary or elaboration on the substantive talks or the communiqué of the China visit...There should be no further reiteration of the maintenance of our defense commitments...There should be no further elaboration of the Communiqué language on U.S. forces on Taiwan." Rogers concurred and suggested that China be increasingly referred to as the PRC, and Taiwan as the ROC.[23]

Looking back at Nixon's 1967 "Asia After Vietnam" article in *Foreign Affairs*, some of his ideas seem prophetic. He wrote, "the world cannot be safe until China changes. Thus our aim, to the extent that we can influence events, should be to induce change. The way to do this is to persuade China that it must change...and that its own national interests require a turning away from foreign adventuring and a turning inward toward the solution of its own domestic problems."

Following his election he continued to reach out to Beijing and that along with the end of the Cultural Revolution, and the realization that she was vulnerable to a nuclear armed Moscow, forced China to realize that she was unable to go it alone. Washington appeared to be the balance needed against Soviet threats, and provide her time and space needed for domestic development, the stepping stone to becoming a major player in the world community.

CHAPTER VII

NORMALIZATION INTERRUPTED:
ABM, SALT AND PEACE IN VIETNAM

The Nixon visit had done little to resolve the war in Vietnam, and this became obvious on March 30, 1972 when Hanoi launched a major offensive across the demilitarized zone. While the White House had anticipated a spring offensive, it was surprised by the size of the invading force, numbering over 120,000 troops.[1] Nixon responded and on April 16 ordered the resumption of intensive bombing in the north including Hanoi and Haiphong harbor. While this risked compromising some of the progress made during his Beijing visit, he wanted the PRC to know that resolution of the Vietnam War was his first priority. While maintaining peace talks in Paris, Nixon changed the conduct of the war, reducing the number of combat troops on the ground, replacing them with increased air attacks. On May 8, he notified Beijing that he was going to mine all North Vietnamese ports, and to intercept any vessels carrying supplies to the North Vietnamese troops in the South as a means to quickly end the war. He reassured Beijing, as he had in the past, that America had no interest in winning a war, she simply wanted to insure that the South Vietnamese could determine their own political future.[2]

As Nixon and Zhou had compartmentalized Taiwan and the PRC, Nixon aimed to do the same with Vietnam and the PRC. While showing his commitment to the survival of South Vietnam, he did not want to jeopardize the improved relations with the PRC. Beijing, too, wanted to maintain good relations and since the agreement called for increased bilateral trade, she invited forty American businessmen to visit the Chinese Export Commodities Fair in Canton in the spring and fall of 1972. The meeting resulted in an increase in bilateral trade from 5 million dollars in 1971, to 95 million in 1972, and to over 800 million in 1973.[3] During trade talks, Zhou indicated that China would like to have her exports receive MFN status. However, the administration had already decided that MFN would not be awarded until other issues were resolved. Foremost was a resolution of American business claims against Beijing since 1949 following her seizure of all American companies' properties and products.[4]

The Shanghai Communiqué also called for greater "people-to-people" contacts. To facilitate travel, Rogers had the visa requirements for China eased and quickly US congressmen lined up to visit Beijing. The first were the two leading Senators, Mansfield, a Democrat, and Scott, a Republican, and did so with their wives from April 18-May 3. They would later be followed by congressmen Boggs and Ford in June who met privately with Zhou. The premier was concerned about America's upcoming presidential election, and statements made by the Democratic Party nominee, George McGovern, and his campaign pledge to reduce the Pentagon's budget by $30 billion. Zhou hoped this did not occur, since he saw such a move would weaken America's involvement in Europe thereby permitting Moscow to increase pressure on Beijing. Neither congressmen made any comment, but the message had been heard.[5] "People-to-people" also permitted a visit by the PRC's table tennis team including a meeting with Nixon. The doors were open, and reciprocal visits grew in number.

With the China piece in play, Nixon turned his attention to the Soviet Union, the other part needed for his multi-polar foreign policy. As announced the previous October, Nixon prepared for his summit in Moscow. The ongoing SALT negotiations in Helsinki and Vienna, first begun on November 17, 1969 and pushed along by a May 20, 1971 agreement, were put on a fast track. The lengthy negotiations were fueled by the asymmetrical weapons systems which would pose some problems in Congress, but supported by the Pentagon. Finally, on May 12, the Soviets indicated that agreements could be reached, and ten days later Nixon arrived in Moscow for his fourth visit to the Soviet capital, the first as the Vice President in 1959, and as a tourist in 1965 and 1967. This time he came as the first American president to visit the city. On the flight to Vnokovo airport, Kissinger spent time with the secretary of state explaining to him the background of the weapons talks, which had proceeded without Roger's involvement. On May 26, Nixon and Brezhnev put the finishing touches on two treaties. The ABM treaty, whose details had been agreed upon in 1971, permitting both sides to have only two Anti-Ballistic Missile sites, one to protect its capital and the other as an ICBM launch area. The site could contain up to 100 interceptor missiles and 100 launchers to insure retaliation if necessary. The US decided to develop only one protected site, that being its launch area in the Mid-West. The treaty would be reviewed in five years, and every five years thereafter. Following ratification, the ABM treaty came into force on October 3, 1972.

SALT was the other five year agreement, and it called for limitations, but not reductions. The treaty froze land-based and submarine launched offensive weapons at their current level of production for five years. Critics of the treaty quickly pointed out that there were imbalances. SALT left the Soviets ahead in ICBMs (Intercontinental Ballistic Missiles) and SLBMs (Submarine Launched Ballistic Missiles). On the other hand, the agreement maintained Washington's superiority in long-range bombers, short-range bombers and missiles launched from aircraft carriers as well as missiles supplied to   NATO allies. There was also no mention of MIRVs (Multiple Independently Targeted Reentry Vehicles), a single warhead which could contain multiple missiles, defying efforts to accurately assess America's missile stockpile. This improvement would take the Soviets nearly five years to match. While many in Congress were concerned about conceding any advantage to the Russians, MIRVed weapons helped the legislature approve the ABM agreement along with the SALT treaty.

On the last day of the summit, May 29, both sides signed a Basic Principles of Relations Between the US and the Union of Soviet

Socialist Republics (USSR). It was a contract for détente. Of the eleven principles three contained the core agreements. The first called for both sides to maintain peaceful coexistence and not interfere in either country's internal affairs. The second emphasized the importance of avoiding military confrontation which could lead to nuclear war. The third promised that both countries would work to "promote conditions in which all countries will live in peace and security." While Washington did not give much weight to the agreement, Moscow certainly did. To Brezhnev and the Politburo, the Basic Principles, a formula used between NATO countries and the US, meant that Moscow was equal to Washington in international circles. Further, it was evidence that the White House had accepted "peaceful coexistence" as the bases of relations between the two superpowers. This was most important to the Kremlin since she knew that she was unprepared for an American attack, and would spend the next six years building an armed force equal to the US. Shortly after the summit, the two countries signed an Agreement on the Prevention of Nuclear War. The idea was to talk before taking action, meaning that America did not have to immediately respond in the event of a Soviet attack on Europe. Only Britain, among the NATO countries, would sign the agreement.[6]

The ratification debates on the ABM and SALT talks enabled those congressmen, who were furious about being kept in the dark, an opportunity to express their displeasure. And while the treaties would finally be ratified on October 3, 1972 they were done so with a resolution designed by Senator Henry Jackson requiring all subsequent arms control agreements guarantee at least parity in all arms treaties. However, Jackson was not through. He did not believe in détente, opposed any concessions to the Soviet Union, and wanted to force Moscow to change her emigration procedures, as he had indicated in the previous congressional session. Anticipating that détente would produce more legislative activity involving Soviet relations, especially trade, Jackson would wait for the right opportunity to amend a much desired administration bill to force Moscow to alter her emigration practices.

As planned, Kissinger returned to Beijing on June 20, three days after an apparently innocent break-in at the Democratic Party headquarters at the Watergate, an office-condominium complex. Few people would care about the event until after the Nixon's reelection in November. Meanwhile, Kissinger met with Zhou Enlai and, as promised earlier, shared information about Nixon's Moscow summit. The NSC advisor assured Zhou that "we do not do reciprocal things in Moscow. The reason we do it with you is because of our evaluation of the relative intentions of the two allied Communist countries."[7] Kissinger gave him copies of agreements signed in Moscow, except for the SALT treaty. He spoke about Moscow's interest in having an agreement not to use nuclear weapons against each other. While this sounded logical, if agreed to, America could then not use nuclear weapons to defend Europe against Soviet aggression. His explanation implicitly rejected Zhou's suggestion that all countries agree to not being the first to use nuclear weapons.[8]

Discussion moved to a solution to the Vietnam War, but without much progress. America was not willing to remove Thieu from power, while Hanoi had this as a *sine qua non* for peace. Zhou was not impressed by Washington's willingness to withdraw nearly all her forces, but not her support to Saigon. In what Zhou called America's "tail" in South Vietnam, it did not require a large troop deployment, only a commitment to defend Saigon in the event of an attack. Kissinger said the "tail" was only needed until the Vietnamese accepted a ceasefire upon which Washington would withdraw her last troops in exchange for the return of American prisoners-of-war.[9]

As usual with talks between Kissinger and Zhou, most areas of the world were topics for discussion, especially India. The premier was quite concerned about Delhi's efforts to dominate the subcontinent. Zhou saw this as India's first step to seize West Pakistan, similar to her success in East Pakistan. Kissinger agreed and believed that by making Islamabad stronger, both economically and militarily, any Indian effort to seize the country would absorb so much of her strength, that she would be unable to control the rest of the subcontinent. But Kissinger admitted that he had a problem implementing this strategy. The Democratic Congress was still allied to India, and would not support West Pakistan. Washington had tried to set up a consortium of Greece, Iran, and Turkey to provide Islamabad with American weapons, but with limited success. Ignoring the illegality, Washington did make arrangements with Paris to sell airplanes to Pakistan. Zhou admitted that China too was selling her weapons. If these efforts failed, Kissinger believed that Pakistan would become "a vassal of India and therefore free India to move into Southeast Asia or other parts."[10]

Meanwhile, the Brezhnev-Nixon summit had ended and both sides agreed to a trade agreement. All that was needed was legislation granting MFN status to Moscow's products, and a presidential determination of Soviet eligibility for credits. The credit issue was simple. Moscow had sufficient funds as evidenced by her $750 million purchase of grain over a three year period. This would be called by critics the "great grain robbery," since the Soviets also purchased sixteen million tons of corn and wheat unknown to the White House. These agreements nearly depleted the entire grain and corn surplus in the US, resulting in Americans paying more for their grain products than did Soviet citizens. Since the grain and corn were export commodities, MFN was not required. Once Congress learned of the extent of the purchase, they believed they had been fooled, and this did not settle well with some congressmen who still had to consider granting MFN product status to Moscow. Nonetheless, on October 18, the two countries signed the trade agreement granting Soviet products MFN status. In return, Moscow agreed to repay Washington for goods supplied during World War II.[11]

For the agreement to come into force it needed congressional approval, especially that of Senator "Scoop" Jackson, and his Ohio congressional colleague in the House, Charles Vanik. Jackson took the lead, and wanted MFN granted only if Moscow guaranteed free emigration for her people, especially the Jews. Jackson hoped to use the emigration issue, which did affect more Jews than other nationalities, to raise money from the Jewish community for a presidential campaign in 1976. Since the Soviet Union had educated and provided medical care without cost to its people, Moscow did not want to see its best and brightest fleeing to the West without compensation. In August 1972, Moscow imposed an "exit tax" on all emigrants. The tax varied widely from $5,000 to $25,000 per person. Jackson wanted to force the Soviet Union to renounce the tax. Jackson and Vanik introduced legislation in their respective houses linking trade to emigration. Simply put, an exit tax meant no MFN. The White House was silent. The second session of the 92nd Congress was coming to an end. Nothing would be passed, so there was no reason for the administration to show its hand. March, 1973 would be early enough to fight the renewed Jackson-Vanik legislation. The White House also knew that Beijing was closely following the MFN debates.

The main show during the fall and early winter of 1972 was Vietnam. Secretly Zhou Enlai told Hanoi that she ought to conclude a peace treaty under the current president, who seemed to be willing to end the war, rather than gamble and have Nixon lose his re-election bid. The Moscow summit, with its tones of greater cooperation in world events, too spoke to the value of a rapid end to the war. Le Duc Tho, the chief Vietnamese negotiator, made a major concession. President Thieu could remain in power in South Vietnam. Kissinger responded immediately, since this had been the principle stumbling block for four years in the peace negotiations. On October 18th, Le Duc Tho and Kissinger had a draft treaty, scheduled to be signed on October 31. However, Washington forgot that South Vietnam was the nation involved in the war. Kissinger and Nixon had always viewed the war as between the US and North Vietnam, as did much of the world. On the 26th, the NSC advisor announced on television that "peace was at hand" ignoring the 23 changes that Thieu had given him on October 21.[12]

Thieu was furious about being left out of the negotiations, and his intransigence forced the White House to buy time. With the presidential election looming within a week, Nixon did not want anything to interfere with his reelection. And there were opportunities for disruption. Hanoi threatened to break off all talks since American planes continued to bomb North Vietnam, albeit far away from the capital city, while Saigon refused to accept the draft settlement. However, on November 4 the White House caught a break. Realizing that a treaty would not be signed before the American elections, Hanoi asked to have a resumption of talks on November 14.[13] As a result, the elections went on without interruption and Nixon was overwhelmingly reelected for another four years. For those voters who knew about Watergate before the election, it was not viewed as anything sinister, but simply "dirty tricks," nothing unusual in American politics.

Negotiations following the election were acrimonious to say the least. Hanoi felt deceived since she had bargained in good faith, and did not have a treaty. Saigon believed that she had been "sold down the river" and Thieu was not going to agree to any settlement that did not protect South Vietnam. On November 20, he submitted another 44 changes, several calling for a demilitarized zone (DMZ) between North and South Vietnam protected by an international peace keeping force. The result was a resumption of talks on December 4. The DMZ was the new obstacle, and after nine days of arguing, negotiations collapsed without a date to resume. Kissinger believed that Le Duc Tho had kept negotiations alive believing that there was discord between Saigon and Washington, and the imminent return of a Congress more hostile to the president than its predecessor.[14]

Upon his return from the Paris talks, Kissinger met with Nixon and Al Haig, soon to be named as Vice Chief of Staff of the Army. Haig believed that only a massive round of bombings could force Hanoi to make peace. Nixon liked the idea, but decided not to make known his decision to the public. On December 17, Operation Linebacker II, or what became known as the "Christmas bombings," began with the goal of bringing Hanoi back to the negotiating table. The time was chosen because Congress was out of session, and schools and colleges were on winter break, thereby reducing large student demonstrations. Nixon also saw the bombings as a way to convince the conservatives in Congress that he was willing to play hard ball. Once the press learned of the bombings, Nixon explained that they were designed to force Hanoi to release American POWs.[15]

On the day after Christmas, Hanoi agreed to resume negotiations, however Nixon continued the bombing for four more days. Recently released documents from the Cold War International History Project detail Zhou's advice to North Vietnam. He believed that Nixon was "truly planning to leave [Vietnam]. Therefore, this time it is necessary to negotiate [with them] seriously, and the goal is to reach an agreement."[16] Finally, Kissinger's efforts to woo Beijing into using her influence on Hanoi succeeded. Two weeks later, on January 23, Kissinger and Le Duc Tho initialed an agreement which was essentially the same as the one in October. To make the agreement palatable to Thieu, the president promised, without congressional approval, continued military support in his continuing efforts to maintain an independent South Vietnam. On January 27, officials from the US, Republic of South Vietnam, The Democratic Republic of North Vietnam, and the Provisional Revolutionary Government, which represented the pro-Communist South Vietnamese, signed the treaty in Paris. That evening, in a nationally televised speech, Nixon announced that America had "concluded an agreement to end the war and bring peace with honor in Vietnam and Southeast Asia."

Negotiations had taken four years, during which time there were 20,553 additional American casualties bringing the death total to over 58,000. For their efforts, Kissinger and Le Duc Tho would receive the Nobel Peace Prize, much to the chagrin of Nixon who believed he should have been the recipient. On February 12, 1973 the first American POWs returned home, and on March 29, the last troops left Vietnam.

CHAPTER VIII

NORMALIZATION TALKS BEGIN:
TRADE, LIAISON OFFICES,
REPATRIATION OF AMERICAN NATIONALS

With the end of the Vietnam War in sight, Zhou Enlai invited Kissinger on January 3, 1973 to return to Beijing following completion of the negotiated settlement between Hanoi and Saigon.[1] Since his visit to China the previous June, Kissinger had maintained contacts with the Chinese Ambassador to the UN, Huang Hua, through meeting secretly in CIA "safe houses." He also maintained the Paris connection through Beijing's Ambassador to France, Huang Zhen. However, there was nothing as productive as a meeting with Zhou Enlai. Kissinger writes in his memoir that he had "no clear-cut plan for increasing visible contacts. I had intended to propose some modest step, such as an American trade office in China."[2]

The White House also hoped that some progress could be made to further the Shanghai Communiqué including an increase in people-to-people visits, the release of three American citizens, two of whom were pilots shot down in 1968 and John Downey, a government employee who had been the subject of several discussions concerning his release. There was also the issue of claims by private American citizens on property and product seized by the Communists following their assumption of power in 1949. The Chinese had a counter claim concerning assets blocked in the US since 1949. But the most important topic for Kissinger was to work toward normalizing relations, the core element in the Shanghai Communiqué. And this could be facilitated by some sort of "liaison office," a diplomatic step toward formal recognition of China.[3]

Two weeks after Nixon had announced a "peace with honor," Kissinger and his entourage arrived in Beijing on February 15, 1973 for a four day visit. And from the outset, Kissinger would remind Zhou and Mao that the information he was sharing had been given to no other "foreign leader or for that matter to any of our own people."[4] Kissinger urged that the two countries to take steps to proceed rapidly toward normalization, fearing that since America was withdrawing troops from both Vietnam and Taiwan, Moscow might see an opportunity to establish hegemony in the Asia-Pacific region.[5]

Without question the Soviet Union was the primary focus for Beijing, and while the Kissinger-Zhou conversations included their normal *tour d'horizon* approach to the world, Moscow was normally the focus. Time and again, Kissinger reminded Zhou that the Soviet Union wanted Washington to sign a treaty obliging each side "not to use nuclear weapons." While the US was willing to consider certain circumstances in which she would not use nuclear weapons, there were times when they would be necessary. But rather than rejecting the offer, the White House took it under consideration. Kissinger would offer changes designed to "water down" the terms, knowing that the Kremlin would reject them thereby keeping the treaty in abeyance. In analyzing Moscow's position, Kissinger saw three possibilities: the Soviet Union genuinely wanted to reduce world tensions, or to use such rhetoric as a means to reduce Europe's already limited defense preparations, or to gain time to accelerate her own military preparations. Mao believed that Moscow's goal was "to occupy both Europe and Asia, the two continents."[6]

Kissinger believed that there were three motives for Moscow to attack China. One was the assumption that Washington would stay out of the battle. The second assumed that if a Soviet-China battle ended in a stalemate, American would remain neutral. And third, incompetence in Washington which would weaken the West sufficiently to encourage a Soviet attack on China. In examining each of these, the first could "never be our policy." If Russia conquered

China, Japan would join Russia, Europe would be under Soviet control, and America would be isolated.

Zhou did not believe that Moscow could successfully defeat China. He noted that preparations had long been made for the people "to dig tunnels deep, to store grain everywhere, and never seek hegemony. The tunnels were deep for protection from bombing, and were interconnected to enable coordinated military attacks. The granaries would stock pile food and make China better prepared than Russia, which historically had major grain shortages." In the event of an attack, "we must be prepared to withstand that attack; we must be prepared to make it so that they will be able to come in but not go out." Finally, recent developments in international relations had opened China to more foreign visitors and to foreign influence. In turn, the world was learning that China was not interested in dominating Asia, and it was in the best interest of the world to support China, rather than permitting Moscow to extend her influence over all of Asia.[7]

The second scenario, if America saw a Sino-Russian conflict ending in stalemate, Washington "would be forced either into a position of demonstrated impotence and irrelevance to the rest of the world or into a series of delicate and extremely complex decisions.
The third option, America's incompetence, a Sino-Soviet war would be due to misjudgment by Washington, "not the result of a deliberate policy." But were that the case, America "would consider aggression against China as involving our own national security."[8]

Europe was the second item on Beijing's agenda. Zhou was concerned about the ongoing Mutual Balanced and Force Reduction talks (MBFR). Kissinger was more than concerned. He viewed Europe as America's "biggest problem" not Moscow.[9] He saw the MBFR talks as a means for the Soviet Union to weaken Europe's ability to defend herself. Europe was not as strong militarily as she had been. Her recent focus was on economics and the expansion of the European Union from six nations to nine. During the time of these negotiations,

France had lost Charles de Gaulle, West Germany had Willy Brandt who had bargained away part of Germany via his *Ostpolitik* to reach an accommodation with Russia, while Britain's Edward Heath had his hands full with a major miner's strike, and London was not always loyal to Europe. Zhou agreed that a weak Europe meant that Moscow could increase her influence in Asia including Japan, Korea, and Indochina. And this was especially true with India and Pakistan.[10] In his meeting with Mao, on February 17, the Chairman reiterated Zhou's concerns noting that by pushing Russia eastward, she would go beyond China, and assert herself against Japan, and "probably towards you, in the Pacific Ocean and the Indian Ocean."[11]

In an effort to strengthen Europe, the White House had announced that 1973 would be the "Year of Europe." Over the next six months, Washington intended to develop a common economic and military policy with the European countries and design a charter, hopefully including Japan, to strengthen NATO, and become a more serious bulwark against Soviet military actions in either the West or the East. While this sounded very good, the "Year of Europe" would soon be forgotten as the Watergate issue began to strangle the White House. New initiatives were difficult to develop, especially those requiring congressional support from a Congress which was growing more hostile to the president month by month.

Another agenda item was Southeast Asia. As for the future of South Vietnam, Zhou was quite clear: "as far as Thieu is concerned, he has a greedy personal ambition and is bound to fail." Kissinger was concerned that the January 1973 agreement might collapse. Washington viewed the agreement as a means to stop the military conflict, and "that it should start a political process, and we will accept the political outcome, especially if it goes on over a reasonable length of time."[12] While not defining any particular amount of time, Kissinger was really asking Beijing to provide Washington with a "decent interval" before Hanoi's forces marched into Saigon permitting America to "save face." In his meeting with Mao on

February 17, the Chairman said that "the Vietnamese issue can be counted as basically settled." Kissinger agreed adding that "we must now have a transitional period toward tranquility," a view shared by Mao.[13] Nixon's Vietnamization of the war, albeit too late and without congressional approval, did buy time until North Vietnamese forces captured Saigon on April 30, 1975. The two year delay enabled Nixon to still claim that he had achieved "peace with honor."

In addition to pulling her troops out of South Vietnam, Washington had decided to reduce her troop deployment in Taiwan as well as in Korea. Since Japanese aggression was always on the mind of Beijing, Kissinger assured Zhou that there would be sufficient forces remaining to prevent Japan from returning to the Korean peninsula. And America was also available through SEATO, the Southeast Asian Treaty Organization, which was an anomaly, except it was the vehicle which had enabled Washington to become involved in the Vietnam War. Zhou noted that very few countries in Southeast Asia had joined it. Kissinger agreed that it was a "very curious phenomenon," but that it might still have relevance in light of Moscow's increasing interest in India and Southeast Asia.[14]

Since normalization was the main reason for his Beijing visit, Kissinger suggested that each country establish liaison offices in each other's country, but Zhou suggested that both offices could be in Washington. He was soon overridden by Mao on February 17. The Chairman announced that there would be a liaison office in each capital, led by the "Chief of the Liaison Office." He would handle issues concerning trade, cultural, scientific and people-to-people exchanges. This would replace the Paris connection, but leave it in place for future needs. While the Chinese Ambassador to the United Nations would maintain contact with the White House, extremely important issues would still be addressed directly between the leadership in both countries. Nixon was adamant about this arrangement, and told Kissinger that contacts would be done by the two of them, "Alone."[15] On March 17, Nixon announced that America would establish a Liaison Office in Beijing effective May 1 with David Bruce as the Chief. Previously Bruce had served as Ambassador to France, West Germany and the United Kingdom.

One of the most important functions of the Liaison Office was trade, and some headway was made. Two-way exchanges grew from virtually zero in 1970 to over $800 million in 1973, and to over $900 million in 1974. To be fair, China produced most of the volume through her exports. Nonetheless, trade was an issue that excited Congress, and big business, giving some support for Nixon's efforts to forge closer ties to Beijing. The White House and Department of State and Commerce supported a new private enterprise, the National Council for China Trade, established in March, 1973. It travelled to China in November, making it the "first visit of a broadly based, commercially oriented American group to China in more than 20 years." In 1974, the trend continued with more and more American businessmen visiting China, while a few Chinese commercial groups visited America looking to buy plant equipment.[16]

The most difficult issue was expanded trade. China's long time belief in "self reliance" as the basis of her economy, and her fear that increased trade would become a means to influence her politics. On the American side, the constraining issues on trade were the export controls in place since 1949, especially those identified by the COCOM lists. COCOM stood for Coordinating Committee, a secret organization established in 1949 which controlled American exports to all countries including her allies. Since Washington was a member of GATT, and a strong supporter of free trade, COCOM meetings had no minutes, was unknown to the world until 1953, and continued in existence until the mid-1990s.

The reason for the restrictions on trade with America's European allies was the fear of transshipment of materials which could be used by the Communist Bloc for military purposes. And the restrictions were severe considering that straw was prohibited for export since it could be used to package ammunition. And there was another American barrier, tariffs. Congress liked to protect American business, and high tariffs were one solution. Kissinger indicated that the administration was trying to get a trade bill through Congress which would give the administration discretion in imposing tariffs. Between China's penchant for "self-reliance," America's COCOM lists and high tariffs, trade would be slow to develop. [17]Chairman Mao summed it up succinctly, saying at present, trade "is very pitiful."[18] But with tongue in cheek, he suggested that since China had an excess of women, and there were no quotas on women, he was quite willing to give America "a few...some tens of thousands...Let them go to your place. They will create disasters. That way you can lessen our burdens." He continued, in a jocular mood, which masked China's view of women as less than equal, saying "We have too many women, and they have a way of doing things. They give birth to children and our children are too many." Kissinger kiddingly said he would have to study the issue, to which Mao replied, that his visit was a way for China to settle her population problem.[19]

There was little progress in settling the claims issue, principally because Beijing had shown no real interest since the previous July when the issue was first raised, but there was progress in the return of American POWs. Zhou announced that two pilots, Major Philip Smith and Lieutenant Commander Robert Flynn, shot down in 1968 when their plane entered Chinese territory, would be released at the same time as the release of POWs from Vietnam. As for John Downey, whom Washington recognized as being a legitimate prisoner, he was released on March 12.[20] On the final day, February 19, the two sides reached agreement on a communiqué which would be jointly announced on February 22. The document was brief and emphasized that "the time was appropriate for accelerating the normalization of relations." To facilitate that, each side would establish a liaison office in each other's capital, and agreed to broaden their contacts through expanded trade as well as scientific, cultural and other exchanges.

According to Michael Schaller, when Kissinger left Beijing he believed that "with the exception of the United Kingdom, the PRC might well be closest to us in its global perceptions. No other world leaders have the sweep and imagination of Mao and Zhou nor the capacity and will to achieve a long-range policy." Washington and Beijing, "in plain words" have become tacit allies.[21] The National Security Advisor continued in his summation of his trip to Nixon, noting a couple of points. First, that the Chinese leadership would soon change. Mao, at age 80, had "received an invitation from God," while Zhou Enlai was 75 and not in the best of health. For this reason, America should act quickly to consolidate this new relationship. Second, for the Beijing-Washington connection to continue, America had to be strong. A weak US had no value to China, because Beijing needs America as a counterweight to Moscow and Tokyo. Consequently it was incumbent upon Washington to maintain a strong defensive posture.

The president believed that the negotiations with China and Russia were more important than ending the Vietnam War. As he often did, he criticized the press this time noting that "they think it's great we've gone to China, we've shaken hands and everything is going to be hunky-dory. It's not going to be hunky-dory; it's going to be tough 'titties'. So now that we have come this far, the real game is how do you build on these great initiatives."[22] As though Beijing had heard Nixon's remarks, a few days later, the Chinese Communist Party notified its members that "opposition to the two superpowers" would continue to be Beijing's guiding principle. However, the primary target should be "Soviet revisionists, so that China and the US will develop a new relationship characterized by a combination of confrontation and coalition."[23]

Kissinger also met with Ambassador Shen of the Republic of China. Naturally, he wanted to be filled in on all the details, but he learned little. He assured Shen that the liaison offices would have no effect on America's recognition of Taiwan. He further assured Shen that nothing else of importance was discussed during the four day meeting. Talks focused on some trade opportunities, and people-to-people exchanges. All in all, Kissinger told Shen nothing, but suggested that were the opportunity to avail itself, he should be willing to "negotiate" over the future relationship with Beijing.[24]

While the Liaison Office was available on March 15, Kissinger and Nixon delayed sending Ambassador Bruce until May 1. The White House wanted time to "prepare public opinion" as to Washington's new relationship with Beijing. The administration also needed time to prepare Bruce for his new assignment. Since the Liaison Office came under Kissinger's oversight, he wanted to control the operation insuring effective lines of communication with Bruce, as well as appointing the CIA and State Department members of Bruce's staff. The State Department representative would work through Hong Kong, while the CIA person would "be there on condition that he did literally nothing that was not cleared by both Ambassador Bruce and Kissinger." The Chinese would know the identity of the CIA person, so that he would not be viewed as a spy. Kissinger believed that being up front about his identity was important since "total honesty" was the best policy with Beijing.[25]

Two weeks later, Nixon briefed Bruce as to his expectations. The president saw Bruce as a symbol. He told him that he was "not the State Department's ambassador, you are the President's, and I want you to be in on everything." He expected Bruce to be highly visible, meeting with Communist leaders in an effort to assess who were moving up the ranks to replace Mao and Zhou. Bruce shared Nixon's view of the State Department as a sieve for information and agreed to use the back channel to communicate with the White House. He wanted Bruce to tell the Chinese how much the president "appreciated the welcome" he had received, that he looked forward to returning, and welcomed a visit by Zhou to the United Nations. And most important, the ambassador was to tell the Chinese that he "looked upon the Chinese-American relationship as really the key to

91

peace in the world." Continuing, Nixon told Bruce to "always have in the back of your mind that the Russians are their deadly enemies. And they know it, and we know it. And that we will stand by them....That's the commitment I have made....How we do it, I don't know...my point is the Chinese must be reassured they have one heck of a friend here."[26]

CHAPTER IX
NIXON IN TROUBLE, KISSINGER CARRIES ON

The end of the war in Vietnam and the Soviet agreement along with the Kissinger's visit to China augured well for Nixon who had been overwhelmingly reelected by one of the largest margins of victory in American history. However, the Soviet agreement involved trade, and the Jackson-Vanik supporters who showed their hand at the end of the Ninety-Second Congress had regrouped and gained additional support to tie a country's emigration practices to trade. In March, 1973 Jackson in the Senate and Vanik in the House introduced nearly identical legislation prohibiting the grant of MFN trade status to any non-market economy, which denied its citizens free emigration. This applied to Moscow but was equally applicable to any other Communist country. The White House tried to work with Moscow, and received some assurance that the emigration laws would be used only on "unusual" cases involving national security. Ambassador Dobrynin noted that Congress could not be informed since it would imply that Moscow permitted Washington to interfere with her domestic policies.

On April 10, the president sent his trade package to Congress including granting MFN to Soviet products. On the same day, Jackson added his amendment to the bill. Moscow showed a willingness to work with Washington, but the president had lost much of his power. The Watergate investigation had already implicated the president's Chief of Staff, Robert Haldeman, domestic advisor, John Ehrlichman, and the Attorney General, John Mitchell. The only person of note who escaped being involved in Watergate was Kissinger. And to safeguard his foreign policy objectives, on August 22 the president nominated Kissinger to be Secretary of State, while keeping him as his NSC advisor. Congress approved the appointment on September 21, but this did little to diminish the legislature's attack on the Executive Office. The weakened presidency invited Congress to increase its power. Jackson's demands would not be easily met. He insisted upon a specific number of annual exit visas, including a large number for Jews. Following hearings, the House Committee reported the trade bill to the floor on October 3. The House expected to vote on the bill by October 18.[1]

Debate on the bill was suddenly postponed when on October 6, Syrian and Egyptian forces attacked Israel and the Yom Kippur War began. Kissinger asked Congress to postpone debate since any action would undercut his efforts to work with Moscow to end the Middle East crisis. Congress agreed and postponed debate until December. The House passed the Trade Reform Bill with Section 402, the Jackson-Vanik amendment on December 11, 1973. The Senate would consider the bill the following spring.

During the debates, Kissinger was heavily involved in restoring peace in the Middle East. His "shuttle diplomacy" approach made him the mediator between Egypt, Syria and Israel and this would consume the bulk of his time through the end of 1973. The war had also produced a resurgence of OPEC, the Organization for Petroleum Exporting Countries, founded in 1960, but generally benign during the past thirteen years. However, America's rescue of Israel in the Yom Kippur War prompted the OPEC members to show their displeasure and support their Arab brothers by placing an embargo on oil. Japan, and Europe were most affected by the shortfall in production since they were heavily dependent on foreign oil, while America, who too imported oil, was caught off guard with little surplus. OPEC announced a cutback on all oil production at the rate of five percent per month. Gasoline and heating oil prices escalated as the price of a barrel of oil went from about $3 per barrel to $11. No longer was gasoline twenty-five cents a gallon, it was suddenly fifty cents in America, and significantly higher in Japan and Europe. The Common Market failed to work cooperatively, as each nation competed for OPEC oil. The embargo began in October, just before the onset of winter. In addition to bringing an end to the Israeli-Arab war, the new secretary of state took on the task of ending the embargo. Through arrangements with Saudi Arabia, the details which are not known, Riyadh agreed to reduce the cutback from 25% to 15% forcing the rest of the OPEC nations to follow. The end of the embargo on March 18, 1974 did not make a significant decrease in oil and gasoline prices, but it did make the product far more available. Further, Saudi's cooperation showed her to be a good ally, one that America looked to because of her oil, location and religion. Her Islamic Fundamentalism was anti-Communist. As an aside, the crisis introduced the West to layered clothing, and insulated attics, as well as wood burning stoves, which occasionally had the unfortunate effect in some homes burning to the ground.

As the Middle East crisis came to a close the Senate began hearings on the trade bill on March 4, 1974 three days after a Federal Grand Jury indicted Nixon's closest advisors for attempting to cover up the Watergate investigation and lying to the FBI. Kissinger tried to work with Jackson and Moscow to find a compromise. However, Jackson really did not want a compromise, he wanted to be viewed as a hero to his Jewish constituency, whose money he would need for his anticipated run for the presidency. He wanted Moscow to put in writing a guarantee of 100,000 exit visas annually. This was an impossible request. If the Kremlin conceded, and it became known, which would undoubtedly occur, Moscow would appear weak and unable to manage her own internal policies. As Watergate became America's fascination, Congress saw an opportunity to seize greater control of the government and several congressmen introduced legislation to impeach the president. Nixon stonewalled all attacks, but he could not stop the House from voting to impeach. A quick head count of senators supporting impeachment, forced the president to announce his resignation as of August 9, 1974.

As for the bill, it continued on its legislative track in the Senate. In a last effort, Kissinger managed to have Moscow agree to permanently suspend the emigration tax, and permit anyone to leave who was not viewed as a national security risk, but she would not provide any specific numbers. In order to get what was called the Trade Act of 1974 through Congress, Jackson agreed to a compromise. It allowed the president to waive the freedom-of-emigration requirement if he (a) determined that the waiver would substantially promote the objectives of the requirement, and (b) if he had received assurances from the applicant country that its emigration practices would lead substantially to the achievement of free emigration. On January 3, 1975 President Gerald Ford signed the bill into law, and Moscow said that it would not abide by the provisions, viewing it as an intrusion into its internal affairs. America would not grant the Soviet Union MFN until President William Clinton did in 1996.[2]

Watergate also gave Congress the opportunity to further interfere with the president's prerogatives in foreign policy. Nixon decided in 1969 to increase the bombing of Cambodia begun in 1964. He approved the Pentagon's "Operation Menu," a bombing plan whose code names included "Breakfast, Snack, Lunch, Supper, Dinner and Desert," indicating the times of bombing missions. The purpose was to destroy Vietnamese hideouts in the jungles. In an effort to prevent Cambodia from falling into the hands of the Communists, Nixon authorized the bombings to continue after the Vietnamese peace agreement. While the bombings were supposed to be secret, word gradually leaked out and by the spring of 1973, the public learned of the bombings. They amounted to over 250,000 tons of bombs, more than all of the bombs dropped on Japan during World War II. As the public recoiled at the amount of destruction, Congress acted and in May decided to cut off all funding for military actions against Cambodia. A month later, Congress approved the end of all military operations in Southeast Asia. In July, a federal judge adjudicated a case involving four service men who were to be court-martialed for refusing to fly bombing missions over Cambodia. The judge determined that since Congress had given no explicit authority for the continued bombing, it was illegal and Nixon was in violation of the constitution. With that decision, Congress ended the bombings on August 15.

Enjoying its new found influence in what was normally the president's bailiwick, Congress went further and passed the War Powers Act in November. This curbed the right of the president to send troops to foreign lands without informing Congress within 48 hours, and the troops had to be withdrawn within 60 days unless Congress approved an extension. Without America's support Lon Nol's government would fall to Pol Pot's Communist Khmer Rouge. This enabled him to implement his genocidal policies resulting in the killing of over one million Cambodians in what became known as the "Killing Fields."

Beijing had not anticipated that Congress would act so quickly to withdraw support from Lon Nol in June, and the subsequent suspension of bombing surprised Zhou. He had thought that the United States and China were working together to produce a cease fire. The sudden action of Congress upset Zhou and he needed time to interpret the meaning of the events. He cancelled Kissinger's scheduled visit for early August. If Washington's actions were not sufficiently unpleasant, Zhou was personally incensed by the remarks made during a congressional visit to Beijing led by Senator Warren Magnuson. He told the premier that "he need not worry about the bombing; Zhou should be patient; it would soon be over---specifically on August 15; Zhou had Congress to thank for it. Zhou grew visibly irritated." He and Kissinger had agreed that Zhou "had induced Washington to end the bombing as his contribution to the peace process." Magnuson took this all away, in front of a number of witnesses. The Senator continued to repeat that "We stopped the bombing," implying that Beijing had nothing to do with it. Zhou was furious. The surprising change in congressional support, along with Magnuson's bombastic announcement, coupled with a realization that Watergate had crippled the president and reduced America's ability to protect China, postponed any discussion of a Kissinger visit. To save face, the White House sent Beijing a note that the trip should be postponed until "sometime in the fall."[3]

During the entire Cambodian issue, Kissinger had ignored Taiwan for nearly half the year. On August 6, he met Ambassador Shen, essentially to reassure him that his forthcoming meeting in Beijing would not result in Washington's recognition of the PRC. In parrying with Shen, Kissinger made no commitments, but was willing to entertain requests for a future visit to the US by either the foreign minister or the premier. Again, Shen left a meeting knowing nothing more than he had beforehand.[4] However, in late September Kissinger told the American Ambassador to the ROC, Walter McConaughy, a different story. In a prescient statement, he said "We are moving inexorably toward full recognition of Beijing, which is bound to come by 1980 at the latest. There may be some change in 1975 (toward the end of Nixon's second term) but regardless, Taiwan could continue her separate status if that is what she wanted.[5]

In early October, Beijing's Vice Foreign Minister Qiao Guanhua arrived in New York to give a speech at the UN and to have lunch with the new secretary of state. During the talks, Qiao raised the issue of Cambodia and said what difference does it make whether Phnom Penh is "red, pink, black or white;" "what difference will this make in the end for world history." He blamed America's Cambodian policy on Congress and the press, exonerating the White House. Thus, Kissinger would be able to visit Beijing. However, Kissinger was not readily available. His involvement in Middle East process would make him unable to give full attention to China until the fall.

On November 10, 1973 Kissinger arrived in Beijing for his sixth visit to the PRC, now as secretary of state. Following the required welcoming banquet, he and Zhou and their associates met briefly with Zhou who asked questions about Brezhnev's June visit to the White House. The Soviet leader was quite focused on learning more about China's nuclear capabilities, to which neither the president nor Kissinger gave any information. The secretary of state told Brezhnev that such questions were an "inadmissible line of discussion and that we would not pursue it."[6]

At the beginning of the second day, the large group of advisors was divided between those involved in political affairs and those in technical issues including such topics as trade and cultural exchanges. Kissinger and Zhou led the political group and soon focused on their favorite topic, a *tour d'horizon.* In many ways it was a rehash of the important points in their February meetings. Kissinger reiterated Washington's position on Taiwan, namely that there was only one China, America would not support independence movements, and would discourage any military moves against the Chinese mainland. As for normalization, Kissinger was more encouraging and expected full recognition by the middle of 1976, the expected end of the Nixon administration. Zhou asked about the Secretary's success in the Middle East. His two main problems were Moscow and Golda Meir, the head of Israel. Moscow wanted to have a bilateral Soviet-American expeditionary force to move into the Sinai and restore order between Jerusalem and Cairo. The Soviet's threatened to move unilaterally unless America agreed, but this proved to be nothing but talk. Kissinger had managed to bring about a cease fire agreement, but only by constantly battling Golda Meir. His "secret dream is to involve Madame Meir in negotiations with President Thieu." He continued, "If Mrs. Meir only gets ninety-eight percent of what she asks for, she considers herself betrayed" by the US. Although Egypt lost the war, Kissinger believed that Cairo had sent a message, that Israel was no longer viewed as the military juggernaut previously believed by the Arab world. As for Europe's response, there was none of importance and Zhou showed his growing concern about Western passivism which, as mentioned in February, would provide an impetus for Moscow to be more aggressive in her dealings with Beijing. Due to the Cultural Revolution, and the subsequent dislocation among the hierarchy, Zhou felt threatened by the Kremlin. He sought reassurance that America could be called upon to safeguard China against Soviet pressure. India and Japan rounded out the day's topics with no changes in strategies.[7]

During the afternoon of the 12th, the two parties resumed discussions. Zhou questioned the purpose of a growing air force in Taiwan. America had supplied the planes for self defense, and minimized their attack capability since they only had single fuel tanks, not sufficient for round trips to the mainland. The excuse was a bit lame, and Zhou noted that a second tank would permit them to attack and return. The Secretary reassured Zhou that if that were to happen, Washington would cut off all airplanes and airplane parts to Taipei. Further, as he had repeated often, America would not permit Taiwan to attack the mainland. Among other topics was Moscow's efforts to garner MFN, which was tied to the Jackson-Vanik amendment and proving very problematic, and the outcome was uncertain. The Middle East, Japan, and Korea were also fair game including the never ending Armistice Commission talks. Both believed that the negotiators had become quite comfortable and found vacationing in Beijing as a pleasant retreat, not that it helped bring closure to the Korean conflict. At 5:30 Zhou interrupted the discussions and suddenly announced that Mao was waiting to meet with Kissinger, Ambassador Bruce, and Winston Lord, Kissinger's note taker and extra hand.[8]

Ten minutes later, the Chairman greeted his guests, and unlike previous meetings, he took over policy discussions, normally done by Zhou. Mao's physical condition had obviously deteriorated, but, according to Kissinger, "he exuded greater concentrated willpower and determination than any leader I have encountered" except for de Gaulle. The Chairman's health had declined precipitously. He moved with great difficulty and his speech deteriorated to the point that Lord wrote down "what the sounds he uttered might mean, whereupon he would either nod or shake his head before the interpreter was able to proceed."[9] Nonetheless, he was quite concerned that Washington understood several issues. First was Taiwan, and in no uncertain terms, he said that "as for the question of our relations with Taiwan, that is quite complex. I do not believe in a peaceful transition." "I say that we can do without Taiwan for the time being, and let it come after one hundred years....Why is there need to be in such a great haste?" Kissinger responded that Washington could not immediately sever relations with Taipei, and this primarily has to do with America's domestic policies. He still wanted to grant Beijing full diplomatic recognition by 1976, but it would require some sort of formula to accommodate Taiwan.[10]

Tokyo and Moscow were also important to Mao. In the past, he had urged Kissinger to spend more time in Japan during his Asian visit, and was delighted to learn that he would be in Tokyo for nearly three days. Mao wanted to make sure that the US and Japan were friends, in order to prevent Tokyo from seeking support and protection from Moscow. Since Sino-Japanese relations were mercurial, Mao needed American-Japanese relations to be strong, and he was concerned that Japan was afraid of the US and might look to Moscow for support. Kissinger needed to reinforce Washington's commitment to Tokyo

The Moscow talks broached the same issues that Kissinger and Zhou had addressed in February. Mao reiterated an earlier opinion that Moscow wanted "to seize in its hands the two continents of Europe and Asia, and North Africa and elsewhere....they will have trouble doing that as long as countries that are threatened stay united." At this point he toasted everyone, as though as to put an exclamation point on the importance of continued relations with Washington. The remainder of the meeting returned to a *tour d'horizon* approach including India and Middle East, but provided no new revelation nor policy changes.[11]

During the final two days, the Kissinger-Zhou discussions covered a random list of topics, while their aides prepared a final communiqué. Among the topics mentioned were Che Guevara's revolutionary efforts in South and Latin America and in the Congo which Zhou described as "adventurism," the "rashness" of Salvador Allende in Chile resulting in his being overthrown, and uniformed Marines guarding the Liaison Office in Beijing. The problem was uniforms. The Chinese people were annoyed by seeing uniformed foreign soldiers in their capital. Further discussion indicated that the Marines had been in uniform at the outside of the Liaison Office, but that ended on July 4. Since then, a People's Liberation Army soldier fronted the Office, and uniformed Marines remained inside the compound. This would be contrary to tradition since all American posts around the world were protected by uniformed Marines. But the secretary was willing to give way to address Zhou's concern. The premier also urged Washington to help Pakistan build a naval harbor, a suggestion which Kissinger quickly squelched. Congress, with its strong bias toward India, would never authorize funding to support Pakistan. The ongoing talks about private claims and blocked assets, showed little movement, but there was real progress in the people-to-people program with over 20 exchanges scheduled for 1974. By the day's end, the aides had designed a communiqué acceptable to both sides. It broke no new ground, but it did reaffirm all of the commitments made at Shanghai. In addition, both agreed that the work of the Liaison Offices should be expanded and look to increase two-way trade which was of "equal and mutual benefit."[12]

On his last evening in Beijing, Kissinger hosted a banquet in the Great Hall of the People. As had been done during Nixon's visit, a Chinese military ensemble played American and Chinese songs. During the banquet, perhaps due to too many Mai Tais, Kissinger admittedly made a *faux pas*. He raised the issue of Confucius and implied that Mao was a Confucian. "Zhou lost his composure, the only time I knew him to do so....he insisted in an extremely agitated fashion on the absurdity of my parallel." He would not accept the secretary's disclaimer.[13] While Kissinger was aware that there was an ongoing struggle in the Politburo concerning Sino-American relations, he was apparently unaware of its depth. Mao's opponents argued that the new trade agreements challenged the age old Confucian mantra of "self reliance." Many feared how dependent China would become on foreign technology, and the costs of such a change. To retain power, and prepare for his successor, Mao sacrificed Zhou, seen as the principle supporter of change, hiding the fact that he too supported it. While the premier retained his titles, he no longer made decisions. On the few occasions that Kissinger saw Zhou during the following months, he was forced to tell the secretary that he could no longer talk about political issues. Mao ordered the Politburo to criticize Zhou and force him to write a self-criticism, a technique frequently employed during the Cultural Revolution. Further, Mao resurrected Deng Xiaoping, who had been punished during the Cultural Revolution and quickly made him a member of the Politburo.

To understand Zhou's reaction to Kissinger's reference to Mao as Confucius required a knowledge of the Chinese media. A *Red Flag* article in January entitled "Confucius in Moscow" implied an historical analogy that some leaders in China were cooperating with the Soviets along with "Kuomintang reactionaries on Taiwan" to challenge the views of Mao and Zhou. In February, the *People's Daily* published an editorial signaling the beginning of a mass campaign to support Mao as the anti-Confucian and to identify his opponents as supporters of the traitor Lin Biao. In a conversation, Deng Xiaoping explained to the secretary that Confucius "was an expert in keeping up the rights, and very conservative...If we wish to emancipate the people's ideology from old thinking, we must remove Confucius. This is a move to emancipate the people's thinking."[14] A subsequent article in the *People's Daily* indicated that Mao wanted Washington to be patient, maintain relations between the two countries and to publically de-emphasize Beijing's current difficulties lest they help Moscow undermine Sino-American relations. Mao had to separate himself from the view of a Mao-Zhou union and the best way was to remove the premier from public view. An immediate consequence was that steps toward normalization would be put on hold otherwise they would provide fuel to Mao's opposition.[15]

Zhou's decline would continue. In April, 1974 Mao sent Deng to represent China at the UN, not Zhou who was still physically able to travel. But in June, this changed and Zhou entered a hospital for surgery to destroy the cancer that was gradually killing him. Mao had known about the condition for some time, but refused Zhou's earlier request to go to seek medical attention. The operation proved too little, too late. The cancer continued to spread and Zhou would die on January 8, 1976.

In light of the changing tenor in Beijing, the NSC prepared an end of year assessment of Washington's relations with Beijing which confirmed the situation in China. Bureaucratic forces were limiting "the institutionalization of a durable relationship...thus raising for the US the question of the survivability of our relations with Beijing after Mao and Zhou have passed from the scene." What the report called a "sea of trivia," items which lacked consequence, became the fodder for communication between the Liaison Offices. The report concluded that this situation would continue until the Politburo resolved its internal problems and could adopt a consistent approach to Washington. The only positive in the relationship was that trade was expanding, in spite of bureaucratic opposition. That appeared to be the one area in which Mao and Zhou had established solid contacts to withstand the current problems. The report recommended that the secretary of state invite a high ranking Chinese official to lead the trade delegation scheduled for the spring, and that upon his next visit to China, he meet with a broader range of Chinese officials, and get out into the key provincial cities if possible.[16]

Meanwhile, following his return from his November, 1973 meeting in Beijing, Kissinger had the obligatory meeting with James Shen, Taiwan's Ambassador to the US. Shen appeared convinced that Washington and Beijing had an agreement that at some point, China could absorb Taiwan. He noted that the recent communiqué, unlike the Shanghai Communiqué, did not mention the phrase "of interest in a peaceful settlement." Kissinger reaffirmed Washington's defense commitment. Without question, Shen believed that the secretary was using Taiwan as bait to encourage Beijing to work quickly to establish full diplomatic relations with Washington, and the time table was most definitely before the end of Nixon's second term. Kissinger gave no indication that this was the case, when in fact Shen was on target. Shen challenged every phrase in the communiqué until Kissinger finally said that "the PRC's major concern is the USSR not Taiwan. Taiwan was barely discussed...The PRC has more pressing problems which occupy them more than Taiwan." When he asked for advice on what Taipei should do, Kissinger replied "that the ROC has pursued a wise policy, showing great restraint and wisdom. Painful as it may be, the ROC should continue this policy." He had no other suggestions.[17]

The White House continued its preparations to reduce troop deployment on Taiwan to about 2,800 personnel, and remove one of two F-4 fighter squadrons. Rather than send a shock wave through Taipei, Kissinger suggested that the planes be removed in May, 1975 and Nixon agreed. In addition, Leonard Unger, a former ambassador to Laos and Thailand, and who was familiar with Asian affairs, replaced Bruce who was reassigned to Western Europe to work on an Energy Conference. Unger came with formidable credentials which the White House publicized to Taipei indicating that America considered her worthy of a more experienced representative. During his briefing, Unger learned that Washington was concerned about Japan's growing interest in improving relations with the Soviet Union, and Moscow's advances toward Taiwan, both being issues which would grab the attention of Beijing.[18]

In April, 1974 a Chinese delegation under the leadership of the Vice Foreign Minister Qiao Guanhua arrived in New York to attend UN meetings. Deng was among the delegates, but was not scheduled to speak, instead he was to "take the temperature of the Sino-US relationship." Kissinger hosted a dinner party for Deng and during their three hour meeting, used their *tour d'horizon* formula to learn about each other's international interests. Throughout this meeting, Kissinger underestimated Deng. He thought he was on a "training mission on how to deal with Americans...None of us considered Deng as a major, much less a seminal figure."[19]

Moscow's interest in becoming involved in the on-going Arab-Israeli peace talks concerned Deng, but the secretary assured him that neither side wanted the Soviets involved. Syria too was an issue. Since Israel refused to return the Golan Heights to Damascus seized during the Yom Kippur war, Moscow saw this as an opportunity to further increase her influence in Syria. If the Soviets succeeded, they would have bases in Syria, Iraq and Southern Yemen. While Beijing supported the Arabs, she was willing to make concessions in order to keep Moscow from increasing her influence in the Middle East.[20] When the talks moved to India-Pakistan issues, there was no progress. Deng wanted Washington to increase its military aid to Islamabad, and, while agreeing, Kissinger repeated that Congress still supported India and there would be no military aid to Pakistan. Deng was concerned about America's apparent overextension. He warned that "we ran the risk of stretching out our hands to the point where we would wind up with 'ten fleas under ten fingers.'"[21] The final issue of importance was Nixon's upcoming trip to Moscow in June. Watergate was taking its toll on the White House. Nixon had sacrificed most of his top administrators, and Congress saw that it was only a matter of time before they removed the president. Since the Soviets saw the same scenario, Kissinger told Deng that no agreement of consequence would be signed during Nixon's visit, and nothing would be negotiated that would threaten China.[22]

Nixon arrived in Moscow for his final summit with the Soviet leadership on June 27, 1974. He desperately wanted an agreement to offset his declining political image. Brezhnev was not willing to agree to any new arms reductions. He was disappointed that Moscow had been cut out of the Middle East negotiations resolving the Yom

106

Kippur War, and was aware of the fragile future of the American president. At the end of the first day, Brezhnev suggested that the discussion continue at his villa in the Crimea, just outside Yalta. Rather than labeling the meeting as the Yalta summit, with its 1945 connotations, both agreed to call it the Oreanda Summit, the township of the villa. The seven days of talks produced very little except for a Threshold Test Ban Treaty eliminating underground nuclear tests of over 150 kilotons. This was not the significant agreement Nixon had hoped for. Before he left, Brezhnev told him that he would like to continue the talks at a meeting in 1975, the implication being that détente would continue with or without Richard Nixon. Nixon returned home in time for the July 4 celebrations.[23]

On July 15, Kissinger briefed Huang Zhen, Chief of the Chinese Liaison Office in Washington, on the Moscow summit. The meeting had gone as Kissinger anticipated. Brezhnev wanted to have a mutual assistance treaty if either were attacked by a third party. Since this meant Beijing, Nixon refused. The secretary reminded Huang that America had between four and five times as many strategic weapons as did Moscow, much due to Washington's success in developing MIRVed weapons. Simply put, one missile could carry multiple warheads, and Moscow's initial efforts to replicate this had failed. Since Huang still seemed concerned about America's military preparedness, Kissinger assured him that the United States would never be underprepared due to the Pentagon's technological superiority.[24] A week later, unknown to Huang, the National Security Council agreed to implement the recommendations of a February report concerning the sale of nuclear technology for civil uses to Beijing provided she abided by the safeguards established by the International Atomic Energy Agency (IAEA). This was part of Washington's efforts to broaden her trade options with Beijing, a move that had success by year's end, increasing America's exports to $819 million in contrast to $740 million in 1973.

Brezhnev was correct in not committing to any serious agreement with Nixon. For on July 27, the US House of Representatives voted a resolution to impeach the president, ending a two year power struggle between the judiciary and executive branches of government. The resolution indicted Nixon for obstruction of justice. After taking a head count of the senators supporting impeachment, the president announced his resignation on August 8, turning over the keys to the Oval Office to Vice President Gerald Ford. On August 9, in one of his first acts as president, Ford met with Huang Zhen and affirmed his desire to continue the Nixon-Kissinger approach to Beijing. He reaffirmed that in his first foreign policy speech on August 12. "To the People's Republic of China…I pledge continuity in our commitment to the principles of the Shanghai Communiqué."[25] And as evidence, Ford retained Kissinger as secretary since "our personalities meshed. I respected his expertise in foreign policy, and he respected my judgment in domestic politics." In looking back, he said "I think we worked together as well as any President and Secretary of State have worked throughout our history."[26]

CHAPTER X

1974: CHINA ON HOLD,
AMERICA OVEREXTENDED

With Ford's blessing, Kissinger continued to lead the administration's approach to both China and Taiwan. On October 2, he met with Beijing's Vice Foreign Minister, Qiao Guanhua, along with staffs from both countries including George H. W. Bush, soon to be approved as the Liaison Officer in China. Qiao was in New York to deliver a speech to the UN and Kissinger honored him with a dinner. Discussion soon focused on Korea and normalization. Since 1973, talks had revolved around eliminating the UN military command, reducing the number of UN troops deployed in South Korea and completion of a peace treaty, ending negotiations begun in 1953. In June, 1974 Washington had proposed to end the UN structure overseeing the armistice, and replacing it with a joint US-Republic of Korea military command. This would lead to the two Koreas signing a non-aggression pact, while maintaining the armistice agreed to by Washington, Seoul, Pyongyang and Beijing. To insure that the Republic of Korea abided by the armistice, China and North Korea would have to accept the continued presence of American forces in Koreas as an interim measure. Kissinger emphasized that America was "not committed to a permanent presence in Korea." To which Qiao responded that Mao had often said that Korea was "not a major issue," and should not affect Sino-American relations.[1]

On the surface, the only obstacle to closer Sino-American relations was normalization, granting Beijing full diplomatic recognition. However, underlying this was the problem of Washington's continuing relations with the ROC. The Japanese had proposed that Washington simply break off diplomatic relations with Taiwan. However, hidden in this was a Japanese interest in establishing greater influence over Taipei. This "Japanese formula"

109

eliminated the American Embassy in Taiwan, replacing it with one in Beijing. The origin of this formula was the Sino-Japanese joint statement of September 29, 1972 establishing diplomatic relations between the two countries. Included was Japan's recognition that Taiwan was an "inalienable part of the territory of the PRC." Implicit in this was that America's defense treaty with Taiwan, made no sense because Washington could not make a defense treaty with only one part of a country. Qiao favored this approach, but added that while Taiwan effected relations between Washington and Beijing, "it is not of too great significance." "We hope that our relations can be normalized, but we are not in a hurry." Kissinger agreed.

Washington was in no hurry either. The secretary mulled over the ideas of having either a liaison office or a consulate in Taiwan, an issue which could be awkward due to America's defense treaty with Taipei. "Our problem is how to present a new relationship with you, where we have not just abandoned people, who we have had a relationship with-for whatever reason, to insure a peaceful transition." Qiao saw a different picture, there were two relationships: one between Beijing and Washington, the other between Beijing and Taipei. As for the latter, Qiao did not "believe in the possibility of a peaceful transition. But in our relations with the US, that is another question." Aware that further discussion on the issue would bring no resolution, both agreed that it be continued during Kissinger's visit to Beijing in November.[2]

In preparation for this visit, Richard Smyser, a member of the NSC, sent Kissinger a memo entitled "Where Do We Stand in Asia." He noted that over the past year, normalization had become more complicated because the governments involved were weaker. Nixon was gone, Zhou Enlai was ill, and Chiang Kai Shek was having problems with his military. The only good part of these developments was that Moscow "was too inept to pick up the pieces." "The initial objective of normalizing relations without substantial adverse affect at home or in Asia will be difficult and perhaps impossible to reach."

Kissinger wrote "good job" on the report and had the CIA and NSC prepare studies on America's policy toward China and Taiwan.[3]

The CIA report focused on China, and noted that since 1973 the normalization progress "has markedly slowed." During the past year, the Chinese have been more contentious toward Washington, and have pressed for her to disassociate herself from Taiwan. Mao appeared to be the impetus for the change in part to synchronize foreign policy with the leftward movement in domestic policy. Since late 1973, fighting had broken out in the Communist Party hierarchy, sufficient to postpone the Party's 4th National People's Congress for what became two years. The principle conflict was between the Gang of Four led by Mao's wife who called for extreme changes in China against the more moderate followers of Mao led by Deng and the Politburo. The Chairman was also less frightened by a possible Soviet attack, and looked to the Third World as a new source of power to confront Washington and Moscow. But in spite of all this, the White House should anticipate that efforts to reach normalization will continue but at a slower pace.[4]

Military support to the ROC was the subject of the NSC's November 12 report. The purpose of supplying arms to Taiwan was to reassure her that America was still committed to the Shanghai Communiqué formula: to provide the government with sufficient weapons to maintain order in the country were their domestic uprisings, to provide her with adequate protection as Washington reduced her troop deployment, and to remind Beijing, that America was still interested in the long term security of the island nation. Aware that increased weapon support to Taipei would raise concerns in Beijing, the NSC presented a variety of proposals. Beijing would be most pleased were America to cut off all military aid to Taiwan, but this would produce chaos in the country, significantly reduce Washington's influence, and accelerate Taiwan's development of nuclear weapons. The second option which would also accommodate Beijing, would be to freeze Taipei's access to current levels of military supplies. This would be a middle ground solution. The third and fourth options were to offer Taiwan access to more advanced weapons including guided bombs. While this would keep Taipei happy, it would seriously hinder the normalization process with Beijing. The NSC recommended the second option.[5]

Immediately after the Ford-Brezhnev summit, Kissinger left for Beijing for a five day visit along with members of his State Department staff, Ambassador Bush, representatives from the Liaison Office, President Ford's newly appointed assistant Donald Rumsfeld, and representatives of the media. Following their arrival on November 25, Kissinger met with Deng Xiaoping, and early on Kissinger raised the ongoing issue of claims suggesting that he "was indifferent as to whether there is a million dollars more or less in settling the question of locked accounts." He was indifferent to the end result of the settlement process, as long as it finally ended. Both men agreed to spend much of their time on issues involved in normalization, especially focused on the Taipei-Washington-Beijing relationship.[6]

Having set an agenda, the two men agreed to begin as usual with a *tour d'horizon* approach to international relations. America's relations with Moscow had improved, not at the expense of Beijing, Washington had grown closer to Western Europe especially France, and had negotiated two agreements in the Middle East involving Egypt, Syria and Israel. Kissinger reminded Deng that Israel was a problem which effected Congress, America's domestic policies, and relations with Palestine. He had visited India and concluded that her aspirations were "hegemonial…and would like to reduce all neighboring countries to the status of Bhutan," which was a powerless nation surrounded by China and India. This was a situation which Washington was not willing to accept. Both men agreed to disagree over the future of Cambodia with Washington reluctantly supporting Lon Nol, and Beijing Samdech Norodom Sihanouk, the former King of Cambodia.. As events evolved, neither Lon Nol nor Sihanouk could stop Pol Pot from seizing power in Phnom Penh.[7]

Normalization became the principle topic on the 26th continuing the October 2 discussions which had came to a halt over Taiwan. Kissinger declared that America had reduced her forces on the island from over 10,000 to about 3,200, had continued to implement the Shanghai Communiqué, and not supported any two-China solution, or a one China-one Taiwan solution or any variation. To move toward normalization, the secretary saw the problem in three parts: the diplomatic status of Taiwan and its relations to Washington, continued American forces deployed to the area, and Washington's defense commitment.

On the first point concerning diplomatic status, Kissinger was willing to solve the issue were America to maintain a liaison office in Taiwan and an embassy in Beijing. The troop issue would soon be mute since Washington intended to remove all troops from the island, half by the end of 1976, the rest by 1977. This information was confidential and could not be released before the end of 1975. The third issue was the defense commitment. Kissinger admitted that he had not found a solution to this issue. Committed to defending Taiwan, and seeing her as part of China, America was in a bind. How to defend part of a country? Due to American politics and a strong pro-Taiwan lobby, America could not simply abandon the island having supported her since the end of World War II. Washington needed a formula "that enables us to say that at least for some period of time there are assurances of peaceful reintegration which can be reviewed after some interval" thereby avoiding serious congressional opposition. Washington needed time to influence public opinion as to the benefits of leaving Taiwan.

Deng's response was not welcoming. He argued that by switching the positions of the embassy and the liaison office would not solve the problem. "People will come to the conclusion that it is a variation of one China and one Taiwan." Therefore it was unacceptable. As for the defense treaty, "it must be done away with." Deng pointed out that Kissinger had already given the reason, you

113

cannot defend part of as country and not the other part. To go further, Deng suggested that were America to break relations with Taipei, then he assumed that remaining questions involving Taiwan's future would be resolved by China alone.

Kissinger was concerned that both Zhou and Deng had several times quoted Mao as saying that the Taiwan issue "would ultimately have to be solved by force." This solution would not have to be immediate, as Mao had kiddingly said, China could "wait one hundred years," but there would be a solution and probably through force, but in the end Taiwan was a Chinese problem. Deng emphasized the fact that since America appeared to still need Taiwan, until that need ended, there could be no normalization of relations. Before ending the session, Deng threw a curve ball. He extended an invitation for Mr. Schlesinger, the American Secretary of Defense, and sworn enemy of Kissinger, to come to China. No secretary of defense had ever visited China, and the invitation was simply a silly gambit. Were Schlesinger to go to China, the visit would be seriously noted by the Soviet Politburo. Deng was just playing with Kissinger, and nothing came from the invitation. But it did open the door for Kissinger to suggest that Ford be invited to come to Beijing, a suggestion quickly accepted by Deng.[8]

Talks on the 27th broke no new ground. Kissinger repeated what he had said earlier about Nixon's visit to Moscow, and Brezhnev's unsuccessful efforts to have the two countries sign a mutual defense treaty to come to the aid of the other in the event of an attack. Nixon refused, knowing that Moscow could provoke China or NATO into attacking the Soviet Union. Deng was curious about the SALT agreement, and Kissinger reassured him that it only dealt with strategic intercontinental nuclear weapons. Deng continued to discuss Moscow, and feared that her threats to the East were a smoke screen for her real interest in attacking the West. Kissinger saw no evidence that would confirm that position. Rather, Moscow was learning just how under prepared she was for nuclear war. While SALT put a limit of 2,400 launchers, this did not include the weapons NATO had in Europe, nor the nuclear weapons owned by Britain and France. Normalization was a topic for the third meeting of the day, but proved sterile.[9]

On the final day, negotiators from both sides worked on the required joint communiqué. The problem was that little new was accomplished. To add something to nothing, Kissinger wanted to lengthen the news release and both agreed to reference the Shanghai Communiqué as a reason for the meeting, as well as the announcement that President Ford would visit China. In the afternoon, the final talks included an American request for China to update Washington on detained Americans, and to have Beijing urge North Vietnam to provide information on American soldiers missing-in-action (MIAs). At day's end "Deng hosted a Mongolian hot pot meal in the private room of a public restaurant," an "unusual courtesy."[10]

Beijing and Taipei were not the only items on Kissinger's or President Ford's plates. Shortly after taking office, Ford had two issues which had to be addressed before he could implement his own agenda. The first was the Soviet-American trade bill. Senator Jackson's efforts to make the trade bill his bailiwick finally forced Moscow to back out of the agreement. Jackson's announcement that due to his work, the Soviet Union would release 100,000 Jews annually, had never received the Kremlin's approval, and this ended the discussion. There would be a Trade Act of 1974 bill, passed by Congress in December without mention of the Soviet Union. The main result was that Moscow reduced the number of visas granted emigrants in 1975 to 13,000 from a high of 20,000 in 1973.[11]

The other issue was Ford's first Asian trip which after a visit to South Korea and Japan, arrived in Vladivostok, the headquarters of the Soviet Pacific fleet. Kissinger had worked with the Soviet Ambassador Anatoly Dobrynin to set up a meeting to complete the work on a SALT treaty which would extend the 1972 agreement for five more years, or negotiate a new treaty. In his meeting with Nixon

115

in June, Brezhnev refused to deal with the treaty since the president's political life was too uncertain. Nonetheless the summit did keep the door open for further talks, and through Kissinger's efforts, Brezhnev agreed to meet Ford in Vladivostok. The two leaders, from the moment they met, got along well. Soon both agreed to sign an agreement permitting each country to have 2,400 strategic arms, including all land, sea and air based launches, of which 1,300 could be MIRVed. The agreement would last for twenty years. Unfortunately for Ford, the ink had no sooner dried than senatorial opposition developed sufficient to force the administration to accept the agreement as an *aide memoire* signed on December 10, 1974. The successor treaty would have to wait until 1979.[12]

With normalization talks at a standstill, Sino-American relations lost some of their import. But this was not the only issue which contributed to a substantial downturn in America's image as the world's leader. Most Americans were tired of Washington intervening to solve world problems in Southeast Asia, exacerbated by television coverage of America's helicopter retreat from its embassy in Saigon. And America's hand could be seen in the Middle East resulting in an OPEC embargo during the Yom Kippur War, which doubled the price of gasoline and significantly increased the cost of fuel oil contributing to a rapid increase in inflation. Americans were ready to embrace isolationism in order to put their house in order. Most people were trying to come to grips with their new president, who began his administration pardoning Richard Nixon. The vast majority of the people were totally opposed to the president's action considering that most of Nixon's senior administration officials were in jail. Few realized that Ford had willingly agreed to put his political career in jeopardy, in order to save the office of the presidency from being dragged through the courts were Nixon put on trial. The office of the president had lost much of its power and prestige due to Watergate, and Congress showed its metal when it refused to support Ford's SALT treaty.

Beijing too had her difficulties during the final months of 1974 and into the spring of 1975 much due to the declining health of both Mao and Zhou, and a Deng Xiaoping not quite in a position to assert leadership. In the vacuum, Jiang Qing's Gang of Four would try to revive the fervor of the Cultural Revolution and lead Beijing in a new direction not compatible with the environment created by the Shanghai Communiqué. The internal problems in Washington also effected China, since she was dependent on a strong America to maintain world order and to be a counterweight to Moscow. The result of Washington's and Beijing's problems, progress in Sino-American relations slowed, and there would be little serious communication between the two countries until late spring, 1975.

On April 5, Chiang Kai-shek died, and immediately the White House began to discuss who should represent the president at the funeral. The rank of the individual chosen would indicate the importance Washington viewed future relations with Taiwan, as well as a message to Beijing. The first choice was Earl Butz, the Secretary of Agriculture, a relatively minor Cabinet member, which produced an outcry from Americans looking to keep Taipei as an independent country. Ford finally agreed to send Vice President Nelson Rockefeller. This would accommodate the pro-Taiwan faction, Taipei, and not alienate China since she would realize that Washington had to act with dignity and not humiliate an old ally. Rockefeller represented the US at the funeral on April 16.

The following day ushered in two major loses for the US: Cambodia and Vietnam. With the continued withdrawal of American forces from Southeast Asia, Communist forces under Pol Pot and his Khmer Rouge grew in power. With the departure of American troops and supplies, Lon Nol's government fell on April 17. Eight days later, the last Americans left Saigon by helicopter, an embarrassment which was impossible to minimize. Over extension had ended America's participation in Vietnam, an involvement which began at the end of

World War II, and had accelerated under Truman, Eisenhower, Kennedy, Johnson and Nixon.

CHAPTER XI

PREPARATIONS FOR FORD'S VISIT TO CHINA

The geopolitical landscaped had changed by the end of April, and the Ford White House looked for any opportunity to have a foreign policy success story. And one fell into the president's hands. The newly formed government in Phnom Penh under Pol Pot, wanted to extend its influence in the Gulf of Thailand to control several islands whose ownership was disputed by Thailand and South Vietnam. Oil was the issue, and Poulo Wai was the island of interest. Cambodia continued the former government's definition of territorial waters to twelve miles. And since Phnom Penh also claimed Poulo Wai as part of Cambodia, they saw the twelve mile limit extended an additional twelve miles. On May 12, Cambodian soldiers seized a US merchant vessel, the *S.S. Mayaguez*, about nine miles off the coast of Poulo Wai. The National Security Council quickly met, and from the outset the president indicated that he was willing to use military force to free the seamen aboard the *Mayaguez*. The White House reached out to China, but received no official help. However, Beijing indicated that she would not interfere were America to use military force. However, Ford wanted a triumph. Calling the seizure an "act of piracy," the president kept the public and Congress informed of developments, except for telling them of his real plans for a military rescue. The reports of the three days of the *Mayaguez* rescue mission read like a comedy, one mistake after another. From the outset, the US military did not know where the *Mayaguez* was, nor where the sailors on board were. They assumed that similar to the *Pueblo*, the boat had been seized and the crew transported to a land facility. The crew never left the boat, the Marine attack on the island suspected of holding the seaman only resulted in dead Marines, and the bombing of Cambodian ports produced no results. The real problem was that the new Phnom

119

Penh government had not had time to establish an effective communication system with the Cambodian soldiers, and when they finally did, the crisis had ended with the return of all seamen unharmed and well fed. 41 Marines died to free 39 seamen. However, bombings continued after the rescue with Ford authorizing the drop of a 15,000 pound bomb, the largest non-nuclear bomb in America's weapons arsenal. The reason: the NSC wanted America to "look ferocious." Later, congressional investigations would question the logic of the entire operation. Since the public only knew what the White House announced, there was a sense among the people that Ford had shown his mettle, and America was back, following the debacles in Southeast Asia, which was precisely the president's goal.[1]

When Kissinger met with Huang Zhen, Chief of China's Liaison Office in Washington on May 9, America's position in international affairs had changed since their last meeting. She appeared to be weaker as evidenced in her inability to have the Common Market countries work together against OPEC, her failure to ratify a trade agreement with Moscow, and most importantly by the loss of Cambodia and Southeast Asia. Too many Americans had died, and the American public wanted to return to isolationism. One of the first indicators was Congress's willingness to reduce military spending. Seeing this, along with what she had learned about her shortfall with MIRVed weapons, Moscow began a rapid increase in her nuclear arsenal which would reach parity with Washington by 1979. Throughout all of this, America seemed vulnerable, and this was not a position China wanted to see. She needed a strong America to counter any Soviet efforts to expand into Asia.

At the outset of the meeting, Kissinger countered a recent article in the *People's Daily*, that America had entered a period of "strategic passivity." The secretary described Washington's current foreign policy as a "period of reassessment," but this did not include relations with Beijing. America was fully committed to implementing the principles and objectives of the Shanghai Communique. Kissinger

120

continued with the normal *tour d'horizon* of international affairs emphasizing that Washington still had considerable interest in Asia, especially in Korea, where America would not tolerate an attack, and Japan, where America would maintain close relations. He would be meeting with Gromyko in Geneva on May 19 and the agenda was set: the European Security Conference, a new SALT agreement and the Middle East, where there would be no new ground until he met with the Israelis and Arabs.

Of special importance to both men was the upcoming visit of President Ford to Beijing. The Secretary suggested that late November or early December would be convenient, and that a joint communiqué could be worked on prior to the meeting to avoid "any complexities" during the visit. Having the communiqué agreed upon prior to the meeting was a new process which would control press releases and confine the discussion to the topics agreed upon beforehand. Kissinger also was concerned about Ford's frequent misspeaks. Most recently, he told Congress on April 10, that America was "firmly fixed" on implementing the Shanghai Communiqué. On May 6, at a press conference, the president said that he intended "to reaffirm our commitments to Taiwan."[2] Huang and Kissinger agreed to have subordinates meet and establish an agenda for the forthcoming meeting.

On July 3, Philip Habib and William Gleysteen of the State Department, Winston Lord, the Director of Policy Planning, and Richard Solomon of the NSC prepared a lengthy paper examining a number of approaches concerning normalization for Kissinger to consider in preparing for his Beijing meeting in August, and setting an agenda for the upcoming Ford summit. The paper identified three approaches to the summit: "an indefinite postponement, a "sustaining visit", and full normalization." Postponement was quickly eliminated since it assumed that Mao and Zhou would be alive, but this would probably not be the case.

The "sustaining visit" would result from Kissinger determining that Beijing's conditions for normalization were unacceptable. But the need for a summit was in the best interest of both sides, even if there were little or no progress. Deng Xiaoping had already indicated that this could be the outcome when he announced on June 3 that "President Ford will be welcome in China even if there are no agreements on any major questions between the two countries" implicitly including Taiwan. Were this the case, the president might have to return at a later date to move normalization forward. This should produce serious criticism as to why the president should be out of town to work with a country not willing to move forward. What improvement in relations would warrant a second trip? With little enthusiasm, the advisors did not propose to eliminate a "sustaining visit" provided Ford and Kissinger understood the ramifications.

As for a summit with the goal of establishing normal relations, China's concerns would focus on the Soviet Union and Taiwan. The ball really rested in China's court. The American position was clear: Washington would continue to maintain détente with Moscow, and continue to provide Taiwan security. The paper suggested that Kissinger sound out Beijing's commitment to normalization at his forthcoming meeting in China. If nothing were accomplished, the president could point to the fact that America would continue to honor its defense of Taiwan in the event of an attack, and that this was a *sine qua non* of any normalization of relations with China. Further, the summit would show to Americans that he had tried to move forward toward normalization.[3]

Three days later, Kissinger met with the report's authors and blasted them. "I have read your paper and I just won't do it that way. It's exactly the same paper you presented me last year…For political reasons it's just impossible for the U.S. to go for normalization before '76. If there's one thing that will trigger a conservative reaction to Ford, that's it….I don't even agree with your intellectual thesis—that this is the right time to force it." The president was going to Beijing, that was definite. China is "anxious for it but I see no flexibility on Taiwan...Suppose they give us generous terms? What do I do then? Pocket them and say 'We'll have no deal for two years.'" Kissinger saw the real issue as Washington's continued defense of Taiwan in the event of an attack. America had already reduced her troops to 2,500, and anticipated further reductions in 1976. As for continuing to send arms to Taiwan, which Washington intended to do to replace troops, Kissinger knew this was a problem for Beijing. From their viewpoint we were arming one part of their country.[4]

The secretary was also angry about their suggestion that he travel in August. "I am certainly not going in August." Part of Kissinger's angst was his growing awareness that he had lost a lot of power with the arrival of Ford. His Secretary of Defense, Donald Rumsfeld, and Chief of Staff, Richard Cheney, were slowly marginalizing Kissinger's role in foreign policy, and by 1976 would leave him only with the SALT talks which had little hope of progress. Concluding the meeting, he asked for the group to continue to look for a formula which might find "a step toward normalization."[5]

In the Oval Office, the president was basking in some glory. While considering the *Mayaguez* a success, the docking of the last Apollo flight with its Soviet counterpart *Soyez*, and the exchange of astronauts and Russian cosmonauts between each other's shuttle, was seen as an international success and would be later viewed as the high point of détente. Two weeks later, on August 1 Ford flew to Helsinki to sign the Final Act, or Helsinki Accords, along with representatives of 34 other nations including NATO and Warsaw Pact countries. The terms focused on three parts, or baskets as they were called: security, which made inviolate the frontiers at the end of World War II ensuring the Polish-East German boundary and a success for Moscow; economic cooperation with commitments to improve cooperation in the areas of science, technology and the environment; and third, human rights, the most important from Washington's perspective and the least attractive to Moscow. The terms of the latter provision called for all countries to adhere to the principles of the Charter of the UN and the Universal Declaration of Human Rights. This provision would pose serious problems for the Soviet Union down the road, when subject populations demonstrated for change, especially those in the satellite states in Eastern Europe.

Three days after Helsinki, Kissinger received a new report from his advisors suggesting "steps" that could be taken to move normalization forward, but without granting full diplomatic recognition. There were always three major audiences for any progress: Beijing, the American public, and Taiwan, as well as an interested party in Moscow. All of the small steps required reciprocity by China, since she demanded the same for any concession she made. One scenario would be to link a Chinese position of having the US "confirm the principal of one China" to America's view that Taiwan was a Chinese issue and should be solved by "peaceful" means. In addition to language items, bilateral issues could be a source of agreement including a long awaited claims settlement, an agreement to establish branch liaison offices in each country, an exchange of "defense liaison officers," "a hot line" between capitals, and student and research exchanges.[6]

While taking these suggestions under consideration, the secretary's full attention focused on his efforts to negotiate an Egyptian-Israeli agreement following the Yom Kippur War. After months of work, the secretary was able to bring Yitzak Rabin and Anwar Sadat to the White House on September 4, 1975. The two signed the Sinai II agreement requiring both countries to resolve their issues peacefully. Egypt received back as much of the Sinai as she could through diplomacy, Israel received merchant shipping rights through the Suez Canal, and both agreed to a UN supervised buffer zone, and an early warning station maintained by 200 American troops to reduce the possibility of a sudden attack by either side.

While he could bask in the limelight of his success, which he did, Kissinger returned his focus on his own visit to Beijing scheduled for October, and Ford's summit shortly after Thanksgiving. The secretary had already informed Ambassador Huang Zhen that the president's visit would be the beginning of a tour of Asia including the Philippines, Australia and probably Indonesia. He assured Huang that Ford would not stop in India, especially since on June 26, Indira Gandhi declared a state of emergency and had many of her political opponents imprisoned.[7] On September 28, Kissinger met with Beijing's Foreign Minister Qiao Guanhua who was in New York to attend a meeting at the UN. This was a pro-forma engagement and with each principal accompanied by advisors did the normal *tour d'horizon* of international developments.

As usual, Kissinger began with the Soviet leadership and believed that within three to five years there would be a change. A younger group of leaders with different ideas. The Foreign Minister did not agree. Rather he saw that regardless of leadership changes, Moscow would continue to expand her influence worldwide. Qiao was disappointed with the Helsinki Accords seeing them as a means for Moscow to increase her presence in Western Europe, and permit her to extend her military further into the West via the acceptance of the Polish-East German boundary. But his real concern was that with Moscow's success in Europe, she would be free to place more of her attention on Asia, particularly China and Japan, and this was exacerbated by the West's embrace of détente. Kissinger backed off in his support of the Helsinki agreement noting the multi-day European Security Conference and its continued lauding of the agreement, "gave it a greater significance than it deserved." As for the borders that were recognized as permanent, they already were viewed as permanent by the international community. However, Qiao saw the conference as giving "people the idea that the Soviets can station troops in Europe."

After reviewing issues in Africa and the Middle East, Kissinger announced the "real point I want to discuss" was Southeast Asia. He assured the Foreign Minister that America's "only interest is in the independence of the various countries [in the region]." Cambodia was a bit of a problem due to the *Mayaguez*, but both men agreed that in spite of the current vitriolic language at the UN, the issue would gradually die down. The meeting ended with the two discussing Ford's upcoming visit. Kissinger wanted to have some ideas for the communiqué released at the end of the summit, but Qiao said his mind was "blank." Kissinger pressed forward wanting the summit to announce some "steps" toward normalization. He suggested that all aspects of the Shanghai Communiqué were open to discussion, but Qiao was not interested. And after he turned the discussion to the possibility of world war and other topics, the meeting ended.[8]

Three days before Kissinger left for Beijing, he met with the president and gave him some ideas to think about before his summit visit. However, Ford appeared to be more interested in "what will we be doing for 4 ½ days in China?" He recalled that Nixon's first visit to Beijing was a "a tremendous extravaganza. There was massive television coverage. I think it would be good to do something different. What is there that is dramatic?" The secretary suggested a visit to Xian, the ancient capital of China, where excavations were underway on a newly discovered burial site containing terracotta warriors of the Emperor Chin, from 200 BCE. Ford thought "that might attract the television" networks.[9]

In his memoir, Kissinger described his October 19-23 meeting with Chinese leaders as the "most difficult" of all previous encounters. The purpose was to prepare Ford's summit with Mao and Deng, but as the visit progressed, Qiao played a much larger role than Deng, and was more confrontational especially when it came to drafting the communiqué. Upon his arrival, Vice Premier Deng greeted Kissinger and his State Department entourage noting that this was the secretary's eighth visit to China. Once the press had left the reception area, the two men began their ritual *"tour d' horizon."* Kissinger wanted to first discuss the Ford communiqué, then world politics, and finally bilateral topics

Kissinger had brought a draft communiqué including some of the topics discussed with his advisors and gave it to Deng, who agreed to review it and use it as a starting point. He also agreed to permit hundreds of technicians, security people, members of the press, and television people to accompany the president during his visit. With those technicalities out of the way, international relations took the limelight. Beginning as usual with the Soviet Union, Kissinger made the point that China's concerns about Moscow's expansion were focused essentially on Asia, while the US was concerned about Soviet expansion worldwide. This accounted for different strategies and tactics. For that reason, when Gromyko suggested that both sides renounce the first use of nuclear force, Washington refused. Europe was a weak defense partner. She spent little on her own protection assuming that America would use nuclear power to deter a Soviet attack. Deng was frightened that some of that European weakness was due to her perception that America was weak following Watergate and Vietnam, and he wanted America to put forth a stronger image to waylay that view.

Turning from the Middle East, where he had negotiated the Sinai II agreement, Kissinger reiterated Washington's view concerning Korea. Recognizing that there were two different views to ending the stand-off between north and south, Kissinger reiterated America's position that he was open to dialogue with North Korea provided South Korea was present and involved. On the issue of normalization, he wanted some agreements, be they simply bilateral arrangements, to show the American public, Moscow and Taiwan that there was progress toward normalization. This would satisfy Congress, not terribly upset Taiwan, and cause concern for Moscow. Deng was concerned about the growing negativity in the American Congress, especially against the administration. Kissinger cautioned for him not to read too much into the current situation since the Congress presently in session was elected following the disgrace and resignation of President Nixon. His supporters "were very demoralized" and enabled the naysayers to have their day. But the secretary reassured Deng that the normalization process would not be compromised by these developments and in the end he believed that "we will get wide support for the policy that I have described to you."[10]

Deng was still concerned about Europe's weakness. He saw Russia spreading her influence through such "soft" power tactics as the Helsinki Accords which on the surface could give Europe reason to relax her defenses. He was convinced that Moscow's goal was toward the West, not the East. He reminded the secretary of Mao's often quoted "our common aim is to fix the polar bear, deal with the polar bear." He compared America's present attitude toward Moscow as similar to Europe's attitude toward Hitler in the 1930s, a sense of complacency and acceptance. He implied that Helsinki and the SALT agreement were not dissimilar from Munich in1938, and he wanted to raise an alarm in Washington not to be taken in by Moscow's cooperation in détente. He saw this as a ruse to weaken Europe's defenses.[11]

At the opening banquet which followed the meeting, Qiao turned his toast into an attack on détente, reiterating some of his remarks given earlier at the UN. "The stark reality is not that détente has developed a new stage, but that the danger of a new world war is mounting. We do not believe there is lasting peace. Things develop according to objective laws independently of man's will." The foreign minister's classic Marxian rhetoric infuriated Kissinger and he rose, threw away his prepared remarks and defended America's foreign policy as most suited to America's needs. And these needs meant to "resist hegemony wherever it was attempted. In any event, our firm actions had contributed more to thwarting Soviet expansion than the tough-sounding rhetoric of 'others' (a crack at Qiao). While I was speaking, the televisions lights were suddenly extinguished, and American viewers therefore never witnessed the tense exchange."[12]

128

The following afternoon continued a review of international relations including concerns about Communist expansion in Portugal, and the futures of both Yugoslavia and Spain following the death of their aging leaders. But the high point, was an invitation to meet with Mao. At 6:30 p.m., Kissinger, Ambassador George H. W. Bush, Chief of the American Liaison Office in Beijing and Winston Lord met the Chairman at Zhongnanhai, adjacent to the Forbidden City. Mao, as was his wont, liked to challenge prevailing views to elicit new responses. He challenged Kissinger on China's importance in America's world strategy. Washington had five areas of concern and in order of importance they were the US, the Soviet Union, Europe, Japan and China. Washington had stood on China's "shoulders" to get to Moscow and to sign the SALT agreement and other accords. Mao sensed a decline in Sino-American relations because of Washington's growing weakness and consequently China needed to be prepared to "go it alone." As for Taiwan, Mao was in no hurry to solve the issue. In fact, he wanted America to continue its influence in Taipei because China was not ready to change its relationship with the island country. For emphasis he said that "when I go to heaven to see God, I will tell him that for the present, it is better to have Taiwan under the care of the US."[13]

Kissinger agreed that Europe was weak, and argued that Japan would not be ready to assert herself until there was new leadership, but she had "the potential for seeking hegemony." Mao questioned whether or not America would really defend Europe. The American public would not approve of sending troops, and the real question was would Washington use nuclear weapons to defend against a Soviet attack. The chairman saw America's arsenal as a false front. He used the British retreat through Dunkirk in World War II to describe his view of America's commitment to Europe, and if that analogy were true, then China should not expect help from Washington.[14]

Throughout all of this Kissinger repeated that America would "certainly use nuclear weapons" to confront a substantial attack on

Europe. The US had seven thousand troops in Europe and would not stand by and watch them be captured. He urged Mao to agree to "have a minimum confidence in each other's statements. There will be no Dunkirk strategy, either in the West or in the East. And if there is an attack, once we have stopped the attack, after we have mobilized, we are certain to win a war against the Soviet Union."[15] Before ending the meeting, Mao assured Kissinger that he welcomed a visit from President Ford, a statement which made the entire meeting a success.

Winston Lord made a critical assessment of the Mao-Kissinger meeting. He noted that Mao was concerned about China's future. The old guard was old. He was 82, Deng was 71, and Zhou Enlai was 77. Mao looked very sick. Mentally he was still sharp, but he had a great deal of difficulty standing and walking. He was "just about unable to speak, at all, making most of his points on paper or in obscure grunts." He summed up Mao's presentation simply: "The U.S is 'not reliable,' Europe is 'soft,' Japan seeks 'hegemony,' and therefore China will dig tunnels, store millet and oppose the Soviet Union on its own."[16]

During his final meeting with Deng, the focus was on generating a communiqué. Kissinger was most adamant on the need for some sort of communiqué to assuage the critics of Sino-American relations and show that progress was continuing toward normalization. Deng was not interested in commercial, navigation or air traffic agreements. He was willing to include progress on people-to-people and cultural exchanges. At times Qiao intervened and true to his attitude the previous evening in his toast, he noted that Kissinger's language changes in the proposed communiqué were "too marginal to be perceived." Deng was not interested in addressing the issue of MIAs in Vietnam, nor of MFN status for China, nor of spending time in trying to transform the Korean cease-fire into a peace agreement. While both sides agreed upon a Ford visit, the date was left open. Instead, Deng suggested the secretary and foreign minister collaborate on the wording of the communiqué. This promised to be a rocky engagement.

The communiqué and a date for Ford's visit was the agenda for Kissinger's last day in Beijing. However, he would be thwarted in his efforts to find common ground for the communiqué. Qiao was confrontational and defiant. Later, Kissinger would learn that Qiao had joined the Gang of Four which later overthrew Deng, and his attitude was to challenge Deng's policies, not Kissinger's. In reviewing the Chinese draft communiqué, the secretary was annoyed. America needed a communiqué which explained why the president of the US was visiting China, and the Chinese draft gave no hint as to why the president should come. Further, the draft focused on the differences the countries had concerning international relations. Kissinger said that "the document is completely unacceptable, even as a basis for discussion." Qiao insisted that the differences of opinion had to be included, as they had been in the original Shanghai Communiqué. However, four to five pages of differences and a few paragraphs of agreement did not make a communiqué that Kissinger could sell to the American public. Qiao saw that as an American problem and he was equally adamant in rejecting the American draft. The foreign minister indicated that he did not care if there were a communiqué or not. From Qiao's view, Kissinger could take the Chinese view or there would be no communiqué. Since compromise was impossible and Kissinger did not want to cancel the president's visit, the secretary decided to leave the issue alone. When he asked about a date for the Ford visit, Qiao gave him a paper announcing his visit from December 1-6.[17]

Upon his return, Kissinger briefed Ford on the meetings. Relations between the two countries had cooled and he attributed that to a number of factors which could be traced back to 1973. Watergate, along with congressional restrictions on the president's executive authority in foreign affairs, the declining influence of Zhou Enlai and "our goofs" in sending a high-level ambassador to Taiwan indicating our continued support of the regime. Beijing saw America in decline, and was reluctant to make any new commitments. In light of these developments, Kissinger weighed the need for a presidential visit. There would be little tangible progress in the normalization process. And the visit would be a coup for China, emphasizing her importance and, at the same time, annoy Moscow. However, due to the attention given to the China summit, cancellation would be an international event and would be viewed as a crisis in Sino-American relations. Further, Washington would lose its leverage with Moscow, upset the Japanese, give China "a chance to invite all the Democratic candidates (1976 presidential election year) over to say you screwed up the Chinese policy, and worse yet, Beijing would be insulted and that would end any progress on normalization."[18]

In light of this conclusion, Kissinger supported Ford's visit, and reduced it to three days making it appear to be part of a presidential swing through Asia with stops in Indonesia and the Philippines. By visiting China first, the president's visit would give weight to the continued importance of China. As for the communiqué, if one could not be jointly agreed to, a joint press release would serve the same purpose without having either side list all of the areas of conflict. Ford agreed and Kissinger planned to announce the president's visit on November 3, provided the date met with Beijing's approval.

However, when Ford replaced the Secretary of Defense, James Schlesinger, with Donald Rumsfeld on November 2, and on the following day appointed long time friend Brent Scowcroft as Kissinger's replacement as NSC advisor, but kept him as Secretary of State, Qiao was confused and asked for a delay in announcing the date. He did not realize that the fundamental reason for Schlesinger's resignation was Ford's personal dislike of the defense secretary stemming from disagreements beginning in March, 1974 when he was vice president. And as for Kissinger's demotion, the new team of

Rumsfeld and Cheney wanted to reduce his control of American policy and security.

Qiao needed time to assess the implications of these developments. He did not know if this were a coup, or a purge, and what the ramifications were. Did it mean an end to the normalization process? Rather than risk losing all progress on improving Sino-American relations, he approved November 13 as the announcement day for Ford's China visit. Quickly, the administration notified the press.[19]

CHAPTER XII

FROM FORD'S VISIT TO MAO'S DEATH

In preparing Ford for his visit, Kissinger suggested that he indicate that his visit was a step forward toward normalization. He should emphasize that Washington would continue to work with Moscow but, at the same time, she would counter any Soviet efforts to expand. Recognize that Taiwan was an issue, and reiterate the American position that the solution rested with Beijing, but only if it were done peacefully. Kissinger really wanted Ford to try to secure some bilateral agreements, regardless of their import, as a sign of progress. The president could argue that without any tangible evidence of progress, the world would see the relationship as stagnant, not a result beneficial to either side. Finally, he hoped that the president could get a sense of who were the leading figures in line to replace Mao and Zhou.[1]

On December 1, 1975 *Air Force One* landed in Beijing and that evening Ford, and his wife Betty, and daughter Susan, were guests of honor at a nine-course dinner in the Great Hall of the People. During his welcoming speech, Deng noted China's concern about the growing power of Moscow, implicitly suggesting that America needed to regain her strength. On the following day, the president met Mao. The chairman assured Ford that there were no obstacles in China's relations with America, and did not anticipate any in the next few years. Both agreed to work together to confront Russia where necessary. Unlike Kissinger, Ford asked Mao direct questions concerning China's relations with Japan and Europe. Japan's were a bit unsettled, while European-Chinese relations were improving. In responding to his own questions, Ford described relations with Europe as stable and with Japan as much improved. He had visited the country in 1974, and later the Emperor and Empress had made their first visit to Washington. Talks continued and soon resembled the traditional *tour d'horizon* roaming around the world from Angola to Yugoslavia, and from Spain, to Greece to India to Zaire with no area receiving more importance than the others. The common core of the exercise was always the same: what was Moscow doing in each of the geographic areas?

After the Ford-Mao meeting, Kissinger met with Qiao at 11 p.m. for one hour. The topic was the need for a communiqué. Kissinger sought clarification. Were there to be no communiqué, he would inform the press of that decision. Qiao reiterated his position on communiqués: they had to include areas of agreement and disagreement. Kissinger knew that this would produce an outrage in Congress, giving critics of a China policy much ammunition to try to overturn the administration's outreach to Beijing. Watergate started the attack on the White House, and the suggested communiqué would add fuel to their efforts. The secretary was willing to have no communiqué, instead he could issue a statement to the press that relations were basically good and would be gradually improving. But Kissinger wanted more. A couple of bilateral agreements would serve as evidence of improving relations. Qiao said it made no sense to make agreements before relations were normalized. While the two had reached an impasse, Qiao agreed to give Ford further information on America's servicemen missing-in-action (MIAs)[2]

On the following day, Deng, Qiao, Ford and Kissinger along with their staffs met for a *tour d'horizon*. The 2 ½ meeting was simply a replay of previous reviews. China hoped that Ford might add something new concerning America's efforts to rebuild her image as a world power. While the American delegation agreed that her image had been tarnished by Watergate and Vietnam, the US was every bit as strong as before and soon her image should indicate that. On the final day, the same group reassembled and agreed that there would be no official communiqué of the meetings. They also discussed the future of Taiwan. Deng was aware that nothing could be done until after America's presidential election, and repeated that international developments were always in the forefront of China's foreign policy, "and the Taiwan issue second." Ford responded that any unification would have to be peaceful. Deng did not believe in "a peaceful transition." The solution would be done by China, and if it takes 100 years, so be it. Having said his piece, Deng said that there would be no further discussion concerning Taiwan.

As for the MIAs, Deng had good news. Information on seven had been found and China had the ashes of two, Kenneth Pugh and Jimmy Buckley which would be shipped via the Red Cross to America. Unfortunately, the remains of the other five had not been found. After roughly one hour, there was nothing else for the group to discuss. They were afraid to end the meeting for fear that the press would assume that its shortness indicated they were quarreling. So they continued to talk, mostly about Tibet's economic progress, China's agricultural problems and briefly about trade. Ford suggested that Deng send people to visit America's farm belt and learn new techniques to significantly increase agricultural output. As for trade, the growth in 1974, declined in 1975 much due to the ongoing political struggle within the Chinese hierarchy. Deng also feared that in the long run, China would become dependent on foreign imports with their superior manufactures and discourage the Chinese from trying to design competing products. Before leaving, Ford announced that Ambassador Bush, America's Chief Liaison Officer, would be replaced in a few days. He was going back to the US and become Director of the CIA. Deng spoke of Bush's service in glowing terms and hoped his successor would be as useful. Bush's replacement, whose identity was not yet known, proved to be Thomas Gates.[3]

The Ford party left China on December 5 and flew first to Indonesia and then on to the Philippines. The Indonesians wanted to know how much military and economic aid they could anticipate in 1976, while the Filipinos wanted a new agreement concerning

136

America's military bases there. After spending 24 hours in each country, the president flew to Hawaii. Here he gave his "Pacific Doctrine" speech. In it he reaffirmed America's commitment to the normalization of relations with the PRC on the basis of the Shanghai Communiqué. He described the discussions as significant, useful, and constructive. The Sino-American relationship was becoming a permanent feature of the international political landscape, and it benefited "not only our two peoples but all peoples of the region and the entire world."[4]

Third party observers saw the meeting as a failure. There was no progress on normalization, and the only country which came away with any sort of victory was China. Ford's visit was a political *tour de force* for Beijing, and a punch in the nose to Moscow. The visit was the first step in challenging Moscow's exclusive détente relationship with Washington. Strangely, the success of Nixon's 1972 visit rested on his relations with the Kremlin, while this summit's failure to achieve much progress rested on China's relations with Moscow. While there was no ground breaking progress, there could not have been. China's leadership was in crisis, and Ford needed the Republican right to support his campaign for the presidency, and the right supported Taiwan independence. Ford also had to move further right following his pardoning of Richard Nixon, and the rise of the popular conservative Republican opponent, Ronald Reagan. As a result, by year's end the most that could be said was that Sino-American relations were strained, and normalization was postponed indefinitely.

1976 served as the beginning of a time-out period in Sino-American relations. The deaths of Zhou Enlai and Mao Xedong, coupled with Ford's inexperience in dealing with Congress and his focus on reelection, limited any significant progress throughout the year. As for Taiwan, while there were discussions, progress remained elusive. Believing that America had lost some of her international dominance, Beijing's fear of Moscow increased. China's rhetoric attacked Soviet hegemony and described Moscow as the "main source of the perils of war."[5]

Zhou Enlai succumbed to cancer on January 8. He was 78 years old and had been the interlocutor between Beijing and Washington. Thousands of people gathered in Tienanmen Square to mourn his passing. While Mao refused to attend any ceremonies, the western press hailed Zhou for his statesmanship. Zhou's death quickly coupled with Mao's rapidly declining health, pitted Deng against Jiang Qing, Mao's wife, as Zhou's successor. While Deng was known for his moderate stance, the same could not be said for Jiang. She was the leader of the radical Red Guard movement which wanted to restore the spirit of the Cultural Revolution, a move which did not include closer relations with Washington.[6]

Since Deng gave the eulogy at Zhou's funeral on January 15, the White House saw him as the "odds-on-favorite" to become the new premier. Little did they know that the eulogy would be Deng's last major address. Not to say that he was not mentioned in the press. He was through wall posters and newspapers calling him "China's new Khrushchev," and a "leading person in authority taking the capitalist road." Jiang added that he was "an international capitalist agent." As the rhetoric grew, Mao made up his mind. Rather than support Deng, or Wang Dongxing, Jiang's candidate, the chairman chose Hua Guofeng, as his heir. Hua was a relative unknown who was the first party secretary in Hunan whom Mao described as "a dependable leader and a modest, amiable man." The Politburo accepted the recommendation on January 28, and the formal announcement followed on February 3.[7] Jiang was furious, but decided to first eliminate Deng as an opponent after which she would attack Hua.

Three days after the announcement, a Chinese Boeing 707 landed in Los Angeles airport to fly Richard Nixon to China. This was his first public appearance since his resignation, and he made it to pay his respects to Mao. The two "fell upon each other like old friends with great futures behind them."[8] They talked for well over an hour. The meeting was poorly timed from Ford's viewpoint. It revived his presidential "pardon" issue just three days before the New Hampshire primary election, and Ford would have to share press coverage with the visit. And implicitly it criticized the administration's foreign policy which was unable to carry through Nixon's Shanghai Communiqué to fruition. There is no evidence that Mao deliberately chose this time to invite Nixon, he was indifferent to American domestic politics. The chairman had fond memories of his meeting with Nixon, and wanted to relive some of those heady days in 1972 before he died.[9]

Many Chinese people were disappointed in Mao's absence at Zhou's funeral, and his not appointing Deng, the new premier. April 4 marked the beginning of the traditional Qing Ming festival to honor the dead. People began to gather in Tienanmen Square and soon gathered at the Monument to the Revolutionary Heroes placing wreaths for Zhou. Thousands more came into the square holding placards in memory of Zhou. Soon posters appeared protesting Jiang Qing, and supporting Deng. The Communist Party hierarchy saw the peaceful demonstrations as part of a deliberate, planned counterrevolutionary movement. Mao ordered troops into the square on the evening of April 4, to remove people and posters. On the following day, thousands of demonstrators returned forcing the government to call in 10,000 soldiers to restore order and clear the square. Jiang could not have been happier, and continued to tell her husband that Deng was the organizer of these demonstrations. Mao agreed and he removed Deng from all of his posts, but permitted him to retain his party membership, a concession which would later enable him to return to power.[10]

Meanwhile, the new NSC advisor gave Ford a report analyzing the impact of Deng's apparent fall from power, and the emergence of Hua Guofeng. Scowcroft had no real guidance, describing Washington as "passive observers." He recommended that

139

the president stay the course, maintain good relations with China, show willingness to challenge Soviet efforts at expansion, and move toward completing the normalization process.[11] Two weeks later, on May 29, 1976 Kissinger and Huang Zhen met for fifty minutes. The secretary noted that since this was a presidential election year in America, China should not take any campaign statements literally. Candidates may well make statements that do not reflect reality in order to enhance their bid for election. Huang's principal concern, as usual, was Soviet expansion. He was happy to see that at recent NATO and European meetings, there was a growing awareness that Moscow was a threat to international stability, one which needed to be addressed.[12]

A month later, a CIA report reiterated Huang's concerns about Soviet efforts at hegemony. The report, endorsed by the newly appointed CIA Director George H. W. Bush, stated that Russia "will still be the 'main enemy'" to whichever group emerges, the moderates or the ideologues. China was viewed as a "regional, not a global power." In fact one could argue that she was a "lower developed country," similar to those in Africa and parts of Asia. However, due to her size, and overwhelming potential, both Moscow and Washington would work to improve relations. Taiwan was the only major stumbling block in the Sino-American normalization process. But Beijing was aware that she needed to "be patient and willing to wait for further US disengagement from Taipei."[13]

Disengagement was a frequent topic in Washington, especially within the Pentagon. While the White House had intended to continue to reduce America's military commitment to Taiwan, only in December, 1975 did the president give specifics as to the reduction. Ford told Deng on December 4 that military personnel would be reduced from the current 2,800 to 1,400 by the end of 1976. In February, 1976 Scowcroft became the point man on the reduction, and realized that ultimately there would be no American military personnel left on Taiwan, including intelligence personnel. To prevent

140

this, William Clements of the Defense Department suggested that some of the military intelligence staff could be "civilianized," transferred from military to civilian status. Reductions could be limited to 1,100 to reach the 1,400 number, provided about 300 were civilianized. While annoyed at being left out of the Pentagon discussions, Kissinger agreed with the bottom line. He had Ford sign National Security Decision Memorandum (NSDM) on September, 1976 approving a ceiling of no more than 1,400 military personnel, including 300 "civilianized" intelligence agents, on the island after December 30.[14]

While troop reductions were important for Taiwan, the issue paled in comparison to developments on the China mainland. All of Deng's policies were under fire as best seen in mid-July when Vice Premier Zhang Chunqiao, who supported the Gang of Four, spoke to the Senate Minority Leader Hugh Scott during his visit to Beijing. Zhang told him in no uncertain terms that Taiwan "was a noose under the neck of the U.S. It is in the interests of the American people to take it off. If you don't, the PLA (People's Liberation Army) will cut if off...perhaps that doesn't sound pleasant, but that is the way it is."[15] Upon learning of this exchange, Kissinger knew that Scott's abrasive manner was undoubtedly responsible for Zhang's "firing off some cannons," and he did not see it as an indication of a change in Beijing's policies. However, in later discussions with Huang Zhen the Chinese Ambassador made it clear to the Secretary that the Shanghai Communiqué did not preclude the use of force in resolving the Taiwan issue. This hardened opinion was reinforced a week later when Kissinger spoke with Tom Gates, America's new ambassador to the Liaison Office in Beijing. Gates believed that Zhang's outburst was deliberate, and it had been approved to make public Beijing's position toward Taiwan. And were that the case, China was quite willing to stop progress on normalization, the goal of the Gang of Four.[16]

On July 27, a massive earthquake devastated the coal-mining city of Tangshan killing over 200,000 people. The interim government of Hua was unable to rapidly respond.[17] Many of the poorer people in China viewed the earthquake as an omen. They believed that the gods showed their approval of good leadership through strong harvests and military victories. But they showed their disapproval through natural disasters and military defeats. Without question, the earthquake was a sign from the gods, a sign that was frequently followed by a change in leadership. And the change occurred. On September 7, Mao died at age 82. Two days later Beijing announced his death, and with it the beginning of the end of the Gang of Four. Jiang Qing's connection to her husband was the only reason that the radical movement had survived. With Mao's passing, the connection ended and within four weeks the Gang of Four was arrested, imprisoned, and would be put on public trial in 1980. The moderates who assumed power endorsed Zhou Enlai's 1963 announcement that China needed Four Modernizations in agriculture, industry, national defense, and science and technology. The return of the moderates also meant a commitment to improved relations with the West and especially the US.

On October 7, Hua assumed the chairmanship of the Chinese Communist Party. On the following day, Kissinger met foreign minister Qiao who was in New York City to attend a UN meeting. With the arrest of the Gang of Four, Qiao was far less confrontational. The two reminisced about Kissinger's five meetings with Mao, and the accomplishments of the chairman. Naturally, the Soviet Union and its efforts to expand her influence was discussed especially in Africa, an area often neglected by Washington. Soviet hegemonic tendencies toward East and West were reviewed without any new conclusions. Beijing was convinced that Europe was weak, and that Sino-American relations were not among America's top priorities. Kissinger's recent speech to the UN General Assembly noted Washington's priorities as the Soviet Union, Europe, Japan and then China. Part of the reason for that order, was that nothing was going on between Beijing and

Washington. Normalization was on hold and would remain so until well after the elections. The two parted ways having accomplished nothing except maintaining a dialogue.[18]

CHAPTER XIII

NORMALIZATION STALLED: CARTER, DENG, AND THE VANCE VISIT

On November 2, Americans went to the poles and elected Jimmy Carter, former Governor of Georgia, America's new president. Aware that he needed some experienced people in international relations, Carter invited Cy Vance, a lawyer and former Assistant Secretary of Defense under Johnson, to be his Secretary of State. The two agreed that normalization of relations with China should be one of the administration's principal objectives. Vance agreed and wanted to move slowly, get to know the new Chinese leadership, and assess the situation in Taiwan. He also wanted to work with Moscow. Carter chose Zbigniew Brzezinski as his NSC advisor, a co-founder of the Trilateral Commission and having State Department experience. No two foreign policy advisors could have had held more disparate views on American foreign policy goals, and the means to achieve them. The soft-spoken Vance believed that as Secretary of State he was in charge of recommending foreign policy to the president, and wanted to pursue goals through diplomacy rather than continual confrontation. The Polish, brash, egotistical, outspoken Brzezinski was willing to confront Communism and the Soviet Union whenever he deemed necessary. He was a devoted student of Soviet affairs, and later in the 1970s would be the first to predict the collapse of the Soviet Union due to its economy. As Carter's foreign policy advisor during the presidential campaign, Zbigniew had greater access to Carter than Vance, and he used it to ultimately replace Vance as the principle author of Carter's foreign policy.[1] Through much of this, the president appeared not to realize that Brzezinski's goal was to make Carter's world view mirror his own.

144

Carter was unpretentious and open-minded. He liked to hear multiple sides to an issue, while at the same time encouraging a spirit of collegiality. Carter used a Friday breakfast meeting for his foreign policy advisors which normally included Vice President Mondale, Vance, Brzezinski and Secretary of Defense Harold Brown, all of whom understood that the results of the meeting were secret, unless otherwise authorized by the president. However, this approach would frequently be short circuited by Brzezinski, who would share his ideas with the press, ideas which were often in disagreement with those of the State Department. The result was that foreign governments feared that Washington did not know what it was doing. Once a decision was made, Carter would micromanage the outcome. Departments reported directly to him, without any cross communication, and at times this resulted in departments confused as to their role in implementing decisions.

During the transition period between presidents, Kissinger had his last meeting with Ambassador Huang Chen, Chief of the PRC's Liaison Office at the secretary's dining room. He used the occasion to introduce his successor, Secretary of State-designate, Cyrus Vance, and after an exchange of pleasantries, Huang raised the issue of Taiwan, in what became a primer for Vance. Kissinger reiterated the standard American response that Washington supported a one China policy. Huang reiterated Beijing's three point position: America was to sever diplomatic relations with Taiwan, withdraw troops, and abrogate the defense treaty. The groundwork had been laid. Beijing wanted to maintain friendly relations with Washington due to her fear of Moscow, and wanted the US to strengthen its NATO partners, a position Vance reassured Huang was supported by Carter. Throughout the meeting, conversation focused on reminiscing about times past, and at the close, Kissinger and Huang exchanged farewells.[2]

The change in government leadership in Washington and Beijing put a halt to any significant progress in normalizing relations. Early on, Michel Oksenberg, an NSC staffer, suggested to Brzezinski

145

that it was important for Carter to do something to indicate that he wanted to move forward on the issue. There was an imbalance between the president's interest in Soviet-American relations and his apparent indifference to relations with China. Oksenberg also suggested that a committee be formed to establish a strategy to deal with Beijing throughout the year. Brzezinski agreed to both ideas, and soon China specialists, led by Dick Holbrook, Vance's Secretary for East Asia, along with Oksenberg and others met to work out a new China strategy. But, problems among the participants would soon become clear. Holbrooke was exceptionally bright but seriously lacked social skills, and did not like to interact with others.[3] And there was the rivalry between Vance and Brzezinski, with the latter assuming that since he was in charge of national security, he was also in charge of America's foreign policy, the bailiwick of the Secretary of State. Progress in implementing policy was also obstructed due to Carter's inability to establish a good relationship with Congress. This would pose problems since many congressmen feared that the defense of Taiwan would pay the price for normalization.

Taking Brzezinski's advice, Carter invited Huang Chen to the White House on February 8 and introduced him to his China team of advisors. After formalities, both sides agreed that Sino-American relations rested on implementing the Shanghai Communiqué. The president suggested that Chairman Hua or other top officials visit America. After all, Nixon and Ford and many other high ranking American officials had visited Beijing, and it was only natural for China to send representatives to Washington. Huang gave the same response as before: as long as there was a Taiwan Embassy in America, no high ranking Chinese official would visit the US. Americans could visit China because there was no Taiwan Embassy there. Following America's acceptance of China's terms for normalization, China would welcome the opportunity to send her leaders to Washington.

The Taiwan conversation went nowhere new. Huang reaffirmed that if there were no other solution to the future of Taiwan, China would use force to seize the island, "but as to when, it is hard to say." As the meeting continued, it proved to be an opportunity for both sides to reaffirm and restate previous positions. China was totally opposed to nuclear weapons and was concerned about the "Polar Bear" to the north. Carter agreed that nuclear weapons were a danger, and that Europe's military forces needed to be strengthened. He raised the issue of claims and assets, and per usual, assurances were made that it could easily be solved, but nothing tangible evolved. As for China's domestic situation, Huang announced that Hua had "smashed" the "Gang of Four," and the country was following the Four Modernizations first enunciated by Zhou Enlai. If nothing else, and there really was not much else, the meeting served as proof that Sino-American relations were alive and committed to moving forward, albeit slowly.[4]

Taipei was quite concerned about the new administration's talks with Huang. Ambassador Shen believed there was a change in Washington's commitment to the ROC. He sensed it from a Vance press interview when the secretary simply said that the normalization process was under review. To Shen, this implied there could be a change in America's military commitment to Taipei since Vance did not mention security issues.[5] Shen's concern was legitimate. America's Ambassador to Taipei, Leonard Unger, believed that America should continue her "conditioning process," which had been ongoing for several years, to prepare Taiwan for the eventual break in diplomatic relations, and an end to the defense treaty. Without question, the White House had shown little interest in keeping Shen informed of any normalization developments, and told the ambassador that at present normalization was not on the front burner in Washington unlike the Middle East, SALT talks and the Panama Canal.[6]

On the same day, February 16, Unger had dinner with Taiwan's Premier Chiang Ching-kuo, Chiang Kai-shek's son and heir. Concerned about America's apparent change in attitude, Taipei had begun to develop plans for nuclear weapons. The premier was under pressure from Chinese scientists at home and abroad, calling for an increase in national security and in prestige of being a nuclear power. Unger emphasized that Carter was totally opposed to nuclear proliferation, and discouraged Chiang from following such a policy. Chiang backed off, and agreed that moving forward on nuclear weapons was "suicidal." In Washington, steps were quickly taken to terminate all exports of anything that could be used to develop nuclear weapons. On April 29, Brzezinski informed Carter that Taiwan had closed down its nuclear weapons program and had agreed to limit its nuclear program to civil uses of atomic energy. Carter noted "good" in the memorandum's margin.[7]

Talks with Moscow for an extension of the SALT I agreement began in February with a meeting between Carter and Soviet Ambassador Anatoly Dobrynin. Vance continued the talks in the spring, but negotiations were stalled when Carter wanted to tie human rights to arms limitations. By 1978, Brzezinski had the ear of the president, and his almost visceral dislike of Moscow, produced an impasse in talks which would postpone a SALT II treaty until 1979. In response to the Soviet invasion of Afghanistan in late 1978, Carter pulled the treaty from Senate consideration and it laid dormant for over a decade.[8]

In early March, Beijing caught the president's eye. He noted a sharp downturn in exports to China creating the first US trade deficit with Beijing since import controls were lifted in 1971. He wanted to know why. In 1969, two-way trade amounted to $3.9 billion and rose to $14 billion by 1975.[9] However, on Mao's death, America's total China trade was $336 million, slightly less than Washington's trade with Honduras, and one-tenth of her trade with Taiwan. In response to a Brzezinski inquiry, Secretary of Commerce Junita Kreps explained that a large part of the trade was in huge agricultural purchases by Beijing in 1973 and 1974. The 1976 downturn was due to a number of factors including hard currency difficulties, a change in Beijing's government, and the Tangshan earthquake in July, killing over 240,000 people making it the world's deadliest in the 20th century. In addition to these issues, there were also factors of America's making. China preferred to trade with countries with whom she had normal diplomatic relations, especially European countries. The Jackson-Vanik language prevented China from receiving MFN treatment, and gave off the image of Beijing being a second class country. Brzezinski added to Kreps's report that the imbalance was also due to America's growing demand for Chinese products at the same time that Beijing turned to other sources for technology and agricultural products.[10]

Since normalization and MFN did not seem to be on the horizon, Kreps recommended that progress be made on the claims/assets issue as a first step to reduce the imbalance in trade. On March 23, during a *tour d'horizon* meeting between Huang and Vance, the secretary called attention to a Holbrooke proposal on claims which stemmed from discussions in 1973. Simply put, all blocked Chinese assets would be available to reimburse US claimants, and all of the American properties left in China would be used to satisfy Chinese claims. Huang had not anticipated a claims discussion at this meeting, and refused to comment.[11]

On April 29, Ambassador Han Hsu, Huang's assistant, met with Holbrooke to respond to the March 23 offer. In no uncertain terms, he rejected the American proposal. "The blocking of properties of Chinese nationals by US elements after the founding of the PRC is in itself illegal. The Chinese side absolutely does not recognize it." As for the "so-called" properties of American nationals in China, regardless of the amount, would not compare to the "plundering of Chinese resources" by American businesses over a long period of time. The only issue involved is the amount of money America owes China. In view of this interpretation, the question of returning to the

149

1973 proposal was impossible. At the end of May, Brzezinski sent Carter a memo on the claim/assets negotiations and recommended that since the Chinese did not see this as an obstacle to normalizing relations, the administration should "let the matter rest."[12]

Throughout these developments, members of the NSC staff called for the White House to turn its attention to China. Finally, on April 5, Carter ordered a Policy Review Committee to examine Washington's China policy in three areas: what were the broad options toward dealing with Beijing, a strategy to withdraw troops from Taiwan, and an analysis of the sale of defense-related technologies to the PRC. The review would be done by June 1.[13]

Six days later, Vance told Ambassador Huang that the president had appointed Leonard Woodcock to be his representative in Beijing. He had been the head of the United Auto Workers, and whose age, experience and demeanor would work well with the Chinese leadership. Further, his auto worker background should appeal to a Marxist government which theoretically called for the "workers of the world, unite." Vance also wanted to visit Beijing, preferably in August. Huang saw no problem and he would be welcomed in China. The discussion continued for another hour or so with a review of international relations, but nowhere near the degree of detail covered in former meetings with Kissinger.

While the review committee continued its work, Vance had prepared a paper endorsing normalizing relations with China. The present Sino-Soviet rivalry gave America an advantage to have China accept terms she might not be willing to accept if her relations improved with Moscow. Taiwan was coming to accept that normalization would alter her relations with Washington, but the blow could be made easier via continued economic and military support to Taipei. The American public was ambivalent. On the one hand, there was little interest in a "sell-out" of Taiwan, but at the same time there was increasing interest in improving relations with Beijing. All in all, Vance's paper was rather weak in its recommendation which called for "moving cautiously." When Michel Oksenberg of the NSC read the report, he sent it to Brzezinski with the notation "a frankly somewhat diffuse and disappointing paper." But he recommended that the NSC make no comment to the president, but simply forward Vance's report. In his memoir, Vance believed that his report "laid the basis" for Carter's decision to go forward.[14]

Independent of Vance and of the review committee, Brzezinski formulated his own position. It had three aspects: expanding bilateral contacts, common strategic interests in discouraging Soviet expansion, and the normalization process "which should be moved forward whenever opportune." He also told Carter that Beijing was central to the global equilibrium and that he should support a strong China. Carter endorsed some of Brzezinski's ideas in his famous May 22 foreign policy speech at Notre Dame. He referred specifically to China as a "central element of our global policy...and we hope to find a formula which can bridge some of the difficulties that still separate us."[15]

On June 27 the review committee submitted its report on Sino-American relations and representatives from the Departments of State, Treasury, Defense, the CIA and NSC supported the view that Washington should make a major effort to establish full diplomatic relations in the near future by recognizing Beijing, allowing diplomatic relations and the defense treaty with Taiwan to lapse, and remain satisfied that alternative means would exist to sustain the substance of America's current relationship with Taipei. But before moving forward, all wanted to wait for the results of Vance's August trip to Beijing. The group agreed that there were minimum demands Beijing needed to meet concerning its peaceful intent toward Taiwan, either by publically renouncing its intent to use force, or by privately assuring Washington of its peaceful intent following normalization. No one was interested in pursuing collateral activities, and all recognized the political issues of selling "recognition" in Congress, a Congress that was already involved with the Panama treaties, a SALT treaty, and Carter's efforts to bring Egypt and Israel to the peace table. All agreed to postpone any decision until after Vance's visit to Beijing.

During the discussions, differences in the purpose of normalization materialized. Brzezinski saw Sino-American relations in terms of limiting Soviet power. And Secretary of Defense Hal Brown agreed. Vance saw the purpose as recognizing that China would soon be a world player and could not be ignored. He wanted Washington to recognize China for its own potential, not just as a chess piece to be a counterweight to Moscow. Throughout the discussions, Brzezinski tried to minimize the importance of Vance's visit. He suggested that America reduce her military presence on Taiwan before the visit, thereby eliminating one of the secretary's bargaining points. The NSC advisor also suggested recalling Ambassador Unger from Taipei, before the visit, again to reduce Vance's leverage. Brzezinski wanted to reduce Vance's chance of success, so that later he could be the one to go to Beijing, and successfully move the normalization process to fruition. However, Vance received support from Treasury Secretary Blumenthal who believed that Brzezinski's unilateral steps would prove nothing, and that by having patience could be the best negotiating approach.[16] The end product was that Vance would tell the Chinese leaders in August that the administration wished to establish full diplomatic relations, but had to be able to maintain economic and cultural relations with Taiwan, and provide them with needed defensive weapons.[17]

In preparation for his departure to China, Leonard Woodcock, America's new ambassador to Beijing met with Carter and Vance during the first couple of weeks in July. The president wanted Woodcock to deal directly with himself or with Vance, but with no other members of the State Department. Carter shared the Nixon view that the department was a sieve, and was unable to keep secret negotiations under wrap. Woodcock pointed out that normalization could be done without congressional approval, however, future relations and economic issues would be in the hands of Congress. Carter agreed but preferred to keep Congress in the dark as long as necessary. He did believe that once diplomatic relations were agreed upon, he could "sell it to the American people," and that he would take on "the political responsibility for doing so."[18]

At the same time that Vance prepared for his visit to Beijing, there were major changes in the Chinese hierarchy. Chairman Hua Guofeng was not really up to the task of replacing Mao, and knew that he needed help. The best qualified person was Deng Xiaoping who had fallen from power at the hands of the Gang of Four. Now that they were no longer an issue, Hua wanted to bring him back into the administration. Capitalizing on the ongoing meeting of the Third Plenum of the Tenth Congress being held in Beijing from July 16-21, the members agreed with Hua to return Deng to his former positions in the government as well as his being chief of staff of the People's Liberation Army, and deputy chairman of the Military Council. A year later he would, for all intents and purposes, be the leader of China.[19]

While Carter focused his attention on the Panama Canal Treaty, representatives from the departments of state, treasury, defense, the CIA and the NSC worked through a variety of scenarios, several concerning the impact of normalization on Taiwan. A July 26 report suggested that the Nationalist government should be able to control the shock and decline in morale which would accompany the normalization, and that the country's economy was strong. While there was agreement that China would take no military action against Taiwan for at least five years, after that Taipei's military future would be dependent on America continuing to supply the island with defensive weapons. At present, the Taipei government had made no comprehensive plans to prepare the people for normalization, partly because by doing so it implicitly accepted normalization. Once normalization was achieved, the administration believed that Taiwan

153

would move to bolster confidence among the people and minimize any anti-American reactions.[20]

On July 30, Carter convened a meeting of Vance, Brzezinski, Brown, Holbrooke and Oksenberg to work out the basic strategy for Vance's visit. Carter wanted him to be direct in his approach. He should keep in mind the Five Points, known internally as the Secret Pledge, enumerated by Nixon and Kissinger in their 1972 dealings with Beijing. There was one China and Taiwan was part of it, America would not support any Taiwan independence movement but would support any peaceful resolution with China that could be agreed upon, neither side sought hegemony in the Asia Pacific, and that Washington sought normalization. As an aside, earlier Kissinger had promised to reduce America's military presence as normalization progressed. This prompted Oksenberg to note that America's presence on Taiwan was a plus for the Chinese. Washington would keep Taiwan from developing nuclear weapons, from developing relations with Moscow, and from becoming independent.

Throughout the talks, Brzezinski continued to press for including bilateral agreements during the visit, to which both Vance and Brown said "after, not before." The NSC advisor did have the group agree that the *tour d'horizon* approach with Beijing was effective, especially since it could show the Chinese that America shared parallel interests with them, especially vis-à-vis Moscow. The group did agree to prepare a draft communiqué which Vance could take with him to show the Chinese that America was quite serious about establishing formal diplomatic relations. This was a step beyond the Kissinger-Nixon agreement in 1972. The purpose was not to publicize the communiqué, but to show it as evidence of intent. Carter knew that time was needed to prepare Congress for the change, and especially to limit the influence of the Taiwan lobby, which wanted no change in Washington's relationship with Taipei. At the meeting's end, Carter reasserted his direct approach. "I just want to lay it out. Be frank with them…If they are abusive, then Cy can come home. My

154

impression is that the Chinese appreciate candor." Brzezinski was pessimistic about Vance's chances at success and he wrote Vance a memo noting that "he had cautioned the president about undo optimism with respect to the results we can expect from your upcoming visit." He added that the president agreed. To go further, in his memoir, Brzezinski wrote that he anticipated that Vance's mission would produce "very little progress," and that alternative arrangements should be prepared.[21]

Four days before Vance left for Beijing, Carter sent him a note. While emphasizing that negotiations should be reciprocal, he wanted Vance to focus on America's global policy which included an important role for China. As for normalization, in return for full diplomatic relations, Beijing had to agree that it would not publically contradict Washington's statements that the Taiwan problem would be solved peacefully. Finally, he should indicate that America was eager to expand cultural and economic relationships even without normalization, and if this were the only result, it would show the world that the relationship was moving forward.[22]

Carter's willingness to settle for a trade pact or the sale of some goods really undermined the importance of the mission. The president's agenda had neither time nor space to promote normalization. He needed to secure congressional approval for the Panama Canal Treaty, a goal pursued since his inauguration. Add to that were the ongoing talks with Moscow and SALT, and his desire to bring peace to the Middle East, especially between Anwar Sadat of Egypt and Yitzhak Rabin of Israel. And to make progress more difficult, China was undergoing a major leadership change with the rise of Deng Xiaoping as a replacement for Hua Guofeng. In light of these developments, Carter decided to use Vance's visit simply as a sign of his continuing commitment to improving Sino-American relations.

A day later, Ambassador Unger met with Premier Chiang Ching assuring him that normalization would "not undercut Taiwan's security and well being." The Nationalist leader cautioned that Washington ought not expect much from this meeting. The rise of Deng and the ensuing governmental issues would force the hierarchy to take a strong anti-American stance concerning Taiwan and make no concessions, try to drive a wedge between Moscow and Washington, and show no support for a North-South Korean dialogue. Chiang's prescient remarks would prove to be right on target.[23]

On the afternoon of August 22, Vance met briefly with Deng Xiaoping, who Vance believed was the man in charge, and then with the Foreign Minister Huang Hua. At the outset, Vance announced that "President Carter...is committed to normalization." Having made that perfectly clear, he gave the usual *tour d'horizon* of America's foreign policy. Among the topics covered, Vance noted that the administration had strengthened NATO's military forces, a development supported by Beijing, and was negotiating a SALT agreement with Moscow, which would put limits on Soviet ballistic missiles, and benefit China as well as Western powers. In Asia, Washington looked to work with China for regional stability and peace, and to fortify the independence of local states, implicitly including Taiwan. America intended to strengthen ties with Japan, reduce Washington's military presence in Korea, but maintain a defense treaty, negotiate North-South Korean talks with all three sides in attendance, maintain military bases in the Philippines, initiate normalization talks with Vietnam, and seek to strengthen ties with India and Pakistan. He concluded his "round the world" presentation noting developments in Europe and the Middle East.[24]

Africa was the opening topic on the 23rd, and Vance announced a change in America's foreign policy. In the past, Washington encouraged Africans to solve African problems. This did not work out as well as anticipated. The new approach was to work with states where Washington had poor relations most notably Somalia on the Horn of Africa in order to reduce Soviet influence. The US would continue to have strong relations with Kenya, Chad, and the Sudan. As for Rhodesia, Nambia and South Africa, the White House supported efforts to bring about full political participation in each nation's government affairs, and keep in touch with developments in Zaire and Nigeria. All in all, Vance believed that America's objectives in Africa had many common elements with those of China.[25]

At the end of his review, Vance addressed the issue of normalization. Washington recognized that "there is one China and that Taiwan is a part of China." Understanding that, the president was willing "to establish full diplomatic relations with the PRC." This would mean an end to America's diplomatic relations with Taiwan, an end to the Mutual Defense Treaty, and the withdrawal of all American military personnel and military installations. While this would pose some problems in the US, especially among members of the Taiwan lobby and Congress, the president was committed to going forward with normalization provided a "satisfactory agreement can be reached."

Part of that "satisfactory agreement" included America being able to continue her trade and investment practices with Taiwan along with scientific and other private contacts. As for Washington's representation on the island, some government personnel would be required to remain under an *informal* arrangement. (emphasis in original). There would be some sort of office for personnel to work with American business representatives and the like. It would have no diplomatic function, no flags would be flown nor any government seal on the doors. As a final condition, both sides needed to refrain from criticizing each other, especially if it concerned America's statements about the peaceful unification of Taiwan and the mainland. Similar to the Chinese, Americans were very conscious of criticism, and if Beijing implied that it would use force to seize Taiwan, Congress would never approve normalization. The Foreign Minister had said little during the presentation, but at the end simply said that there was no change in China's position.[26]

Huang presented China's view of international relations on the morning of the 24th. Chairman Hua Guofeng had just enunciated them the day before at the 11th National Party Conference of the Chinese Communist Party. And there was nothing new. Hua reaffirmed the Mao-Zhou policies which focused on Moscow's strategy to defeat the West, China's support of an independent Palestinian state at the expense of Israel, maintaining good relations with Japan, and supporting Korean reunification as an issue to be solved solely by North and South Korea. In Africa, he saw Moscow's sending mercenaries into Zaire and Angola, as a first step for greater control of the countries. As for normalization, no new news here either.[27]

In many ways these first few meetings were a dress rehearsal for the principal meeting with Deng Xiaoping. Initially Deng had high expectations for the visit, but the president's overwhelming concern over the Panama treaty and SALT indicated that Vance's meeting might be more for show than substance. Deng had a sense that the visit was to keep normalization on the negotiating table, but not necessarily to reach agreement.

At the outset, Deng noted that he was "internationally a well-known man. I have survived thrice and gone down thrice…that is why I am well known. For instance, you here are all diplomats and I am just a country bumpkin!" Following the banter, Deng reviewed the international scene with China's normal focus on Moscow and her efforts to expand her presence throughout the world. As for normalization, Deng realized that Carter was not ready to move forward. Vance abandoned his prepared remarks and simply gave Deng a copy of the American proposal. Any questions that Deng might have could be addressed when Huang Hua came to the UN for the upcoming General Assembly meeting.[28]

Deng went on the offensive. The America proposal of ending diplomatic relations with Taiwan, removing all troops and military equipment, and letting the defense treaty expire was nothing new. In

158

fact, Washington had added another element, the right to maintain some sort of unofficial office for American government personnel to handle business and personal issues of Americans in Taiwan. America had to realize that it owed China a debt, not vice versa. Deng reiterated China's three points and was willing to accept what was called the Japanese Formula which suggested moving the American Embassy in Taiwan to Beijing, and moving the Liaison Office in Beijing to Taiwan, provided the office had no diplomatic function and no government officials. Picking up on Vance's willingness to postpone any immediate decisions, Deng agreed that a leisurely pace would be beneficial in light of their many common interests. However, this did not mean procrastination for its own end. Regardless of the amount of time needed, Beijing would decide when and how Taiwan would be "liberated" and united with the mainland. With that, the meeting adjourned and the participants prepared for a dinner hosted by Deng at the Summer Palace.[29]

Vance began his final day in Beijing with Chairman Hua Guofeng, a meeting which was more important as a media event than for anything substantial. During the 90 minutes, Hua reviewed his rise to power following the death of Mao, and reiterated Beijing's anti-Soviet views stemming from the times of Peter the Great. He was aware of the past several days of discussions and expected that the talks would continue. Following the meeting, Vance met with the foreign minister. Having been rebuffed earlier about the need for a communiqué, he tried again, but without success. The secretary was willing to settle for a one page summary as a means to show that some progress had been made. However, the foreign minister saw no need for any written record, but suggested that Vance was free to express his views in a press conference with journalists that evening before he returned to America. On the 26th, Vance flew to Japan on his way back to Washington.[30]

On August 28, after he had returned to the US, John Wallach, a reporter for the Hearst newspapers, after listening to the

159

government's official explanation of the visit which emphasized the positive, wrote that China had shown some "unexpected flexibility" on Taiwan. This was completely false, and in a very uncharacteristic move, Deng publically denounced the report. As Carter noted, "the last thing the Chinese wanted was for someone to accuse them of being flexible on a matter of principle."[31] Later, in assessing the Vance mission, Carter believed that part of the reason for the outburst was due to "a surprising incompatibility between Secretary Vance and the Chinese leaders, which I never really understood. This personal estrangement seemed to carry over during the months that followed."[32]

Taiwan's reaction to the Vance mission was as anticipated: concern and fear that Taipei was simply a pawn to be played by either side to achieve normalization. On August 27 Holbrooke and Ambassador Unger met with Chiang Ching and assured him that no deals were made, and no decisions were taken. Two weeks later, Ambassador Shen met with Vance and was given the same information. Shen was concerned about news that America's Embassy in Taiwan would be downgraded. Vance assured him while that was an issue, it was purely exploratory without any conclusion. White House responses did little to assuage Taipei's fears that she indeed would be a pawn.[33]

While the Vance mission failed to move normalization forward, Deng wanted progress, and having little faith in the Secretary of State, he lobbied to have Brzezinski come to China. He knew that he could use the NSC's distrust of Moscow as leverage to have him accommodate Beijing's views on normalization. In order to ingratiate himself with the American public, he hosted a high level American media delegation to China on September 6. Included were Keith Fuller, managing editor of the Associated Press, Arthur Sulzberger, publisher of *The New York Times*, and Katharine Graham, publisher of the *The Washington Post*. While promoting student exchanges, Deng's real message was that America had to accept Beijing's

160

position on Taiwan to move onto normalization. He assured the press that while he would work to resolve the issue peacefully, the matter was exclusively one for Beijing to resolve without outside interference.[34]

During the next several months, every time Deng met an important American politician he repeated the same message, that Taiwan was an internal matter for China. But try as he might, Carter had decided to put Taiwan on the back burner and focus on passage of his Panama Canal Treaty. The main stumbling block to approval was opposition to the gradual transfer of control of the canal to the Panamanians. To secure needed votes from conservative Republicans, the president decided to defer the Taiwan issue until after the senate approved the treaty.[35]

Efforts to have Carter meet with the Chinese Foreign Minister on October 4 failed to materialize. Huang Hua's flight to Canada for a meeting in Ottawa had no room for a Carter meeting. Instead, Vance would meet Huang in New York on September 28, where the foreign minister was to address the UN General Assembly. The meeting began with a review of global issues starting with the Palestinian Liberation Organization's (PLO) resolution to be recognized as the sole representative of Palestinians. Further talks included many states in Africa, SALT, Yugoslavia and Tito's visit to Beijing, ending with a brief discussion about normalization. The White House had not completed its review of prior discussions, but anticipated this would be done "in the near future." When that occurred Vance wanted to make sure that the Chinese understood that all communication with the White House concerning normalization would be conducted only through Ambassador Woodcock. This would eliminate misunderstandings and leaks to the press. Huang agreed.[36]

With Vance's mission viewed with limited success, Brzezinski began a major campaign to carry the president's message to Beijing. The first opportunity came at a farewell luncheon on November 3 for Tsien Ta-yung, Counselor at the Chinese Liaison

Office in Washington. During the lunch, NSC staffer, Oksenberg, suggested that Beijing ought to invite Brzezinski to come to China. Two weeks later, Vice President Mondale, hosted a luncheon for Ambassador Huang Chen, who was being transferred back to Beijing after four and one half years in Washington. While the press took pictures, Huang announced that Brzezinski would be welcomed in China. The NSC advisor quickly responded, "it is a date." During the multiple toasts, Mondale reminded everyone that Washington was fully committed to reaching the goal of full normalization of relations within the principles of the Shanghai Communiqué.[37]

At year's end, the CIA delivered its assessment on policy issues in the post-Mao era. The most important concerned the leadership of China. When Deng was rehabilitated at the opening of the 11th Party Congress, he promised to assume a subordinate position to Chairman Hua, not to criticize the Cultural Revolution nor its creator, Mao Xedong, and most important, not to seek revenge against those who had opposed him in the past. Despite these pledges, Deng appointed a number of people to high ranking positions, securing his vision, and virtually undermining Hua's leadership. As for the Cultural Revolution, he openly criticized it commenting that it would take China "20 to 30 years" to recover from the turmoil. The third pledge was in the process of being undone. Deng had replaced several members of the Politburo, each of whom had profited at his expense during the Cultural Revolution. The end result was that Deng was on the move to take control of China, and Hua and his supporters were trying not to lose more ground.

With respect to economics, while there was agreement to develop the Four Modernizations," there was considerable debate as to which should have priority, and this had postponed any major changes. In foreign policy, Deng favored stronger ties with America and the West, not only to counter Moscow, which was not very important to him, but to improve trade and technology transfers needed for his goal of rapid economic development. In conclusion, the

CIA report saw China as politically stable, and economically needing foreign trade to restore and grow her domestic production.[38]

CHAPTER XIV

BRZEZINSKI'S VISIT, PROGRESS RESUMED

After Vance's August meeting which was viewed as a step backward, coupled with Deng's focusing his attention on increasing his power in the Chinese Communist Party, substantial discussions between Beijing and Washington were put on hold. Instead, during the next several months, in an effort to buy time and keep alive the normalization process, Washington addressed a number of loose ends. One was the sale of military equipment to both Beijing and the ROC, along with the issue of American troop reduction in Taiwan including the number and pace of the American withdrawal.

The trade issue soon became apparent with Deng's increasing power, obvious by his promotion of science and technology, one of the Four Modernizations. Beijing wanted to purchase technology for civilian purposes, but since they could be used by the military, the export control process forbid the sale. During the early years of the Cold War, the US had forced her allies to accept prohibitions on exporting any materials which could be used by the Communist bloc for military purposes. Since this trade restriction was totally in violation of the GATT which promoted free trade, Washington set up a Coordinating Committee including representatives from her allies to restrict trade. COCOM, as the committee was called, was secret until 1954 and remained in existence until the early 1990s. In implementing the COCOM lists of prohibited sales, Congress passed the Battle Act of 1951 which prohibited sales of "arms, ammunition and implements of war" as well as materials and technology which could have military use to any country threatening the security of the US. The Commerce Department and the Department of Defense oversaw all exports to the Communist world, and due to the lists, there were few export licenses granted.

164

This was the State Department's problem in trying to accommodate Beijing's request for technology and scientific equipment. Requests for IBM computers and geophysical equipment were stalled. The hesitation was not only on the basis of military use, but also concern that if Washington agreed to help China, how would that effect Soviet-American relations. On October 31, the NSC noted that if America did not sell China technology, Europe would. Due to business pressure, the White House had approved limited sales to China, recognizing that it would have "limited impact" on Beijing's military capabilities. The NSC encouraged greater trade because of its political value. It would serve as a sign that while normalization was not on the front burner, Washington was still very interested in maintaining close ties with the Middle Kingdom. However, in 1976 the total sales of multi-use materials was $13 million. The NSC wanted greater coordination with the Export Control Boards to help them understand the political value of easing their restrictions on Communist countries.[1]

At the end of January 1978, Leonard Woodcock returned to Washington, a very frustrated head of the American Liaison Office in Beijing. Carter had offered him a number of cabinet posts, but he chose the China assignment since it involved negotiations which would be an easy fit in light of his years of negotiating for the United Auto Worker. When he returned he spoke to his former association and told them "that the US policy toward China was based "on an obvious absurdity." The idea that Washington should recognize Taipei as the government of China made no sense, because all the Nationalist government could do was govern Taiwan. Woodcock's statements made headlines, and he feared that he might have embarrassed the president. Six days later on February 7, he visited the Oval Office, and Carter quickly assured him that privately he shared the same view.[2] Woodcock urged the president to visit China, but Carter refused. Two American presidents had already visited Beijing, now it was time for reciprocity. Mondale and Brzezinski were eager to go, while Vance said that it was a State Department issue. However, Carter was having trouble with Moscow over the SALT negotiations and considered sending Vance to Moscow and Brzezinski to Beijing.[3] Woodcock was hesitant about the timing. Since Washington was not prepared to move forward on normalization, the Chinese might not be interested in meeting the NSC advisor. Furthermore, until the fall congressional elections there would be little support in Congress for a change in Washington-Beijing-Taipei relations.

Since Carter had not made a final decision, Brzezinski put on a full court press and "badgered the president enormously." Vance saw the normalization as a State Department function, and believed that the NSC advisor was not the right person for the job. If the president sent Brzezinski it would give a confusing message to Beijing as to "who spoke for the administration on foreign policy." Further, he saw that normalizations talks should have as their primary purpose improving Sino-American relations, while Brzezinski saw the relationship in a larger framework as effecting Sino-Soviet relations, a view Vance feared could compromise the discussions.

As part of his offensive, Brzezinski secured support from Secretary of Defense Brown since both favored the sale of military technology to Beijing. The NSC advisor took it into his own hands to arrange for the Chinese to "receive a NATO briefing on global strategic problems, thereby initiating a tacit security relationship with them."At the same time, he began holding meetings with the Chinese Liaison Mission, all the while trying to ingratiate himself with Beijing and use his initiative as evidence that he was best suited to carry the president's message to China. [4]He continued to raise the visit issue with the president whenever the opportunity arose. He reminded Carter that Ambassador Huang had extended him an invitation to visit Beijing. On February 27, Brzezinski sent Carter a memo "Trip to the Far East" reminding him that he had suggested that he take a consultative trip to China. According to Raymond Garthoff, the deciding factor for the administration was Moscow's backing of a

Cuban intervention in Africa, especially in Ethiopia. The White House wanted to use a China visit as a signal to Russia, that Washington could use improved relations with Beijing as leverage against Moscow.[5] In view of this thinking and a supporting memo from Brown, the president finally decided on March 12 to send Brzezinski to China

Immediately, memos flew around Washington between senior NSC and State Department staffs. A principle issue was when should the White House push for normalization: before or after the November elections, but in either case, it should be done in 1978. 1979 would be consumed with SALT negotiations, and preparation for a second term for Carter, postponing normalization until 1981; an alternative no one supported. On March 13, the NSC presented a paper calling for normalization in 1978 which would have the benefit of forcing the Soviets to be more cooperative with Washington in other areas. To counter criticism that America was abandoning Taiwan, the US could accelerate weapon transfers of air and naval equipment to Taipei including Hawk missiles and fighter planes. As a first step in this process, Brzezinski's visit should be billed as a consultative meeting to discuss global issues, but it would also serve as a signal to Beijing that America was serious about completing the normalization process.[6]

Three days later, Oksenberg sent Brzezinski a memorandum noting some Chinese signals that she was interested in moving forward. Among these were her granting several visas to permit reunification of two divided families, Chinese military attaches appeared more willing to interact socially with their American counterparts, and earlier the Chinese had featured Edgar Snow on the front page of the *People's Daily,* reminiscent of the missed signal in 1972 that China was ready to improve relations with Washington.[7]

On March 17, Congress passed the first Panama Canal Treaty, and the administration immediately notified the Chinese Liaison Office that Brzezinski was ready to visit Beijing. On March 21

Ambassador Han Hsu of the Chinese Liaison Office met the NSC advisor in the White House. Brzezinski wanted to know if his visit would be welcomed and, if so, when was an appropriate time. Assuring him that he would be most welcome, Brzezinski suggested a two to three day meeting the middle of May. He gave a suggested agenda, the first day being a review of global developments, the second day could have time for a visit around Beijing, and the third a day of conversation, implying normalization talks. Six days later, the White House received approval for a Brzezinski visit from May 20-23.[8]

With his visit confirmed which included a meeting with the Foreign Minister, Huang Hua, the next issue was whether to press for normalization before or after the November elections. The consensus was after the elections. On May 2, the president told Brzezinski to "go as far as he could toward normalization without a final agreement." In weighing the chances that the NSC advisor would have in securing China's agreement to move forward, there was no guarantee of success, but there was a consensus that "our chances are as good as any we are likely to face for the next two years."[9]

Not everyone agreed with this assessment. Vice President Mondale's Chief of Staff Richard Moe was a naysayer, who believed there was no reason to rush toward normalization. The president had already used considerable political capital with the Panama Canal Treaties, angered others with his decision to reduce America's military presence in Korea, and his cancellation of the B-1 bomber and the neutron bomb. All of these issues had constituents who would like to show their displeasure, and normalization could be the issue. In addition, if all of the disparate groups gathered together, SALT would also be in jeopardy. Recommendation: wait until the second term for normalization.[10]

May 16 Carter gave final approval for Brzezinski's visit. On the following day, he told the NSC advisor that "you should state that the US has made up its mind on these issues."[11] He also gave

Brzezinski instructions of what he hoped to accomplish. In his memoir, the NSC advisor notes with "Mike Oksenberg's help, I drafted for myself the president's instructions, which he revised and signed.". The two principle issues were America's strategic relationship with China and normalization. As for the former, he was to assure Beijing that she was a central part of America's global policy. As an example, Brzezinski was to review Washington's policies vis-a-vis Moscow, Africa, the Middle East, India and Korea. As for the latter, the White House was ready to move forward to remove obstacles to normalization. He could tell the Chinese that America accepted their three conditions, and expected them to accept the "American formula" which included a non-governmental office in Taipei, a peaceful solution to Chinese-Taiwan relations, and acceptance that America would continue to supply Taipei with needed military equipment. Informally, Brzezinski could mention that there would be a further troops reduction on Taiwan, increased technology exports to Beijing, and an invitation to Chinese trade and military delegations to visit the US.[12]

Armed with recommendations, and his own ideas, Zbigniew Brzezinski landed in China on Saturday, May 20, 1978 to begin part two of the Nixon-Kissinger effort to establish diplomatic relations with the Middle Kingdom. Six years had passed without implementing the goal of normalizing relations between the two countries. But this did not mean that there had been no progress. To the contrary, communication had continued in spite of enormous political changes. A president forced to resign replaced by a new-comer to the Oval Office, the end of the Vietnam War, a new president in 1976, coupled with the deaths of Mao Zedong and Zhou Enlai, and the fall and rise of Deng Xiaoping. Yet positive steps were taken concerning prisoner issues, troop reductions in Taiwan and Korea, and sharing strategies involving global issues most importantly against the "Polar Bear" to the north. In addition there were ongoing talks about shipping nuclear technology to Beijing, and limiting its sale to Taipei, and at the same time trying to assure Taiwan that her security was not being compromised on the altar of securing diplomatic relations with China. Brzezinski had all this baggage along with the recent, less than successful, Vance mission to Beijing.

Met at the airport by the Foreign Minister Huang Hua along with numerous Chinese officials, Brzezinski and his ten member entourage, including his wife, were quickly driven off to a government guest house. After a couple of hours to recoup following the lengthy flight, the NSC advisor and Huang, along with their staffs, met for three hours. Following the prepared agenda, Brzezinski began with the customary *tour d'horizon* which was a lengthy account of America's global interests and would consume the balance of the afternoon. From the outset, he emphasized Carter's commitment to normalization, along with an interest in consulting on issues of parallel interest as well as identifying areas where separate interests could reinforce one another's goals. Without question, Moscow was a focus of Brzezinski's review including a detailed analysis of American-Soviet military preparedness. He believed that the Soviets wanted to achieve a strategic balance with Washington through SALT, which she believed would give her an advantage in putting pressure on Western Europe. Moscow wanted to radicalize the Middle East, destabilize southern Africa especially Rhodesia, Zaire and Angola, penetrate the Indian Ocean, and eventually surround China. To counter these moves, America would maintain sufficient military capabilities, especially in NATO and other areas of strategic and political importance through advanced weapons technology. To prove his point, Brzezinski showed his audience a chart, which "reveals many military secrets of the US and the Soviet Union." Concluding, he added that at present America was developing a significant force in the US for rapid global deployment to confront any attempt to threaten America's interests.[13]

Sunday morning began with a visit to the Mao mausoleum, followed by a meeting with Foreign Minister Huang Hua who gave the Chinese world view. Using a Marxian approach involving inevitability of historical development, Huang saw the rivalry between Moscow and Washington as the main source of "untranquility" with the Soviets on the offensive and America on the defensive. This was due to Russia's continued efforts for world hegemony. The result would be the inevitability of war. Huang saw Washington as sending the wrong messages to Moscow. In an effort to show good will to Moscow, especially during the SALT talks, Carter cancelled development of the neutron bomb, for which he received no corresponding concession. Everywhere Huang looked, he saw evidence of Soviet attempts to expand its influence. This included all of Europe, the Middle East, Africa, India, Southeast Asia, and the recent coup in Afghanistan. He applauded Washington for its growing ties with Japan, but believed that America should withdraw all of her forces from Korea, and let the two Koreas work for unification without foreign influence. As for the issue of normalization, Huang reiterated the three principles but did add that he was willing to accept the "Japanese Formula" which permitted America to maintain a liaison office for non-governmental and commercial contacts in Taiwan. Beyond that, there was no room for additional accommodation.[14]

In response, Brzezinski mentioned areas in which he disagreed with Huang namely in his assessment that the two superpowers' rivalry was over world hegemony. That was a not the goal of America. He also did not see war as inevitable, and said "there is not such a thing as a neutron bomb." Since it had not been exploded, he was technically correct. Further, America had no intent to leave Korea. But rather than dwell simply on negatives, Brzezinski also suggested that the president was quite willing to have several members of his cabinet go to China to share information on energy, trade and commercial relations as well as areas of health, education and welfare. In addition, Ben Huberman, who was part of Brzezinski's entourage, was working out details for a top level visit by his boss,

Frank Press, the president's advisor on science and technology. The NSC advisor hoped that this offer might show good will and quicken the pace toward normalization.[15] At the close of his remarks, Huang told him that he was invited to meet with Vice Premier Deng Xiaoping later in the afternoon.

When Deng asked Brzezinski were he tired, he said "I am exhilarated," and he was. Similar to Kissinger's reactions in meeting Zhou Enlai and later Mao, Brzezinski described Deng as "a man tiny in size, but great in his boldness." He immediately took to the vice premier noting that he was "bright, alert and shrewd, he was quick on the uptake, with a good sense of humor, tough and very direct."[16] As an explanation as to his exhilaration, he quickly explained how he had flown all around China, but never landed until now. "I feel a little bit like the American astronauts before landing on the moon. They went around it many times and in the end they landed." From the outset, as he had with Huang, Brzezinski repeated the new mantra: President Carter has made up his mind, and he repeated this four times during the two and one half hour meeting. His mission was twofold: consultative so that both countries could exchange global views, widen areas of cooperation and to reaffirm America's commitment to normalization. He made it clear that he was not going to engage in negotiations at this meeting, but that Ambassador Woodcock would be prepared to do so in June. While accepting Beijing's three terms concerning Taiwan, he needed Deng not to contradict Washington statements that the future of Taiwan would be done through peaceful means. This was a very important domestic issue. If Beijing could restrain from criticizing White House summations of talks and negotiations, congressional and public approval would be far easier to secure.[17]

The vice premier raised some concerns about America's downgrading of Taiwan's importance. She might not have the ability to defend herself against Soviet infiltration, or worse, Taipei might produce her own nuclear weapons, now banned by America.

172

Brzezinski countered that America had "ways to deal with it. We have taken such things into account." Trade was also an issue for Deng. While Washington talked about science and technology as fields for information exchange, the COCOM lists and Battle Act prohibited any meaningful cooperation. The Commerce Department had refused time and again to grant export licenses for computers and infrared scanning equipment.[18]

Deng continued to describe Soviet-American relations in terms of Washington's failure to realize that Moscow was always on the offensive. If she conceded an issue in Africa, she would counter with a move in the Middle East. Brzezinski grew tired of the criticism. He decided "this was the time for a little dig of our own." He pointed out that "over the past thirty years, America alone has challenged Soviet hegemonic designs and that is roughly twice as long as you have been doing it, so we have a little bit of experience."[19]America and the Soviet Union had worked well together particularly during World War II. But in a different way, Moscow's constant efforts to embarrass the US had forced America to grow and expand faster than she might not have otherwise. Yuri Gagarin's space flight pushed America to send a man to the moon, the Cuban missile crisis set the basis for the Non-Proliferation Treaty in 1968, and Russia's continued claims that her Five Year Plans were successful, prompted Washington to encourage new economic programs as well as those which developed nuclear energy for military and civilian needs. In each instance, America won the competition. What Deng saw as a negative, the constant Soviet challenge, he failed to see that capitalism thrives on competition.[20] At the end, Deng made a most unusual gesture of friendship and invited Brzezinski to an informal dinner at Fang Shan restaurant, overlooking a small lake in Peihai Park, in the middle of Beijing. Afterwards, they attended a performance of the Beijing Opera.[21]

On Monday, his last day in Beijing, the NSC advisor began with a visit to the Great Wall followed by a meeting with Chairman

Hua Guofeng prior to dinner. At the outset, Brzezinski presented Hua with a piece of the moon, and the flag of the PRC, which was raised on the moon and brought back by the astronauts. In contrast to Deng's bluntness and sense of urgency, Hua was soft-spoken, relaxed and graceful which suggested an inner peace. He was self assured, and had a "masterful overview of the global situation" without using any notes.[22] Similar to Huang and Deng, Hua was quite concerned about the Soviet goal of world domination, including "subjugating China," and warned America to be prepared to counter Moscow's efforts to secure air and naval bases worldwide.

As for normalization, Hua repeated an earlier Chinese response that if Carter had really "made up his mind" it would not be difficult to resolve outstanding issues. He noted that the president wanted China to not contradict White House statements that the Taiwan issue would be peacefully resolved, and, at the same time, permit Washington to continue to supply Taipei with weapons. "What will be the result of these actions? I think it is still the creation of one China and one Taiwan, or two Chinas." One solution was to stop sending Taiwan weapons, and this could facilitate a peaceful resolution of the problem. Continuing, he described his efforts to secure a peace treaty with Japan, but Tokyo did not want to include an anti-hegemony clause, which was designed to curb Soviet expansionism. Moscow supported Tokyo's refusal, and Hua hoped that since America supported China's position, Brzezinski might be able to raise the issue during his visit the next day to Japan. Brzezinski readily agreed. During the talks Deng alluded to his interest in visiting America, saying that he believed that he had only three years to live. Brzezinski read this as a sign that China was ready to move forward on normalization.

As a postscript, continuing his Asian trip, Brzezinski met with the Japanese Prime Minister Fukuda, assured him of America's continuing support and encouraged him to sign a peace treaty with Beijing. In October 1978, the two countries signed a treaty including an anti-hegemony clause, bringing an end to negotiations begun in 1972. As anticipated, Moscow criticized the treaty as a threat to the Soviet Union.

Discussion about the two Koreas brought no forward progress. America insisted she be part of any North-South Korean discussions. As for the Middle East, disagreement continued. China saw the only way to peace was if America pressured Israel to withdraw from occupied territories and recognized the national rights of the Palestinians. While not opposing the idea, Brzezinski countered that unlike China, the White House and Congress were often in conflict, and none so often as over issues concerning Israel. Solution of Middle East issues were a domestic issue in Washington, and Hua should not expect much progress. In conclusion, Brzezinski said that Ambassador Woodcock was authorized to begin negotiations in June during which time America would continue her economic relations with Taiwan. Both sides agreed to maintain secrecy concerning the substance of their talks, and future negotiations.

In analyzing China's terms for normalization, Beijing apparently was giving America a choice. Either to continue arms sales to Taipei after normalization without receiving a Chinese statement of intent to peacefully resolve the future of Taiwan, or, America needed to cancel her arms sales, in return for a declaration of peaceful intent. From Hua's view, to sell arms, and expect China to promise a peaceful resolution to Taiwan would produce a "two Chinas" resolution.[23] At the end of the session, Brzezinski hosted a dinner banquet where he gave a lengthy toast reinforcing America's commitment to normalization. In his concluding remarks, he mentioned that a "secure and strong China" was in America's interest and, according to his memoir, the phrase was "much highlighted by the world press, and the Chinese media."[24]

Before his return to Washington, his aide and admirer, Michel Oksenberg, prepared an appraisal of Brzezinski's Beijing visit. He began "without question, we leave China with a substantially better relationship than existed prior to your three days in Beijing." "You made a favorable impression simply being yourself. The Chinese admire people who think strategically and conceptually, and you clearly demonstrated those qualities...You demonstrated an inner toughness...you have an open and precise mind. Your youthful spirit and zest for life runs counter to disciplined, tempered Chinese mannerisms, but are characteristics which the Chinese admire in Americans...They know innovation flows from enthusiasm." "On the negative side, by no means outweighing the positive side, I suspect you came across as somewhat vain, perhaps overly confident, and somewhat prone to verbosity" He later added: "Cy behaved with greater dignity than you."[25]

In comparing Vance to Brzezinski, he saw the difference between the two presentations as "strikingly great. You have given the Chinese a stake in your own political success in the US. By so doing, I suspect you have become their preferred interlocutor...[and] if any concessions are to be extracted from them concerning normalization, they clearly will prefer to give you the credit for it." In assessing the Deng-Hua relationship, he believed that it was "more collaborative and complementary than competitive...We should not assume that Deng is in charge." Whether his view of Brzezinski was accurate or not, Oksenberg would learn by December how clearly off base he was on the Deng-Hua relationship.[26]

There was a different assessment of Brzezinski's mission by Dick Holbrooke. He saw the visit as successful and his handling of normalization as productive. However, he would not have revealed to the world talks about security issues. In addition, the continued repetition of the president "having made up his mind," may have created a credibility problem "if we are not able, in fact, to carry through on normalization in the next few months." There were several important points made indicating that America had changed her strategy since the Vance visit which had focused on Soviet-American cooperation, to a more competitive relationship. Areas of agreement

176

were far more important between Washington and Beijing than differences. In summary, however, "the Chinese posture toward you was not very different from that taken toward Vance. Both Huang and Deng continued to portray US policy as weak, inadequate and naïve...They left little doubt that if China were to take additional actions these would be taken independently of the US." As for normalization, Huang for the first time implied a "linkage between the completion of normalization and their willingness to cooperate with us in our common concern about the Soviet Union." The Chinese had also shown a willingness to refrain from any mention of forceful liberation of Taiwan, simply noting that it was an internal matter.[27]

Upon Brzezinski's return to Washington, Deputy Secretary of State Warren Christopher met him as a symbol of solidarity between the two departments, and in the afternoon the NSC advisor visited the president. When he entered the Oval Office, Carter "jumped up from his chair...rushed toward me, grabbed my arm, pumped it warmly and gave me a bear hug. He then called in a photographer to have a picture taken of the two of us." The president would write in his memoirs that his visit "was very successful."[28] And added that he thought that he was "overwhelmed with the Chinese" and had been "seduced" by them.[29] During the meeting, Brzezinski gave him a brief overview of the major topics covered with the Chinese leadership, noted the conundrum which Beijing had presented with the issue of America wanting to continue to send arms to Taiwan, and expect China to accept America's desire for a peaceful resolution of the island's future. He cautioned the president that the administration had to be careful in what it said about relations with China and that Woodcock should be well prepared for his June negotiations.[30]

One unfortunate result from Brzezinski's visit was a renewed confrontation with Vance. In an interview with *Meet the Press*, reporters quizzed him about the Soviet Union, not China. The NSC advisor gave what appeared to be an analysis of America's foreign policy vis-à-vis Moscow, Beijing, concerns in Africa and the Indian

Ocean. All in all, it appeared that he had replaced the Secretary of State as the spokesman for Washington's foreign policy. While he admits that when he read reports in *Newsweek*, *The Washington Post*, and *The New York Times*, "I really felt pained and almost sick when I read it." Vance was furious and hurt, forcing the president to upbraid Brzezinski for his description of the Soviet Union as responsible for worldwide problems, including the Middle East and threatening China by placing troops on her border. "All this simply went a little too far." However, he noted that within a day, the "President and I rode together to attend a NATO summit meeting...and in the course of the drive, 'he kind of casually allowed that he feels better today about my interview.'" The summit meeting was held at the State Department auditorium, and only Carter and Brzezinski spoke, with Vance sitting in the front row, saying nothing. "It made me feel rather awkward. I do not wish the relationship to deteriorate."[31]

Taiwan was most anxious to learn about the results of Brzezinski's visit. On May 29, as soon as he had returned from a visit outside Taipei, President Chiang met Ambassador Unger. In response to Chiang's question about normalization, Unger assured him that there had been no real progress, but Washington was still committed to establishing diplomatic relations with Beijing. Chiang repeated his policies announced in his inaugural address given a week earlier, namely, that Taiwan would base its foreign policy on "self reliance, no negotiation or compromise with 'Communist enemy' and opposition to normalization."[32] On the following day, the Assistant Secretary of State Richard Holbrooke briefed Ambassador Shen repeating Unger's message to Chiang. Shen was not convinced. He believed that Washington had accepted China's three demands and all that remained was a date to establish relations. Holbrooke continued the White House policy, of no news about normalization. He also had to lie to Shen about the possible sale of military items to Beijing, information that the ambassador had learned from the Japanese press. Holbrooke assured Shen that America would act "deliberately and responsibly."[33] Shen's sense was correct, Taiwan was a pawn in the Sino-American game of chess.

CHAPTER XV

JANUARY 1, 1979 BEIJING IS CHINA'S CAPITAL

Following his return, Brzezinski assumed control of Sino-American relations. He micromanaged Woodcock's approach and negotiations with Beijing. "I worked on every line of the communiqués going to Woodcock."[1] Secrecy was the by-word to an extent reminiscent of the Kissinger-Nixon approach to Beijing and Moscow. While Vance was in the loop, his department was not. With instructions written by Brzezinski and approved by Carter, Vance met with Foreign Minister Huang on June 2. Early in the conversation, Huang recounted a remark made by Deng at a dinner meeting in Beijing. He was getting older, and wanted to visit the US, but could not as long as Taiwan maintained an embassy there. This was the second time that Beijing had used Deng's age as a sign that China was ready for normalization.

On June 7, Carter gave a major address at his alma mater, the Naval Academy in Annapolis. He told the midshipmen that he was frustrated by Moscow's lack of cooperation to address problems in areas such as Ethiopia, the Persian Gulf, Yemen and Kampuchea. He wanted to increase collaboration with Moscow as well as with emerging nations, the countries of Eastern Europe and with the PRC. He concluded with a very strong statement, "the Soviet Union can choose either confrontation or cooperation. The US is adequately prepared to meet either choice. We would prefer cooperation."[2] Without question, the president's speech left many confused. On the one hand he supported détente, and on the other confrontation. Many commentators thought the speech was a patch work of Vance and Brzezinski advice, without any clear direction. All in all, according to Raymond Garthoff, the speech reinforced the belief of some administration officials and political pundits, that no one was in charge of foreign policy.³ As for international reaction at the highest levels, Americans were confused, Russians angry and the Chinese happy.

Having alienated Moscow, Carter wanted to move forward on China, sooner than later. On June 13, he met with Vance, Brzezinski, Secretary of Defense Brown and Chief of Staff Hamilton Jordan and made several significant decisions. First and foremost was setting the middle of December as the goal to realize normalization, followed by congressional action before deliberations on SALT. Woodcock would conduct negotiations, and suggest that talks be every ten days. He was to emphasize Washington's acceptance of the three principles and her need to maintain some personnel to continue "non-official" relations with Taiwan following the closing of the American embassy in Taipei. Woodcock was to encourage China to announce that she would pursue a peaceful resolution of Taiwan, accept America's continued sale of defensive weapons to Taipei, and encourage Beijing to simply say that the resolution of the Taiwan question was an internal matter. At some point, Chiang and Japanese Premier Fukuda needed to be notified, probably about three weeks before the official announcement. As for the actual implementation of normalization, the group anticipated it would take between three and six months.⁴

While Woodcock began normalization negotiations, Washington considered issues relevant to Taiwan. On June 30, the White House decided not to send Taipei sixty fighter-bombers. Recognizing that Deng had assumed control of the science and technology modernization program, Carter agreed to send Dr. Frank Press to lead a science and technology delegation to Beijing around the middle of July. Discussion also focused on the process of terminating the Mutual Defense Treaty with Taiwan, with the conclusion that it automatically ended with normalization. As an alternative, the president could extend the treaty for twelve months prior to termination in accord with terms in the treaty, or he could take any action he liked within the twelve month period including immediate termination, and could do so without senate approval.[5]

An additional issue was Vietnam's recent request for normalization of relations with Washington. While Vance showed interest in the overture, Brzezinski told Carter to ignore it. Vietnam was a complicated issue. Hanoi was a Soviet satellite, while China supported the government of its neighbor, Cambodia. Vietnam wanted to move into Cambodia, prompting Beijing to increase her support of Phnom Penh. Brzezinski saw Hanoi's request as nothing more than a Soviet effort to abort the Sino-American negotiations, and he warned Carter not to be distracted by Hanoi's overtures. The president finally agreed in October to defer Hanoi's request, and in November decided to ignore the issue.[6]

Woodcock made his initial presentation on July 5 designed to address three issues in sequence. The three were the nature of Washington's post-normalization presence on Taiwan, Sino-American public statements when normalization achieved, and American trade with Taipei following normalization. Foreign Minister Huang led the Chinese delegation. He was an experienced negotiator, a "Long Marcher," and an ally of Deng. He wanted Woodcock to make an opening statement on all three issues. To maintain a positive beginning, Woodcock decided to make a lean presentation, sufficient to appease Huang and broad enough to leave room for negotiations on each point.[7]

While negotiations continued in Beijing, Washington mounted a public relations campaign to prepare the American people for normalization. Holbrooke spent considerable time in New York meeting with influential editors and businessmen to point out the advantages of a new Sino-American relationship including its strategic and trade benefits. On August 17, when he met Ambassador Chai Zemin, newly arrived head of the Chinese Liaison Office in Washington, he noted Deng's meeting with Congressman Wolff's delegation to Beijing, and the positive feelings they had following

Deng's presentation. Holbrooke hoped that China would continue to take steps to promote a sense of good will between the two countries, steps that would be reported in the American press. Chai agreed, and said that China's view on normalization was "the sooner, the better."[8]

Washington was also encouraged by Deng Xiaoping's continued rise in power. He was westward looking and had given several indications of his desire for normalization, and to quote Chai, "the sooner, the better." Deng had replaced some senior party officials with men of his own choosing, wall posters were frequently attacking Deng's enemies, he had initiated a purge of Lin Biao's supporters who continued to support close relations with Moscow, and had already announced that he intended to terminate the Sino-Soviet treaty signed in 1950. Further, he had just signed a Treaty of Peace and Friendship with Japan following six years of negotiations. He asked for America to launch a satellite on behalf of China, and had encouraged Chinese students to participate in an exchange program with Washington. There were also promising discussions about trade. At present, China bought wheat from the US, and indicated that following normalization she would like to buy scientific and technological equipment as well as satellite technology, mining equipment, and energy products. All in all, while Deng had opposition, including some led by Hua Guofeng, he was moving forward towards his goal of implementing the Four Modernizations.[9]

Negotiations in Beijing were at times bogged down over America's insistence on continuing to supply Taiwan with defensive weapons following normalization. To date there had been four meetings between Woodcock and Huang. Carter decided to make his position clear before the next meeting scheduled for November 2. Carter met Ambassador Chai Zemin on September 19, and said that American trade would continue to include "some very carefully selected defensive arms…in a way that …does not endanger the prospect of peace in the region." As Carter had maintained the American position, Chai did the same. Beijing saw the sale of weapons to Taipei as a violation of the spirit of the Shanghai Communiqué. The president also reiterated his administration's position on China not publically contradicting America's call for a peaceful resolution of Taiwan's future.

Meanwhile, after fourteen months of discussions between Israel, Egypt and the United State and thirteen days of frequent acrimonious discussions arbitrated and negotiated by Carter, Anwar Sadat and Menachem Begin signed the Camp David Accords on September 17. This was a Framework Agreement which would set the parameters for a 1979 Peace Treaty between the two countries, a first between an Arab country and Israel. With this resolved, the president focused most of his attention on completing normalization. On October 3, Vance met with Foreign Minister Huang Hua.

Huang's global view was seen through eyes tainted by fears of the omnipresent Soviet effort to broaden its influence to achieve global hegemony. He saw the success of the Camp David Accords, not simply as a peace treaty, but as a means to stymie Moscow's efforts to promote instability in the region. He had mixed feelings about SALT, was pleased with Washington's upgrade of NATO weapons, and both men agreed that little progress had been made in any part of Africa, thus giving the Soviets an opportunity to expand their influence in the entire continent. Huang viewed East and Southeast Asia as a mixed bag. The Sino-Japanese Treaty was a plus, as was America's improved relations with the Philippines. However, there was the issue of increased Soviet influence in neighboring Vietnam, and America's unwillingness to have North and South Korea enter unification talks without Washington being present. As for Sino-American relations, Huang reiterated the standard formula concerning Taiwan, but noted that "in what way Taiwan will be liberated, it is entirely China's internal affair." Not included was language about the use of force, and this was important since Huang was reading from a prepared statement approved by China's leadership.[10]

On October 11 Carter met with Brzezinski and Woodcock and decided to submit a draft communiqué on normalization to the Chinese as a way to show America's intent. Carter proposed January 1, 1979 as the date to begin the new relationship. Woodcock would introduce the draft at the November 2 meeting with Huang. The draft included language indicating that the "liberation of Taiwan is China's internal affair" without foreign interference. Article 10 stated that Beijing hoped that the reunification process will be completed peacefully, and Article 14 reinforced the peaceful aspect of reunification. As for America's role, she would withdraw all US forces and military installations from Taiwan, and that Washington would continue commercial, cultural and other unofficial relations with Taipei. At no point, and quite deliberately, did the communiqué address the issue of America continuing to send defensive military equipment to Taiwan.[11]

Since the White House intended to upgrade Taiwan's defense capabilities after normalization, the NSC decided to finally listen to the Department of Defense's pleas for inclusion in the discussions, a request dating back to February 1978. By September, senior military commanders began to question the wisdom of drawing down American forces and weapons on Taiwan. If that were to be the case, the navy wanted to counter the force reduction by reinstituting nuclear powered warship visits to Taiwan, a practice stopped six years earlier. The White House realized that part of the problem was the secrecy involved in the negotiations and Carter told Secretary of Defense Brown to meet with the Joint Chiefs of Staff and explain America's China policy. The military had to understand that normalization had many benefits, but one of the costs was the force reduction on Taiwan. That was sufficient information for the time being for the military to know. At the same time, the White House moved forward on approving Taipei's requests for more advanced weaponry including aircraft, missiles, launchers, and 400 laser-guided bomb kits.[12]

Woodcock characterized his November 2 meeting with Huang as the "most business-like" to date, without any of the negativism which had occurred in prior meetings, especially those involving Vance. The Foreign Minister wanted more information about America's post-normalization relations with Taiwan. They raised five questions. China wanted to know about an "interim period" which Washington had indicated between the issuance of the communiqué and the time needed to alter relations with Taiwan. The question was how long was the interim period and when would it begin. Beijing wanted to know the nature of future American relations with Taiwan, including cultural and trade. What would be the makeup of the American non-governmental liaison office in Taipei? What are the implications of the "legislative adjustment" needed for implementation of the communiqué? And finally, what did America mean when she said she would continue the same access of Taiwan products to the US? Since Deng and Huang were on a trip to Southeast Asia, Washington did not need to immediately respond to the questions. But there was complete agreement that Woodcock's next instructions needed to include answers to each of the questions, and the information should be forwarded to him by November 10.[13]

However, November 10 would come and go. This was not due to normalization, but to a major change in China's leadership. Since the summer, Deng had been moving up in the party leadership. In May, he made a subtle attack against Hua Guofeng. Hua was Mao's chosen successor, and he used this endorsement in trying to lead the Communist party and China. Deng had embraced Zhou Enlai's Four Modernizations, and he quickly secured control of the science and technology component. For China to implement these reforms, the government had to change its economic policies. Foremost was her emphasis on state control of all aspects of the economy. A guaranteed job did not guarantee quality work. Deng wanted China to privatize some of her state owned enterprises, invite foreign capital, and foreign businesses to build factories in special economic zones which would

186

guarantee tax breaks, have foreigners train China's youth in the operations of capitalism, and encourage them to seek profit in new businesses. This was a definite challenge to the Communist approach to the economy which required state ownership of the means of production. It also challenged the time honored view that China should be self reliant, not dependent on others for survival or success.

In May, 1978 Deng began to criticize the "two whatevers." These were the trademarks of Hua's manner of governance. The two were: implement Mao's decisions, and follow his guidelines. Since Deng wanted to distance himself from Mao, without attacking him, he could achieve the same end by identifying Hua with Mao's policies. The gambit worked, and Deng began his climb to the top.

Aware that China was far behind the West, Deng called for radical changes in China's educational system, a significant increase in the number of Chinese students studying science and technology abroad, modernization of a professional army, expanded cooperation with foreign corporations to exploit China's natural resources and to rely on foreign capital to finance importing Western technology. His efforts did not go unnoticed. An October CIA report described Deng's changes, and an NSC memo reinforced that view but believed that truly hard decisions, such as modernization might be delayed in light of the political struggle.[14] However, a subsequent assessment on November 30 quoted a Japanese reporter's meeting with Deng. Here the Chinese leader said "I have told you before that it would only take one second to complete the Japanese Peace and Friendship Treaty. If we expend the same effort it would only take two seconds for the Sino-US normalization. This is our hope." And were this to occur soon, "I could fulfill my wish to visit the US."[15]

Foreign trips by Hua and Deng set an example for other senior Chinese officials, and when they returned, especially from European capitals and Tokyo, they were excited by what they had seen. The outside world was far different than anticipated, and there was a genuine desire for China to catch up with the West. Much due to

187

Deng's rising popularity, the Communist party formed a Central Party Work Conference on November 10, to prepare for the Third Plenum of the 11th Party Congress. Deng's travels in late November removed him from the opening sessions, but when he returned on November 14, he called for major changes in China's foreign and domestic policies. His summer work in replacing some of the party hierarchy with his own people, coupled with a changing view by some of the old guard due to their visits abroad, gave Deng the support he needed to seize the party leadership. On November 25, Hua and the other members of the party leadership agreed to accept Deng as the party leader. In preparing for his opening speech at the 11th Party Congress, he told his writers that he would call for major reforms and "the basic point is: we must acknowledge that we are backward, that many of our ways of doing things are inappropriate, and that we need to change."[16]

Meanwhile, Carter had sent Woodcock his final demands on normalization in late November. There were three proposals, which the president believed could be difficult for Beijing to accept, but they were necessary. The three were: America would maintain its defense agreement with Taiwan for another year, China would not contradict America's announcement that the future of Taiwan-Chinese relations would be peacefully resolved, and that the US would continue to sell Taiwan military equipment following the end of the defense agreement. The timing could not have been worse. Deng was in the final stages of consolidating his control over the party and government, weighing possible military action against Vietnam, and considering future relations with Washington. In light of these issues, Deng rejected Carter's demands.[17]

On December 4, Woodcock met with Han Nianlong, filling in for the ailing Huang Hua. The meeting proved to be most significant. Han accepted the answers to Huang questions asked on November 2, but more importantly he agreed to issue a joint communiqué on January 1, 1979 announcing the establishment of diplomatic relations between the two countries. In response to Carter's three demands,

China would not contradict statements by Washington expressing hope for a peaceful resolution of the Taiwan-China issue, but would say in a separate statement that the resolution of the problem was an internal affair. Beijing had no real problems on America maintaining cultural and commercial ties with Taiwan after normalization, and while Beijing objected to the sale of military equipment to Taipei, this would not "prevent normalization." The meeting ended with Han indicating that Deng would like to meet with Woodcock soon.[18]

On December 12, the last day of the Central Committee Work Conference Deng made the final presentation. He called for the party to practice a greater democracy, to correct the wrongs done to people during the Cultural Revolution, to "evaluate" Mao Zedong as a revolutionary leader and his role in the Revolution, and the need for radical change in the fields of management and economic policy.[19]

On the following day, Deng met with Woodcock. The State Department had sent him a memo on Deng and his desire to quickly come to closure on normalization. Deng was 74 years old, and time was of the essence. He looked to normalization as a means to counter Soviet and Vietnamese pressures on Beijing, as well as giving China easy access to foreign capital, expertise and technology. As a reminder to Woodcock, Deng needed normalization to at least appear as a step toward eventual reunification, a development which the ambassador had viewed in June as taking a long time.[20]

The Deng-Woodcock meeting on December 13, was brief and to the point. The two met in Kiangsu Hall of the Great Hall of the People at 10 a.m. Deng questioned why the defense treaty could not be terminated at the same time as the announcement of normalization. The ambassador explained that the treaty had a one year termination clause, however he anticipated that all American troops would be removed within four months. Deng suggested that Washington not include Article 10 in the final agreement, which noted the one year period needed for termination, but he had no problem with America including the issue within its statement accompanying the

189

communiqué. He also asked that during the one year termination time that Washington not sell weapons to Taiwan before 1980, much to the dismay of the Joint Chiefs of Staff who were still smarting for not being involved in the negotiations. Deng added that if weapons were sold, "Chiang Ching-kuo would strut his tail feathers and this would increase the chances of conflict over the Taiwan Straits." Aside from that issue, Beijing and Washington agreed to make simultaneous announcements of the resumption of diplomatic relations effective January 1, 1979.[21]

The Chinese version of the communiqué included an anti-hegemony clause, not in the American draft. Since the phrase was implied in the Shanghai Communiqué, and this was the basis of the normalization agreement, Washington chose not to include it in their communiqué. Both agreed to set up their embassies by March 1, and make an announcement on December 15. Before leaving, Woodcock expressed Carter's invitation for a high ranking Chinese official to visit Washington, and Deng quickly responded that he would lead the Chinese delegation for a January visit. On the 14th, during a meeting with Woodcock, Deng agreed that he would make his first visit to America on January 28.[22]

While excited, Carter was ill prepared for such a rapid conclusion to years of negotiations. Deng's willingness to accept the draft with minor changes and his eagerness to have the announcement on December 15 put the White House in a frantic mood. No one knew about the negotiations, they had remained secret. When Vance learned of the developments the "news came as a shock."[23] He was not involved in the final stages of the Brzezinski-Woodcock-Carter discussions being in Geneva negotiating the SALT agreement with Gromyko. Vance did a quick round trip to Washington arriving on December 15 just in time for the announcement. Congress too was unaware and Carter hastily called a meeting of senior congressmen and informed them of the impending announcement. While some criticized the decision, they all knew that constitutionally the president

190

had the sole power to recognize and establish diplomatic relations with a foreign country or its government. Also in the dark were America's Asian and European allies, the American public, and the Soviet Union. America's Ambassador to the UN had to be told to expect China to take Taipei's seat, a situation for which he had no foreknowledge, and Taiwan, which was being most effected, needed to be informed.[24]

At 2:20 a.m. on December 15, Ambassador Unger informed President Chiang of the Republic of China of the impending announcement of the Sino-American rapprochement. Unger assured the rather shocked Chiang that Washington intended to continue her traditional relations in trade, travel and other practical ties, except for the Mutual Defense Treaty which would be terminated in one year. After the termination, Taipei could resume purchases of "carefully selected defensive weapons" from the US. After assuring Chiang of Washington's continued loyalty, Unger added that he did not expect Taiwan to view the normalization as contributing to world or regional peace. Chiang took the presentation "rather badly," warning of dire consequences in Taiwan as the people saw themselves betrayed.[25]

On the following day, Chiang gave the official government response. America had broken its word in promising to maintain diplomatic relations with Taiwan. Washington "cannot be expected to have the confidence of any free nation in the future." As for the ROC, it "shall neither negotiate with the Chinese Communist regime, nor compromise with Communism, and she shall never give up her sacred task of recovering the mainland and delivering the compatriots there. This firm position shall remain unchanged." [26]

In order to soften the effects of the announcement, Washington decided to sell Taiwan some of her pending arms requests which might help her psychologically, and to defuse some of the congressional opposition to normalization. She would also supply spare parts needed for earlier orders, as a sign of a long term commitment. As for the withdrawal of American forces, this would proceed in an orderly manner and be accomplished by April 30, at the same time the defense department would gradually reduce her military-to-military contacts. Since Taipei was a military supply center for American forces in Asia, the so-called War Reserve Materials would be transferred elsewhere by December 31. While both countries' embassies would end by January 1, as well as other ancillary government organizations, the consulates could remain operational until February 28, 1979 in order to provide alternative non-governmental means to fulfill their duties.[27]

To further ease the impact on Taipei, on December 30 Carter issued a memorandum to all US departments and agencies notifying them that all treaties and agreements between the two countries "shall continue in force." This memo in essence removed most of the legal effects of Washington's de-recognition of Taipei.[28] However, President Chiang Ching-kuo did not see the importance of Carter's memo and indicated this to Deputy Secretary of State Warren Christopher during his visit to Taiwan. Taipei did not trust America to defend the island, especially since she had to cut back on sending military equipment, and as a result refused to agree to the non-governmental relationship Carter wanted. This would slow talks for several weeks. While Taipei complained, Washington looked to draft legislation that would insure continued commercial, cultural and other relations with the people of Taiwan on an unofficial basis. The White House also approved draft legislation to establish an American Institute in Taiwan, which would serve as a center for non-governmental relations. On January 26, the president would send his proposals to Congress.

Moscow too was surprised, not by the fact of negotiations, but by the speed of a final agreement. While SALT talks had been slowed over the issue of encrypted telemetry and its effect on missile verification, they nearly came to a standstill following the December 15 announcement. Moscow had not opposed normalization, but she was insulted by the reference in the communiqué concerning the Sino-

American mutual opposition to "hegemony," a euphemism for the Soviet Union. Gromyko also saw the timing as inappropriate considering that the SALT talks were close to an agreement. Moscow was also concerned about stories in the press about a possible Carter-Brezhnev summit in mid-January, a couple of weeks before Deng was to arrive in Washington. Brezhnev had no intention of having his summit upstaged by a Deng visit. According to Vance, Gromyko's sudden interest in many aspects of telemetry was designed to postpone SALT talks until well after Deng's visit. And the tactic worked, postponing a SALT agreement until June 18, 1979.[29]

During the negotiations there had been agreement that the claims/assets issue could be easily solved. With the anticipated announcement on January 1, Beijing wanted to start the process and soon staked its claim to all of the ROC's public assets within the US including the embassy, the chancery, Twin Oaks and the Chinese Procurement and Services Mission facilities in Washington. The White House agreed that Beijing had a legitimate claim to "real property of the Government of China used for public purposes."[30] And by December 28, ownership of all but the Twin Oaks property had been transferred to China. The massive mansion was purchased by Taiwan in 1947 and used as a convention site and cultural center. When Carter announced that he was ending diplomatic relations with Taiwan, Taipei sold the estate to a private group called the Friends of Free China Association, co-chaired by Senator Barry Goldwater. Later Taipei would re-purchase the Twin Oaks effectively keeping it out of Beijing's hands.[31] This re-purchase would become an issue in the spring during debate over the Taiwan Relations Act.

In addition to physical property, the White House was concerned that Beijing would try to seize Taiwanese bank accounts, and "big ticket items" such as generators or airplanes that Taipei had ordered and paid for. The administration hoped that Taipei had anticipated these issues and had taken care of them. At the same time, Taiwan had to leave enough capital in America to underwrite normal

193

economic relations. Unger sent the State Department a memo indicating the above problem, and suggested a solution. Namely, that Washington consider assets generated by the economic efforts of the people of Taiwan as property of the people of Taiwan.[32] These would be issues needing resolution after January 1.

Why after nearly eight years of talks, and lots of procrastination and delay was Deng so quick to accept nearly all the terms in the American draft, when many of them had been discussed for months without resolution? Deng was in a hurry. He was 74 years old, some of his dearest colleagues were dead including Mao and Zhou. He was also aware that the Soviets were close to signing the SALT agreement, and the consequences of that could affect the normalization talks. So he wanted to bring closure to a relationship which would open major trade opportunities as well as foreign capital for infrastructure and foreign investment in manufacturing. Further, timing was important. He could use the normalization announcement as the final piece in his ascendency to being the leader of China. He was scheduled to make the opening address at the 3rd Plenary Session of the 11th Central Committee of the Communist Party of China. The December 18-22 gathering was a triumph for Deng. He elevated a sufficient number of his supporters to insure that his new economic policy would be approved. They were supporters of Deng's oft quoted expression: "it doesn't matter whether the cat is black or white, as long as it catches mice." This was a criticism of Mao's emphasis on ideological correctness as a substitute for performance. Deng called his economic program "socialist modernization," a program that over the next two decades would make China a dominant player in the global economy. As for party members who supported the "two whatevers," they were relieved of most of their economic and political responsibilities. Hua Guofeng, while not demoted in title, lost his power and was forced to engage in "self criticism." His role was ceremonial until Deng removed him in 1981.

While Deng was insuring his place as the new leader of China, President Carter was in pain. He had a severe case of hemorrhoids and described his problem in two pages of his dairy. Several days before Christmas, the inflammation began, and after several sleepless nights he mentioned his condition to Sadat during a Christmas conversation. The Egyptian president had Egyptians pray for that his hemorrhoids would be cured "because he was a good man." On the day after Christmas, they were cured. "I was tempted to make a public announcement thanking the Egyptians but decided we've had enough publicity with my ailment."[33]

With that crisis resolved, and with little fanfare, on January 1, 1979 Carter announced the beginning of diplomatic relations between Washington and Beijing. At the same time, he announced the termination of the 1955 Mutual Defense Treaty with Taiwan effective January 1, 1980. In China, Beijing officially adopted the Pinyin system for spelling and pronouncing Chinese names and places in Roman letter, including government documents and correspondence. Pinying had been long used in Chinese schools and on street and commercial signs. Americans would need some time to learn that Peking was now Beijing. On the sidelines sat Brzezinski who was enjoying a Carter congratulations, something the president rarely did. He told his NSC advisor that he was the "driving force behind the entire effort...Whenever I wavered, you pushed me and pressed me to go through with this."[34] Twenty-seven years later, he proudly told some former colleagues at a State Department Conference held in September 2006 that the president had chosen him to be the point man on the negotiations because they "could not be entrusted...to the State Department...And I daresay that it probably wouldn't have been successful if it had been undertaken otherwise."[35] After all those years, Brzezinski could not let go of his dislike for Cyrus Vance.

CHAPTER XVI

DENG XIAOPING AND JIMMY CARTER
BREAK BREAD IN THE WHITE HOUSE

Following the announcement the administration focused its attention on Deng's visit. Economics would be a major topic of discussion and on January 8, the Treasury Secretary convened a meeting with heads of all agencies dealing with trade along with representatives of the CIA and NSC. First item was resolution to the claims/assets issue which involved settling America private claims against China, and Chinese assets blocked in the US. The other important topic was granting China MFN product treatment. The latter involved the Jackson-Vanik language, and the reaction of Moscow were Beijing alone given MFN. Other issues included the role of the Export-Import Bank (Ex-Im) which currently had no free cash, and a textile agreement which would permit Washington to be selective in China's exports. While there was little support for a joint US-Chinese Economic Committee, when Brzezinski gave his recommendation to the president on January 26, he suggested that a committee had merit in addressing bilateral issues and that the president should raise the idea during his meeting with Deng.[1]

With only two days to go before Deng's arrival, Brzezinski and Vance each gave the president what they believed he should discuss with the Communist leader. While both men urged the president to emphasize the need for Deng's cooperation to "help us sell normalization to the Congress and the American people," the issue was more important to Vance. Brzezinski, as could be anticipated, focused on an emerging triangle, Washington-Beijing-Moscow and saw that Carter's talks could bring the former closer together to counter Soviet efforts at global hegemony. While some people suggested that Washington should treat China and the Soviets in a "evenhanded" manner, one supported by Vance, the NSC advisor wanted a balanced approach. "Evenhanded" he labeled as a mechanical measure, which could at times reward "intransigence by one party and ignoring restraint or accommodation by the other." A "balanced" approach recognized that there were differences in America's relations with each country. Brzezinski wanted the president to convince Deng that America was a "credible counterweight to the increased Soviet military power in Asia." Both men suggested that the president not raise the issue of human rights. Deng had already made his position clear at an earlier meeting with an American congressional delegation led by Senator Nunn on January 9. He told the Senator that any such discussion "would be acrimonious. I have my own interpretation."[2]

Both advisors also prepared a brief note about Deng's personality. Vance saw him as "feisty self-confidently outspoken, direct, forceful and clever." While he had power to make many decisions, he was "sensitive to potential criticism from the Politburo," and other critics in Beijing. Brzezinski emphasized that the president be willing to challenge Deng's statements with which he did not agree. Toughness toward China would indicate that he was willing to be tough toward Moscow. He warned that the Chinese place a great emphasis on words, both formal statements and in conversation. Simply put, Carter should be aware of what he was saying and how his words could be interpreted.[3]

On January 28 Deng, his wife Zhou Lin, Woodcock and his wife Sharon, and Deng's staff boarded a Boeing 707 for the US. The *Time Magazine* 1978 Man of the Year, with his photo on the January 1, 1979 issue, landed about ten hours later, at Andrews Air Force Base. Upon landing he exuberantly declared that he had always wanted to "visit America before going to see Marx."[4] After checking in at the Blair House, where he and his wife would be staying during their Washington visit, Deng, his wife, several senior members of his staff drove out to Brzezinski's home in McLean, Virginia for a private supper along with Woodcock, Oksenberg, Vance and Holbrooke. The

197

supper was an informal affair, with Brzezinski's children acting as wait staff. At one point during some small talk, Brzezinski told Deng that Carter was having some difficulties with the China lobby over normalization, and "I asked him facetiously whether he had similar difficulties in China. In a flash, Deng responded 'Yes, I did: there was some opposition in the province of Taiwan.'" Before returning to Blair House, Deng mentioned that he would like to talk with the president about Vietnam. Brzezinski quickly interpreted the request as meaning that China planned action against Hanoi, and would like to have the support of the White House. Of course that would also mean, that Washington was supporting an attack on a Soviet satellite, which would be Deng's purpose, and a position which Carter could never support. But rather than saying anything negative, Brzezinski notified the president of Deng's intentions. [5]

On the 29th just before 11 a.m. Carter and Deng met along with their staffs. The Carter-Deng meetings would involve three sessions, and both men agreed that the first should be a "get to know you" moment, and then the president should give an overview of America's global view including Soviet-American relations. The second session would be the standard *tour d'horizon*, and the third, bilateral issues including claims/assets issues, MFN, science and technology issues, cultural exchanges and consular arrangements. Following an exchange of welcomes, Carter spoke about America's intent to maintain her strength and influence to help others. This included supporting democratic processes worldwide, and shifting power from Moscow to include other emerging countries including China. As for the Soviet Union, America had maintained military parity while Moscow had shown herself to be "weak politically, economically, ideologically, and their inferiority complex caused a potentially unstable attitude toward the rest of the world." The president also emphasized two issues of particular concern, the instability in the area from Southeast Asia, north through the Indian Ocean to Africa, and Moscow's rapid increase in military strength. In conclusion, Carter wanted America "to join with China to use the positive elements in the world to deal with the negative ones."[6]

Deng agreed with Carter's view of the Soviet Union as the cause of "untranquility" in the world.[7] This produced situations which could produce common cause between Beijing and Washington. Deng's real purpose in his presentation was to encourage America to be more vigorous in confronting Moscow's hegemonic designs. As usual, he saw Soviet influence spreading everywhere in the Middle East, Turkey, Africa, India, Iran, Afghanistan, Pakistan and Vietnam while America stood by doing nothing. Deng concluded that while not recommending a formal alliance between Beijing and Washington, he believed that the two countries should coordinate their activities and work together to stop the spread of Moscow's influence worldwide. To make sure that he was not giving the wrong impression, he emphasized that China did not want war. She was in the beginning of a 25 year plan to implement the Four Modernizations, and war would postpone progress considerably. China needed a long period of peace.[8]

Vance and Deng led the second session which at the outset included a review of America's relations with Turkey. In 1974 the Turks invaded Cyprus, dividing the island between Greek Cypriots and Turkish Cypriots. America imposed an arms embargo on Ankara, and while later lifted, relations remained strained. True to form, Deng wanted America to improve relations to prevent Soviet expansion. Since the day's agenda called for military preparedness, Secretary of Defense Brown joined the conversation. He spoke about the relative strengths of the Warsaw Pact and NATO forces. Ever since the combined effect of Watergate and the military defeat in Vietnam, the American public had little taste for combat, and thus there was growing support for decreasing the defense budget. In light of that, coupled with Moscow's realization in 1972 that she was far behind in missile development, the Kremlin had moved rapidly to not only bridge the gap, but to take the lead in weapons production. Brown indicated that ten years earlier, the Warsaw Pact was behind NATO in military preparedness, but now she had reached parity, and Moscow had increased her force commitment to the Warsaw Pact countries. As far as could be seen, while the Soviets feared an attack against her satellite states, she had no desire to initiate a war. Both sides realized that a conventional war would quickly become a nuclear war initiated by whichever side was losing, and neither side was willing to take the first step towards such an outcome. In many ways, nuclear weapons had created a nuclear peace. Brown asked Deng about China's ability to respond quickly to a Soviet attack. While admitting that Beijing's early warning systems were not adequate, the Vice Premier believed that in light of the lengthy border between the two countries and the limited military troops the Soviets had stationed in the Far East, that an attack was not imminent. With this, the session adjourned for a lunch prepared by Mrs. Vance.[9]

At the last session of the day, Deng and Carter exchanged views on global problems. The president highlighted Washington's progress in strengthening NATO, working more closely with Egypt, Indonesia, Yugoslavia and Romania. As for the Soviet Union, Carter did not want to form an alliance with China but there were "many areas in the world where we can act in concert." In addition to his concerns noted the previous day, Deng opposed Washington's continued support of Israel in opposing Palestine and the Arab world. He also cautioned Carter, that while he had no problems with Washington signing a SALT agreement, he warned that Washington ought not expect the Soviets to live up to its terms.[10]

As the meeting closed, Deng asked Carter for private meeting on Vietnam. Immediately, the president invited Mondale, Vance and Brzezinski to join him and meet with several Chinese representatives including the vice premier and Foreign Minister Huang. What prompted the need for an immediate meeting was Vietnam's invasion of Cambodia on December 25, 1978. She had rapidly advanced and captured Phnom Penh, Cambodia's capital and headquarters of the Khmer Rouge, best known for its infamous "killing fields."

Vietnam's relations with Cambodia were centuries old. Vietnam's unification in 1975 and its subsequent purging of ethnic Chinese minorities forced Hanoi to look to Moscow for support. At the same time, the Khmer Rouge, led by Pol Pot, overthrew the American supported Lon Nol regime in Cambodia, and looked to Vietnam and ultimately Moscow for support. However, when the Khmer Rouge initiated genocidal attacks on the Cambodian people, Vietnam decided to distance herself from Pol Pot. The Khmer Rouge rounded up Vietnamese, executed them and tried numerous cross border attacks into Vietnam. Pol Pot believed if he attacked Vietnam, he would unite the Cambodian people under his leadership. The December attack attracted few Cambodians; they feared and hated the Khmer Rouge. Hanoi denounced Pol Pot's government and attacked Cambodia in December and early January forcing the Khmer Rouge to literally take to the hills. Beijing had watched the fighting and concluded that it was supported by Moscow and designed to have Vietnam assume control over Cambodia and all of Indochina, giving the Soviet Union a stronghold south of China. Given these developments and Beijing's line of thought, Deng's request to seek America's help made sense.[11]

While understanding China's perspective, the president had no intention of having America become involved with Vietnam again. From the outset, Deng made it clear that he intended to take military action against Hanoi to teach her a lesson. The attack would be limited and done quickly enough to eliminate any Soviet counter move. Deng asked Carter "for moral support in the international field." The president was not about to be innocently dragged into the fray. "It would be difficult for us to encourage violence. We can give you intelligence briefings" concerning Moscow's movements, but that was the limit of support. "I have no other answer for you." At the close, Carter appeared to have left open a door, when he suggested a private meeting between the two the following day.

The state dinner was critiqued as one of the finest put on by the Carter White House. And to add to the brilliance of the occasion was Richard Nixon. The Carter people had suggested that the former president attend in light of the success of his multi-polar diplomacy which recognized China as a global player. Following the dinner, the dignitaries went to the Kennedy Center where Deng went on stage and hugged and kissed a group of students who performed several songs in Chinese. The audience was moved to tears, and Deng's actions would be remembered when the vote on normalization came before Congress.

Carter suggested that bilateral relations be the topic for the second day of talks emphasizing that normal trade relations could now begin. The first obstacle was the claims/assets issue. Both quickly agreed that a solution could be easily found through a joint commission led by Treasury Secretary Michael Blumenthal and the Chinese Foreign Minister Huang Hua. Following resolution of that issue, Deng wanted to sign a long-term trade agreement, and Carter agreed but added the caveat that it would have to be approved by Congress. And there was a stumbling block, the Jackson-Vanik amendment requiring a country to permit free emigration. Deng saw no difficulty. Already Chinese were going to Canada and Hong Kong in considerable numbers. Indicating that he saw no problem with the amendment, he kiddingly said "if you want me to release 10 million Chinese to come to the US, I'd be glad to do so." Carter parried that in return he would send Beijing 10 million journalists.[12]

Both sides agreed to sign civil aviation and maritime agreements at a later visit by Commerce Secretary Kreps and Blumenthal. While both men endorsed the idea of increased student exchanges, Deng cautioned that China needed more time to provide housing adequate for American students. Carter wanted a journalist exchange program of up to 10,000 for each side. Deng said "that would be a bit too much." Because of limited travel conditions in China, there was no need of such a large contingent of journalists.

And as for censorship, each side agreed to give journalists freedom for reporting. The ongoing negotiations about consular and embassy locations and services had just ended, and an agreement would be signed on the following day. Carter wanted Deng's reassurance that he would work to resolve the issue of Taiwan's reunification in a peaceful manner. Deng noted that there were only two reasons why force would have to be used: Taipei's failure to talk with China over a sustained period of time, and a Soviet attack on Taiwan. Carter urged Deng to let Congress know of his intent not to use force. Before concluding this meeting, both men agreed to communicate directly or through their ambassadors. Hopefully this would prevent leaks to the press.[13]

At the end of the session, Carter and Deng held the promised private meeting over Beijing's desire to attack Vietnam. The president believed that a "token" Chinese action would not be considered "as significant punishment." But it would end Beijing's image of being peaceful, produce negative reactions throughout the world, and raise questions in America about China's approach to resolving the issue of Taiwan. Further, the invasion would force Hanoi to seek greater help from Moscow, a goal antithetical to China's interests. Deng's response was similar to what he had told the president earlier. "China must teach Vietnam a lesson." The action would only last 10-20 days, and he would appreciate continued intelligence briefings from Washington concerning Soviet and Vietnamese actions.[14]

On the last day, Deng met with members of Carter's cabinet for breakfast. The topic was trade, and the impediments to free trade. The claims/assets issue was still unresolved, and Most Favored Nation (MFN) status needed congressional approval. Deng believed that while Taiwan had a healthy trade with America, China's would be "ten times greater." Each of the cabinet members attending spoke about the how they could assist Deng in his modernization program. Following the meeting, Deng visited Congress and was asked about China's emigration policy in light of the Jackson-Vanik constraints.

203

The Vice Premier quickly repeated an earlier response he had made, "Oh, that's easy! How many you want? Ten million, fifteen million?" That ended congressional concerns about China's emigration practices.[15]

Following the meeting, Chinese and American officials signed a number of bilateral accords including agreements on science and technology, culture, consular relations which permitted America to later open consulates in Shanghai and Guangzhou, and China to do the same in Houston and San Francisco. There were also agreements on student exchanges, agriculture and space technology. Deng and Carter also exchanged acceptances of invitations to visit each other's country. On February 1, a joint press communiqué indicated that there had been a meeting and noted the signed bilateral agreements.[16]

With genuine enjoyment, Deng continued his American visit and the first stop was Atlanta, Georgia, the home state of Carter, where he captivated his audience of 1,400 with his knowledge of the Atlanta revival following the Civil War. He compared Atlanta's growth, from being part of the American South, "a relatively backward area" to now being a pacesetter. He saw China in the same terms, and anticipated that she too would come out of her "backwardness." Stop two was in Houston, where he visited the Ford factory, the LBJ Space Center, and a rodeo in Simonton, thirty-seven miles outside of Houston. Here, a young girl on horseback galloped up and presented him with a ten-gallon hat. The photograph of Deng wearing the hat became a symbol of his visit. "It signaled to the U.S. public that he was not only good-humored, but, after all, less like one of 'those Communists,' and more like 'us.'" On to Seattle, the last stop on his tour and what proved to be the last time he would stop in America. He arrived at dinner time on February 4, and on the following day visited the Boeing 747 plant, from where China had just purchased three 747s. Unfortunately Deng caught a cold which forced him to cancel a couple of other scheduled engagements, and he left for Tokyo on February 5.[17]

Deng's visit forced Americans and Chinese to view each other in a much different light. Since much of his trip was televised, Beijing produced a documentary movie which presented a very favorable view of the US. The film showed not only factories, and highways, but families in neighborhoods and how they lived with modern furniture and fashionable clothing. All in all, the visit was a major stepping stone in developing stronger Sino-American relations.[18]

CHAPTER XVII

CHINA ENTERS AMERICA'S ECONOMY

The White House had little time to bask in its success. With normalization now a done deal, the hard part began: implementation, with Taiwan as the first item on the agenda. This would soon be followed by claims/assets issues, a trade agreement and MFN for China's products.

As Deng's plane left from Seattle, Deputy Secretary of State Christopher explained to the Senate Foreign Relations Committee the administration's new policy contained in Senate 245, the China Omnibus Bill, and its House counterpart, which would later become the Taiwan Relations Act. The provisions were those agreed to during the Woodcock-Huang negotiations in Beijing and included America's commitment to maintain commercial, cultural and other relations with Taiwan on an unofficial basis. The vehicle for doing this would be through the American Institute in Taiwan. The administration had pressed China to agree to a peaceful resolution to reunification of Taiwan and China, but no promises were made. The administration assured the senators that these new relations and military restrictions would not reduce America's regional military posture.[1]

During these initial debates, Washington had urged Taipei to accept the non-governmental arrangement Carter had offered on December 30, but without success. On February 10, Washington sent Taiwan an ultimatum, either except the arrangement or accept a complete rupture in relations between the two countries. A couple of days later, Taiwan established a Coordination Council for North American Affairs, a counterpart to the American Institute in Taiwan, with headquarters in Washington and branch offices in eight other American cities. Several congressmen wanted more security for Taiwan, and forced the administration to accept a strengthened bill.

206

During the next two weeks both Foreign Minister Huang and the Chinese Ambassador Chai Zemin complained to Woodcock that the Taiwan bill was not in the spirit of the normalization agreement. Christopher assured both that there was no inconsistency between the bill being worked upon in Congress and the normalization agreement.[2]

On March 29, 1979, Congress adopted the Taiwan Relations Act and Carter signed it on April 10. Through the Act, America committed herself to help maintain peace, security and stability in the Western Pacific, and continue commercial, cultural and other relations with the people of Taiwan. The terms included an "expectation that the future of Taiwan will be determined by peaceful means," and that America would continue to provide Taiwan "arms of a defensive character and to maintain the capacity of the US to resist any resort to force or other forms of coercion…on the people on Taiwan." Beijing's reaction was predictable. Foreign Minister Huang had told Woodcock that if the bills became law, "great harm would be done to the new relationship" between the US and China. However, during the period between congressional approval and the president's signature, China raised no protest. Beijing knew that any additional comment would fall on deaf ears.[3] With the signing, Senator Hollings, Chairman of the Senate Budget Committee in the 96th Congress, finally released funds initially budgeted for the American Embassy in Taiwan to the American Institute in Taiwan, a private organization. He had held the monies as a sign of his personal opposition to the Act until the president signed the agreement making it law.[4]

While Congress considered the Taiwan Relations Act, Deng did what he had told Carter. China attacked Vietnam on February 17. Concerned that Moscow might become involved in the conflict, since the Soviets viewed Hanoi as an ally, Carter immediately sent a note to Brezhnev. The US had told China to withdraw her troops from Vietnam, and the Vietnamese to withdraw their forces from Kampuchea. On the following day Brezhnev responded. He was fairly convinced that America was not only aware of the impending attack, but had given tacit approval to it. He saw a connection between Deng's White House visit and the invasion and wondered why the president would assume that Moscow would use restraint in reacting to the Chinese attack considering the importance of the upcoming Moscow summit.[5]

From the standpoint of Beijing, the attack against Hanoi was a "milestone" in Sino-Soviet relations. It was the first time Beijing had challenged a Soviet ally with force. While Beijing won the near month long conflict, its victory showed up its weaknesses. Considering the size differential and China's supposed modern military technology, the Chinese army performed poorly. There were significant command issues as well as logistics, indicating that the Chinese military was not ready for modern warfare. Deng would address that issue shortly after Zhao Ziyang replaced Hua Guofeng as Premier in 1980.

Meanwhile Carter convened a special committee to debate the merits of Treasury Secretary Blumenthal's plans to visit Beijing, and the message it would send Moscow. After a couple of days, all agreed that he should take the trip as planned on February 24. This would give Beijing evidence that Washington wanted to go forward and implement some of the bilateral agreements signed during the vice premier's visit.

The secretary's stay in Beijing proved quite successful. He negotiated a claims/assets agreement, stemming from talks begun in 1977, wherein Beijing agreed to pay $80 million over a period of six years commencing October 1, 1980. The terms represented 41% of the amount unilaterally determined by the Foreign Claims Settlement Commission as the value of American claims. It was better than nearly all other claims settlements. But the agreement had only been initialed, and still needed to be signed. In analyzing the reasons for China's willingness to move forward after so many years of no progress, Blumenthal believed it was because Carter permitted the secretary's planned visit to go forward as a sign of good will, in spite of China's invasion of Vietnam. Deng wanted to focus on modernization and settling the claims/assets issue would open the door to much needed trade. [6]

The Treasury Secretary's visit proved to be a gate-opener. Once China withdrew her forces from Vietnam on March 16, most of the cabinet members who had met with Deng prior to his leaving Washington flew to Beijing. Congressional committees soon followed, along with representatives from the US Conference of Mayors, and on November 2, St. Louis, Missouri, and Nanjing became the first of several cities to sign a "sister cities" agreement.

With the first hurdle resolved, Blumenthal and other cabinet members focused on multiple issues, none more important than completing a trade agreement with China, followed by granting Beijing MFN. Ambassador Woodcock urged Washington to capitalize on China's eagerness to sign an agreement. Seizing the moment, Carter sent Secretary of Commerce Juanita Kreps along with a small negotiating team to Beijing on May 5. During the next ten days, Kreps signed the claims/assets agreement, initialed a trade agreement, and signed four agreements on scientific and technological cooperation, as well as one on trade exhibitions. The only stumbling block during the talks was Beijing's request to be identified as a "developing nation," thereby being eligible for America's generalized system of tariff preferences (GSP). The process was not simple. Under the Trade Act of 1974, for a Communist country to be a GSP beneficiary country, it had to have received MFN treatment, be a contracting party to the General Agreement on Tariffs and Trade (GATT), and be a member of the International Monetary Fund (IMF). Since she was party to neither of these organizations, a GSP designation was not available. The NSC believed that rather than fight Congress over a GSP recognition, the battle should be waged over MFN. [7]

Throughout the trade talks, China frequently mentioned that she needed credit. At a meeting on May 30 between Blumenthal and Vice Premier Kang Shien, and his commercial team, Blumenthal noted that Japan had extended Beijing a two billion dollar credit line which could be used to purchase American products. However, before America would extend credit, Beijing had to repay monies loaned by the Ex-Im Bank following World War II. The total amount was $26.4 million, but part of the materials purchased ended up in Taiwan, so the exact figure needed to be determined. Once that was done, and the loan paid, Congress would be able to approve Ex-Im Bank credits following a signed trade agreement.[8]

Negotiations had been ongoing since Kreps's visit and due to Congress's calendar, a signing needed to be done by July 15 if the trade agreement were to come before Congress in 1979. On July 7, delegations from both sides signed the agreement in Beijing. It provided that in order to establish bilateral trade relations on the basis of non-discrimination, both parties should grant each other most-favored-nation treatment, establish commercial and trade institutions, protect each other's patterns of trade, copy rights and trademarks and resolve bilateral trade issues through negotiations. Once approved the agreement would stay in force for three years. However, the agreement needed congressional approval, and since nothing was moving forward, the Chinese believed that America "had reneged on a commitment" to quickly make the treaty into law.

In part, the delay was prompted by the annual congressional recess in August, enabling many members to return to their districts to address local issues. Further, there were several members of the administration who wanted to maintain an "even-handed" relationship in Washington's dealing with Beijing and Moscow, while other wanted to "tilt" to China. As the delay continued, Blumenthal and Vance raised the issue of granting MFN for the Soviet Union. They thought the president should use his waiver authority under the 1974 Trade Act to grant MFN to each country. However, the president deferred. Brzezinski supported the president fearing that by tying the two countries together, both could lose congressional support. He wanted the senate to focus on Beijing and not be distracted by debating the merits of MFN for each of the Communist powers.[9] In light of these factors, Carter decided to await the return of Vice President Mondale from his scheduled trip to Beijing in August before taking any action on the MFN agreement.

China had not been the only hot topic on the administration's plate. In addition to the Middle East, a pet project of the president, there was SALT. Congressional concern over SALT and its weapons limitations versus loss of security had been ongoing since the beginning of the year. There were simultaneous talks between Soviet and American negotiators in Geneva and in private talks between Secretary of State Vance and Ambassador Dobrynin. The president was concerned about negative effects from China's invasion of Vietnam on February 17. To combat this, he gave an address at the Georgia Institute of Technology on February 20. His message was clear: without a SALT agreement with Moscow, "each crisis…each point of friction…would take on an added measure of significance and an added dimension of danger. It is precisely why we have fundamental differences with the Soviet Union that we are determined to bring this dangerous dimension of our military competition under control."[10]

Talks begun in January began to reach points of agreement by May. With the end in sight, Brezhnev and Carter agreed to meet in Vienna on June 15, the first summit between the two countries since Vladivostok in 1974. Both leaders knew that the only reason for their meeting was to sign the SALT II agreement. There would be little else to discuss, especially in the light of Brezhnev's declining health, which Brzezinski described as bordering on senility.[11] On June 18, 1979 the two men completed a process begun in 1972, and signed SALT II, a protocol, and a statement of principles for SALT III. The treaty restricted both countries to an equal overall total of strategic nuclear launch vehicles enabling Washington to redress a Soviet advantage existing since SALT I. The agreement was to last until December 31, 1985.

While there were no other agreements, Vance viewed the summit as having "tremendous political and strategic importance." Brezhnev's health indicated that there soon would be a leadership change in the Soviet Union, and SALT II could "strengthen the more moderate elements" in Moscow during the transition. Four days after the signing, Carter submitted the treaty to the senate for ratification where it was attacked by Republicans. To make matters worse, in late September, the White House discovered a Soviet military brigade in Cuba. Quickly, anti-Communist forces rallied, accusing Moscow of violating agreements made during Kennedy's presidency. Beijing joined in as well. In early October, Vance went to Beijing and during his talks, Vice Foreign Minister Han magnified the Cuban brigade issue, suggesting that it was a trial balloon to see how America would react. He saw the affair in terms of the 1962 missile crisis, a parallel which Vance quickly squelched. When the secretary returned to Washington he met with Dobyrnin, and learned that troops had been there since 1962 and were part of the agreement ending the missile crisis. There were no additional troops, but the rumor was sufficient enough to sidetrack and slow down the hearings on SALT II.[12]

With the Sino-America claims/assets issue resolved and the bilateral trade agreement signed, Vice President Walter Mondale decided to accept an earlier invitation to visit Beijing. His visit, like Deng's, would be the first since normalization of a high ranking official to the Chinese capital. Similar to Deng, Mondale's visit would also include stops outside the capital in Xian and Canton on his way to Hong Kong and Tokyo. The vice president anticipated a busy schedule including the standard review of global issues with Deng and perhaps Hua Guofeng, along with the opening of the American Consulate in Canton, and signing agreements on civil aviation, hydroelectric power contracts, and expanded cultural exchanges. In preparation for his visit, he received reports from the CIA and Ambassador Woodcock cautioning him that Deng might not be in China's leadership in the near future. Woodcock interpreted Deng's repositioning of his supporters into key positions as a prelude to his retirement. Both reports saw Deng's departure within three years, followed by a period of turbulence as China looked for a leader to continue to bring Beijing into the 20th century.[13] With 2014 hindsight, one is reminded of Mark Twain's famous remark "the report of my death was an exaggeration."

Following his arrival on August 26, Mondale met with Deng on the following morning. The first issue the vice premier raised concerned the delay in congressional approval of the trade treaty. The vice president realized that Beijing thought that America had "reneged on a commitment" to approve the treaty. In part, China's angst was due to the treaty's commitment to MFN, a much needed provision to move forward on the Four Modernizations. Mondale solved the problem. He immediately notified Brzezinski and told him to talk to Robert Byrd, the Senator Majority Leader whose job it was to determine the time line for debate on senate issues. When informed of China's concern, Byrd guaranteed that the treaty would be on the floor of the senate by November 1. This settled the issue. The next item on the agenda dealt with China's ability to purchase American products. Washington was willing to have the Ex-Im bank extend Beijing a $2 billion credit line, which could be increased. The offer was contingent on China agreeing to use part of the money to pay off $37 million worth of claims, which were loans to the ROC. Deng refused to accept the terms, if the $37 million were part of the offer. Mondale explained that American laws required Ex-Im lending be contingent on the recipient having paid off prior debt. Deng saw the issue as a Taipei problem, not Beijing's. Both men agreed to let the experts work out the details.

Mondale offered the availability of reimbursable assistance. This was available only to China and not the Soviet Union, because the US had determined that China was a "friendly country." This label was very useful since it would enable Beijing to enter into negotiations for such items as hydroelectric projects and technical

213

support all on a reimbursable basis, so no upfront monies. Without the "friendly country" designation, this could not be done. Mondale offered OPIC guarantees. This Overseas Private Investment Corporation insured American business ventures in developing nations. American businesses would be far more willing to invest in a Communist country, friendly or not, knowing that their investment was covered by insurance. The vice president believed that $200 million would be initially available for loans to businesses including the sale of digital enhancement equipment as well as the newest executive jet commercial aircraft produced by Lockheed. While pleased with the offer, Deng wanted more. He wanted an advanced computer, a request China had made for a couple of years. Mondale's hands were a bit tied because of America's participation in COCOM, but he believed that a distinction could be made between selling product to a Communist country, i.e. the Soviet Union, and a "friendly country." This required some follow up work by Mondale. Capitalizing on a "Santa Claus" moment, Deng asked to purchase war planes and large-scale maps of the eastern part of the Soviet-Chinese border. Mondale was non-committal, but would bring the request back to Washington. In conclusion, Mondale noted a possible impasse in a civil aviation agreement. China would only permit one airline company as a carrier, and at present Pan American had the contract. Since America was a capitalist country, competition was the byword for success, and Mondale wanted at least two American companies permitted to land in China. Experts would meet to find a solution.

In the afternoon, Mondale spoke to students at Beijing University extolling the new relationship between China and America. He emphasized the "parallel and strategic interests" the countries shared, and added that "any nation which seeks to weaken or isolate you in world affairs assumes a stance counter to American interests."[14] During the evening, the vice president and his staff attended a cultural event where he listed to students sing "two Chinese classics: Jingle

214

Bells and Do Re Mi" in English, a response to the students at the Kennedy Center singing songs in Chinese to Deng and his entourage.

On his final day in Beijing, Mondale met with Premier Hua Guofeng and extended the president's invitation to visit America, an offer reciprocated by Hua. The premier congratulated him for being the first foreign official to speak at the university since 1949. He was also very impressed by Mondale's statement that "any action that tried to weaken or isolate us took a stance that runs counter to U.S. interests." That sentence gave Hua a stronger sense of confidence in America's commitment to China relative to the Polar Bear. He asked Mondale if he had ever read *Peter the Great's Last Will and Testament*. An odd question, but one that Chinese officials had mentioned before. The will stated that God had called upon Russia to establish her rule over all of Europe. The reason: the nations of Europe were "fast approaching a state of utter decrepitude" and as a result could be "conquered by a new race of people when it has attained full power and strength." "We look upon our invasion of the West and the East as a decree of Divine Providence."[15]

With this thinking ingrained in the mind of the Chinese leadership, Hua's concern made sense, and indicated a new shift in Beijing's thinking. No longer did the Sino-Soviet conflict focus on ideology as it had for nearly thirty years, now it was mainly geopolitical. Deng's Four Modernizations were proof that Communist economic thought was passé. In response, Mondale reviewed America's growing military strength including its new MX mobile missile which carried ten warheads rather than the normal three, a Trident submarine with missiles capable of attacking the Soviet Union, and the modernizing of NATO's weapons with Pershing II and Cruise Missiles to counter the Soviet SS-20, recently placed in Eastern Europe.

Mondale addressed the Ex-Im Bank credit issue and means to circumvent the banks' rules which required all prior loans be repaid before new credit could be extended. The debt was incurred by the

215

Nationalist government, and while not a significant amount, Deng refused to pay off a debt he saw as belonging to Taiwan. Mondale mentioned to Hua that Deng's obstinacy would postpone America's offer of a $2 billion Ex-Im bank credit line. In search of a solution to this conundrum Hua suggested that America could finance individual projects and when they came on line the monies generated could pay off the loan. With MFN, this would become easier since Beijing could sell products to America and raise her own capital. Mondale saw the logic and agreed to bring the idea back to Washington. At the close of the meeting, Hua asked to speak privately with Mondale. The premier wanted to know about Washington's interest in selling China advanced military weapons including fighter planes. He agreed to add this to his list of topics he would bring to the president's attention.[16]

His visit to China received glowing reports and threw the Washington bureaucracy and Congress into high gear. The vice president had come home having promised China a number of economic programs, most requiring congressional approval. Included in the economic package was a trade agreement, OPIC, Ex-Im budgeting, product licensing, in addition to a genuine security relationship with Beijing. The visit would later lead to agreements in September 1980 on maritime affairs, civil aviation links, and textile issues, as well as a bilateral consular convention.

With all of the goings-on with China, Taiwan had fallen under the radar. In September, The American Institute in Taiwan notified its Washington office of the impact of normalization. Most affected were the people who believed that their security had been compromised, a fact that would be reinforced with the knowledge that the US Mutual Defense Treaty would expire on December 31, 1979. The island's power structure was "basically unaffected," and Chiang Kai-shek was aware that he had no alternative but to maintain strong relations with the US. In the short term, Taiwan should continue on its course with a solid economy. The problem lied with the death of Chiang, since he had designated no heir, and with his demise, Beijing may be prone to push for an early rather than a later inclusion of Taipei as a province of China.[17]

Fall 1979 started off well for the president. On October 23, he sent the China trade bill to Congress. Accompanying the bill, Carter sent a note addressing the Jackson-Vanik language and determined that the requirements of the Trade Act of 1974 would be met and China could be awarded MFN. That was the highpoint for Carter, for on November 4, Iranian students attacked the American Embassy in Tehran, seizing about 50 staff members. This would become Carter's nightmare lasting 444 days until Ronald Reagan's inauguration in 1981 resulted in their release. Carter called the hostage crisis "the beginning of the most difficult period of my life.[18]

"Difficult" was hardly the word to describe Carter's last three months in 1979. Between trying to use his political capital to sell Congress on the SALT agreement, and trying to find a way to rescues the hostages, he learned about a Soviet invasion of Afghanistan. Carter was surprised although the CIA had advised the White House on December 22 that an invasion was imminent within 72 hours. The president overreacted. He characterized the invasion as "the greatest threat to peace since the Second World War." The first casualty of the invasion was Carter's withdrawing the SALT II agreement from senate consideration on January 4. He asked Senator Byrd to keep the treaty on the calendar rather than sending it back to the Foreign Relations Committee, in the event Moscow quickly withdrew from Afghanistan. While this was viewed as a dramatic step, in fact the White House knew that confirmation would be seriously contested by men who were angered by several White House decisions: canceling the B-1 bomber, postponing the development of the neutron bomb, accepting missile parity with Moscow, and giving up America's long standing arms policy which guaranteed superiority. Carter's actions ended SALT II ratification, but both sides agreed to honor its terms, and did so for the next seven years until Ronald Reagan initiated Strategic Arms Reduction Talks (START).[19]

Meanwhile, since November 1, Congress had debated the China trade bill. The invasion of Afghanistan, and China's denunciation of the attack carried weight in the legislature. Further, her early support of UN sanctions on Iran, and her endorsement of the president's Olympic Games boycott gave the administration sufficient votes for Congress to pass the U.S.-China Trade agreement with its grant of most-favored-nation (MFN) status on January 24, effective February 1, 1980. The passage opened the doors not only to trade, but to the president making a determination on April 2 that it was in the national interest for the Ex-Im bank to guarantee, insure, extend credit and participate in the extension of credit for the purchase of any product or service for sale or lease to China.[20] The door was open for trade, and the promise of normalization of relations spelled out in the Shanghai Communiqué had come to fruition nearly eight years after its signing. The road from Geneva to Warsaw had finally reached its end in Beijing and Washington, enabling China to become part of the American economy, and a potential ally in Washington's efforts to prevent Soviet expansion.

CHAPTER XVIII

CONCLUSIONS

Given the mindset of Washington in 1954, that Communism was evil and had to be contained, who would have anticipated that the French defeat at Dien Bien Phu and the subsequent Geneva Conference would provide a platform for the first meeting between representatives of the US and PRC since 1949. While the initial talks concerned repatriation of detained nationals, they would slowly expand to ultimately include establishing diplomatic relations between the two countries. To be sure, progress was erratic and governed by internal politics in Beijing and Washington as well as by reactions to world events. A real stumbling block for the US was Taiwan. Chiang Kai-shek's Nationalist government fled to Taiwan and announced that it was the only legitimate government of China. This was a view accepted by the American public and supported by a China Lobby including anti-Communist congressmen led by right-wing Republicans, military leaders who had fought with the Nationalists against Japan, and big business which saw Chiang's return to the mainland as a as a means to restart their businesses nationalized by the Communists. Mao's early efforts to threaten the island only gave ammunition to the China Lobby encouraging Eisenhower to protect Taiwan though a mutual defense treaty, which would become a problem in later negotiations.

The China Lobby's influence in Congress would hold up real progress toward normalization for 18 years, followed by another six years following the Shanghai Communique. But the Lobby was not the only obstacle. The American public had to be re-educated into seeing that by supporting Beijing, Washington would have an ally against Moscow. In addition, the White House had to reassure the electorate that she was not abandoning Taiwan, although that would be Taipei's conclusion.

219

While intermediaries continued to meet in Geneva and later in Warsaw over repatriation and mutual claims/assets issues, there was no real communication directly between Washington and Beijing. Mao misinterpreted Moscow's view of Sputnik. Khrushchev saw it as a sign that the Soviet Union could compete with America, enabling him to improve relations with Washington. Mao saw Sputnik as an opportunity for the Communist world to challenge the West for world dominance. The Chairman's description of America as a "paper tiger" angered Moscow sufficiently that she cut off all support for China's nuclear program. This development along with the embarrassing failure of the Second Five Year Plan forced Mao to step down from being head of state.

After waiting several years, Mao organized the Cultural Revolution as a means to return to power, a revolution which produced total chaos and turmoil throughout China. At the same time, America was losing interest in a war in Vietnam, an area most American had never heard of before 1966. Worse, videographers brought the horrors of battle into family's television sets giving Americans their first view of real warfare. People were frightened and none more so than America's young people who would be called into military duty and sent to Vietnam. Students took to the streets to protest the war. In light of these developments, normalization talks were put on a back burner.

Mao's victory over Lin Biao coincided with Richard Nixon's phoenix-like return to power as America's new president in 1968. The new occupant of the Oval Office had a very different foreign policy, one which gave China a significant role. Multipolarity involved five centers: China, Japan, Russia, Europe and the United states. To Nixon, China was important, especially due to her size, potential and genuine distrust of Moscow. The president intended to use that distrust to play Beijing and Moscow off one other for Washington's gain. As for China, she saw Nixon's multipolarity equally useful, for she could have an ally against the "Polar Bear" to the north.

For his policy to work, Nixon needed direct contact with Mao and Zhou. The chairman was open to talks but Washington missed his subtle signal of interest when he stood next to the American journalist Edgar Snow in the October 1970 national celebrations in Tienanmen Square. Meanwhile White house efforts to reach Beijing through Pakistan, Romania, and France failed, but an American Ping Pong team succeed in April 1971. "Ping-Pong" diplomacy became a new phrase in diplomatic lexicons, and gave the White House an entry to Beijing. While Secretary of State Rogers should have been the lead person in the negotiations, he was completely shut out from high level discussions with both Beijing and Moscow. Not only did the president view his department as an information sieve, he also had a natural predilection for secrecy, one equally shared by Kissinger. The NSC advisor would do the leg work to have Zhou extend an invitation for a presidential visit. In February 1972, Nixon, Kissinger, their families and staffs, along with a brigade of correspondents and journalists arrived in China. The television coverage in America challenged the old view of China stemming from early movies of Chinamen chasing people with machetes, and the ugly images emanating from the Korean and Vietnam wars. Instead, Mao's blue jacket became a need-to-have item among celebrities and others.

The Shanghai Communiqué, much ballyhooed within diplomatic circles, made little impact on the American people. To most, Chiang Kai-shek was still the leader of China. But he was not, and he feared that this was the first step to Beijing's efforts to reunite the 23rd province to the mainland. The Shanghai Communique, while important, was not the same as mutual diplomatic recognition. Rather it was a promise to work toward recognition when each country would have an embassy in the other. In 1973, the American Embassy was in Taiwan, and the communiqué required that it be moved to Beijing, leaving no American government site on the island.

From 1972-1976, Sino-American relations moved forward through Kissinger's repeated visits to Beijing. Throughout his talks, he reassured Zhou that America recognized that there was only one China and Taiwan was part of it, America would not support any Taiwan efforts at independence, and would not support any Taiwan attack on the China mainland. In spite of these assurances, Taiwan remained a stumbling block during the negotiations, and would remain so until the American flag flew on top of the American Embassy in Beijing.

As for the *tour d'horizon* discussions, in which each side reviewed global affairs, China always played the "poor backward country" card vulnerable to Soviet aggression. America responded, as Beijing had hoped, by giving her highly classified military information on Soviet forces as well as providing her with nuclear and scientific technology. Although China gained the most from the exchanges, Washington viewed Beijing's support of a stronger American naval presence in the Asia Pacific, as a plus. Furthermore the exchanges of information identified areas of mutual concern as well as disagreement. Both wanted to stymie Soviet expansion in Southeast Asia, and Africa. In the India-Pakistan power struggle, China supported Islamabad, as did the White House albeit surreptitiously due to congressional support of "democratic" Delhi. Both wanted Japan to be strong and linked to America. As a result of Beijing's constant description of a weakening Europe, made more vulnerable by the Helsinki Accords, America stepped up her support of NATO. Areas of disagreement included the process of bringing peace to Korea, and the Palestinian-Israeli issue. While Beijing's foreign policy always began with Moscow, Washington had a more global approach. In addition, the *tour d'horizon* produced a greater sense of trust, identified the whereabouts of detained nationals resulting in their repatriation, kept trade talks alive and basically produced an atmosphere which when both sides were ready, could quickly forward to complete normalization talks.

While Nixon's resignation reduced Kissinger's influence, it was not a principle factor in slowing talks to nearly a standstill. Much

222

was due to Beijing's caution toward dealing with the new President Gerald Ford, Zhou and Mao's deaths followed briefly by the Gang of Four, which was totally opposed to normalization, the emergence of the relatively unknown Hua Guofeng, Ford's election campaigning, and Jimmy Carter's victory. All of which spelled a time out in normalization talks.

And these developments did not include America's free trade impediments especially the 1949 COCOM lists and the 1951 Battle Act, both of which seriously restricted trade with Communist countries. In addition there were the normal trade barriers to protect home industries. Changes would require cooperation between the departments of state, commerce, defense and agriculture. And this did not include changes needed in Ex-Im Bank regulations so that China could borrow money to purchase American goods. The Chinese renminbi was not accepted as currency by the US. And there was an ongoing concern in China. At times Zhou represented the old school and believed in "self reliance." He feared that by importing Western products and technology, China would become dependent on the imports and not focus on developing her own manufactures. Fortunately, when Deng took over negotiations, he was open to new ideas and new products to implement the Four Modernizations.

When Carter entered the White House, China was not high on his to-do list. While he would call for better relations with Beijing in his 1977 Notre Dame speech, and send Vance on what turned out to be a good will visit to China, the president remained busy with the Panama Canal Treaty, SALT II talks, and efforts to end the Egyptian-Israeli conflict. Finally in May 1978, he "made up his mind" and sent Brzezinski to talk with Deng, who too was now ready to establish diplomatic relations. Hua's limited ability along with the arrest of the Gang of Four enabled Deng to climb to the uppermost level of China's government and party hierarchy. To be recognized as China's leader, he needed to negotiate the beginning of diplomatic relations between Washington and Beijing.

The December 15 announcement did not resolve all issues related to the resumption of relations on January 1, 1979. Carter needed to address the problem of Taiwan. In early February he sent Congress a bill which became known as the Taiwan Relations Act. It provided security to the island, including continued shipments of selective weapons, as well as an American Institute in Taiwan, a private organization which would address commercial, cultural and other non-governmental issues. Of even more importance was trade legislation. In October Carter sent Congress a trade bill which addressed the issue of MFN by assuring Congress that the requirements of the Trade Act of 1974, calling for free emigration, was met and China could be awarded MFN. China's support of America's condemnation of the Moscow's invasion of Afghanistan, and her support of UN sanctions against Iran won her sufficient votes to pass the bill effective February 1, 1980. Meanwhile the two sides reached agreement on the claims/assets issue, access to the Ex-Im Bank and treaties concerning a variety of issues including one on textiles, which had been a subject of negotiations for years. By the fall of 1980, the important loose ends had been resolved.

After six years of on-again, off-again talks, Carter's decision that he "had made up his mind" corresponded with Deng's desire to establish diplomatic relations. He knew that they would provide a counter to Soviet threats against China, and at the same time permit him to start the process of modernization. Deng believed that a country of nearly a billion people should be a world player, and he intended to make her so. Normalization was but the first step to China's regaining her world prominence lost 150 years earlier in battles with the West. Equal relations with Washington would enable China to become part of the world's economy and provide her additional protection from Moscow. As for America, recognition gave Washington a sometime ally against Soviet expansion, but more importantly paved the way for a breathtaking growth of two-way trade over the next three decades.

The road from the Geneva Conference to Deng's triumphal visit to Seattle is an interesting example of the quirkiness involved in diplomacy. This is the story of how unintended consequences evolved through each country's reactions to global events, senses of security, and unpredicted changes in leadership. From the outset, Beijing wanted diplomatic relations with Washington with a guarantee that Taiwan was part of China. At the outset, the White House had no intention of granting recognition to the Communist regime, and was dedicated to the defense of the Nationalist government and its claim of Taipei being the capital of China. Yet Beijing-Washington talks persisted, often with postponements and little progress, but they continued and in so doing gave each side time to reassess its view of the other.

When Carter and Deng arrived on the scene, both knew that recognition was mutually beneficial, and that the future of Taiwan should no longer be a stumbling block. While some would say that Taipei paid the price for recognition, in the end she would maintain her independence with a promise of support from Washington, a situation not dramatically different from when the American flag flew from the US Embassy in Taipei.

As a postscript, on June 26, 2014, China sent her first ministerial level official to Taiwan.

NOTES

PREFACE

[1]Warren I. Cohen, *America's Response to China: A History of Sino-American Relations* (New York: Columbia University Press, 1990), 203.

CHAPTER I: FROM LONDON TO GENEVA

[1] *Foreign Relations of the United States, 1952-1954* (Washington, D.C.: Government Printing Office, 1985), 14: 29n4. Hereafter all volumes in the series will be cited as *FRUS*, volume subject, volume number, and pagination.

[2] Ibid., 82-86.

[3] Ibid., 114.

[4] Ibid., 115.

[5] Ibid., 243.

[6] Ibid., 247.

[7] Ibid., 338-339.

[8] Richard W. Prussen, "Over the Volcano: The United States and the Taiwan Strait Crisis, 1954-1955," in *Re-examining the Cold War: U.S.-China Diplomacy, 1954-1973*, ed. Robert Ross and Jiang Changbin (Cambridge: Harvard University Press, 2001), 49. Hereafter cited as Ross, ed.

[9] *FRUS*, 14:414 n2, 3.

[10] Ibid., 417-418.

[11] Ibid., 431-443.

[12] Zhang Baijia and Jia Qingguo, "Steering Wheel Shock Absorber, and Diplomatic Probe in Confrontation: Sino-American Ambassadorial Talks Seen from the Chinese Perspective," Ross, ed,,178.

[13] *FRUS,* 14: 462-475.

[14] Ibid., 485-489.

[15] Ibid., 501-505, 512-513.

[16] Ibid., 666-667.

[17] Ibid., 945-946.

[18] Dwight D. Eisenhower, *The White House Years: Mandate for Change, 1953-1956* (New York: Doubleday and Co., Inc., 1963), 465. Hereafter cited as Eisenhower, *Mandate*; *FRUS*, 14:929.

[19] *FRUS*, 14:1033ff.

[20] *FRUS, 1955-1957, China*, 2:7 n4.

[21] Ibid.,162-163; Eisenhower, *Mandate*, 469-482; *China Daily*, April, 2005; Gong Li, "Tension Across the Taiwan Strait in the 1950s: Chinese Strategy and Tactics," Ross, ed., 150-153.

[22] *FRUS, 1955-1957, China*, 2:26-30.

[23] Ibid., 149-151.

[24] Ibid., 278-279, 296-297, 442-443.

[25] Gong Li, Ross, ed., 152.

[26] *FRUS, 1955-57*, 2: 566, n2.

[27] Ibid., 507-508, 531.

[28] Ibid., 570.

[29] Ibid., 582-585, 614 n4.

[30] Ibid., 648-658, 678-679.

[31] Ibid., 685-687.

[32] *FRUS*, 1955-1957, 3:1.

[33] Ibid., 44.

[34] Steven Goldstein, "Dialogue of the Deaf: The Sino-American Ambassadorial-Level Talks, 1955-1970," Ross, ed., 207; http://history.state.gov/milestones/1953-1960/china-talks.

[35] *FRUS*, 1955-1957, 3: 85-86.

[36] Gong Li, Ross, ed., 153; http://www.nytimes.com/2009/11/04/world/asia/04qian.html?_r=0)

[37] *FRUS*, 1955-1957, 3: 90-94.

[38] Ibid., 103-105.

[39] Ibid., 275-277, 321.

[40] Goldstein, Ross, ed., 234.

[41] http://digitalarchive.wilsoncenter.org/document/117034.

CHAPTER II: GENEVA TO WARSAW, 1957-1969

[1] *FRUS, 1955-1957, CHINA*, 3:558-566.

[2] Ibid., 643-644, 657-659.

[3] *FRUS, 1958-1960, China*, 19: document 14, June 27, 1958.

[4] Ibid., document 23, August 2, 195812.

[5] Ibid., document 68, September 4, 1958.

[6] Ibid. Document 89, September 14, 1958. If interested in the initial Beam-Wang discussions see *FRUS, 1958-1960, China*, 19: documents 92, 93, 96, 97, 102, 119,120,123,126,covering the period through September 25, 1958.

[7] Ibid., document 140, September 29, 1958.

[8] Ibid., document 146, October 1, 1958.

[9] Ibid., document 165, October 7, 1958.

[10] Gong Li, Ross, ed., 167-170.

[11] Nancy Bernkopf Tucker, *China Confidential: American Diplomats and Sino-American Relations, 1945-1966* (New York: Columbia University Press, 2001), 160.

[12] Zhang Baijia and Jia Quingguo, Ross, ed., 191.

[13] *FRUS, 1964-1968, China*, 30: 35.

[14] Roderick MacFarquhar, *Sino-American Relations, 1949-1971* (New York: Praeger Pubs, 1972), 45; Goldstein, Ross, ed.,, 229.

[15] *FRUS, 1964-1968, China*, 30: 232-234.

[16] MacFarquhar, 222-234.

[17] http://millercenter.org/president/speeches/detail/4038.

[18] Goldstein, Ross, ed., 193.

[19] *FRUS, 1964-1968, China*, 30:509-513.

[20] Ibid., 630-635.

[21] Richard Nixon, *Foreign Affairs*, vol. 46, no. 1, October 1967, 113-115.

[22] http://www.youtube.com/watch?v=5aD5rgDpQqc.

[23] Maurice Meisner, *Mao's China and After: A History of the People's Republic* (New York: The Free Press, 1986), 399.

[24] *FRUS, 1964-1968, China*, Document 331.

CHAPTER III: NIXON REACHES OUT TO BEIJING

[1] http://www.presidency.ucsb.edu/ws/?pid=1941.

[2] *Cold War Flashpoints*, Cold War International History Project, Bulletin, Winter, 1998, 155.

[3] *FRUS, 1969-1976, China, 1969-1972*,17: 7.

[4] Chen Jian, "The Path Toward Sino-American Rapprochement, 1969-1972," *Bulletin, Supplement 1*, (German Historical Institute, Washington, DC, 2004), 32.

[5] Tucker, 227.

[6] Chen Jian, 31.

[7] *FRUS, 1969-1976, China 1969-1972*, 17: 22-23).

[8] Foster Rhea Dulles, *American Policy Toward Communist China, 1949-1969*(New York: Thomas Y. Crowell Co., 1972), 240-243.

[9] Raymond Garthoff, *Détente and Confrontation: American-Soviet Relations form Nixon to Reagan* (Washington, D.C.: The Brookings Institution), 246.

[10] *FRUS, 1969-1976*,I, *Foundations of Foreign Policy, 1969-1972*, 78-79.

[11] Garthoff, 247.

[12] http:digitalarchive.wilsoncenter.org/document/117752.

[13] Li Zhisui, *The Private Life of Chairman Mao: The Memoirs of Mao's Personal Physician,* trans. Tai HJung-chao (New York: Random House, 1994), 514.

[14] Joseph Harrington and Bruce Courtney, *Tweaking the Nose of the Russians: Fifty Years of American-Romanian Relations 1940-1990*(New York: Columbia University Press, 1991), 291.

[15] Chris Tudda, *A Cold War Turning Point: Nixon and China, 1969-1972* (Baton Rouge: Louisiana State University, 2012), 25-26.

[16] Harrington and Courtney, 288-290.

[17] Tudda, 26.

[18] Garthoff, 248.

[19] *FRUS, 1969-1976, China, 1969-1972,* 17: 53.

[20] *FRUS, 1969-1976,* 34: 240n6.

[21] *FRUS, 1969-1976, China, 1969-1972,* 17: 67 n1, 43n2; Henry Kissinger, *White House Years* (Boston: Little, Brown and Co., 1979), 182.

[22] Tudda, 29.

[23] *FRUS, 1969-1976, China, 1969-1972,* 17: 80.

[24] *Cold War International History Project Bulletin, Inside China's Cold War,* Woodrow Wilson International Center for Scholars, Fall 2007-Winter 2008, 405.

[25] *FRUS, 1969-1976, China, 1969,* 17: 88-89; Garthoff, 249.

[26] http//digitalarchive.wilsoncenter.org/document/117154-55.

[27] Chen Jian, "The Path toward Sino-American Rapprochement, 1969-1972", German Historical Institute, Washington, D.C. 2004, *Supplement* 1, 34; Michael Schaller, *The United States and China: Into the Twenty-First Century* (New York: Oxford University Press, 2002), 370)

[28] Zhisui, 515.

[29] Tudda, 39-41.

CHAPTER IV: 1970: FROM WARSAW TO BEIJING TO WASHINGTON

[1] www.presidency.ucsb.edu/ws/?pid=2835.

[2] *FRUS, 1969-1976, China, 1969-1972,* 17:165, 171.

[3] Goldstein, Ross, ed., 233,249.

[4] Chen Jian, 35.

[5] *FRUS, 1969-1976, China, 1969-1972,* 17:188-191.

[6] MacFarquer, 249.

[7] Schaller, 171; Chen Jian, 36.

[8] Schaller, 171; Chen Jian, 37.

[9] Kissinger, 699.

[10] Ibid., 701.

[11]Robert Dallek, *Nixon and Kissinger: Partners in Power* (New York: Harper Collins, Pubs., 2007), 265; Henry Kissinger, *On China* (New York: Penguin Books, 2012), 229; *FRUS 1969-1976, China,1969-1972*, 17: 251.

[12] Tudda, 62.

[13] *FRUS, 1969-1976, China, 1969-1972*, 17: 255; Dallek, 266.

[14] Dallek, 266-267.

[15] Kissinger, *On China*, 231.

[16] MacFarquhar, 250.

[17] Michael Schaller, "Détente and the Strategic Triangle: Or, 'Drinking your Mao Tai and Having Your Vodka, Too,'" *Re-examining the Cold War: U.S.-China Diplomacy, 1954-1973*, ed. Robert Ross and Jiang Changbin (Cambridge: Harvard University Press, 2001), 341-344; Zhisui, 558, Chen Jian, 342.

[18] Dallek, 268.

[19] MacFarquhar, 254.

[20] Department of State, *Director of Intelligence and Research, Intelligence Brief, April 14, 1971* in http://www2.gwu.edu/~nsarchiv/NSAEBB66/#docs.

[21] *FRUS, 1969-1976, China, 1969-1972*, 17: 301.

[22] Nixon, 549-550.

[23] Garthoff, 259.

[24] Nixon, 550.

[25] Kissinger, *White House Years*, 723.

[26] Ibid., 724; *FRUS, 1969-1976, China, 1969-1972*, 17: 318.

[27] Kissinger, *White House Years*, 703.

[28] Gong Li, "Chinese Decision Making and the Thawing of US-China Relations," *Re-examining the Cold War: U.S.-China Diplomacy, 1954-1973*, ed. Robert Ross and Jiang Changbin (Cambridge: Harvard University Press, 2001), 345-346; Tudda. 75-77.

[29] http://www2.gwu.edu/~nsarchiv/NSAEBB66/#docs.

[30] *FRUS, 1969-1976, China, 1969-1972*, 17: 332-333,

[31] Dallek, 290.

[32] H. R. Haldeman, *The Haldeman Diaries: Inside the Nixon White House* (New York: G. P. Putnam's Sons, 1994), 317; Kissinger, *White House Years, 727,*

[33] *FRUS, 1969-1976, China, 1969-1972*, 17: 340,346.

CHAPTER V: KISSINGER IN CHINA-OVERWHELMED IN MEETING ZHOU ENLAI

[1] Dallek, 290-291.

[2] Haldeman, 316.

[3] http://blog.nixonfoundation.org/2014/07/president-nixons-america-multi-polar-world/

[4] Dallek, 293.

[5] Nixon, 553.

[6] Kissinger, *White House Years*, 745.

[7] Kissinger, *On China*, 239-241.

[8] *FRUS, 1969-1976, China, 1969-1972*, 17: 368-370.

[9] Ibid., 361-363.

[10] Ibid., 410-411.

[11] Ibid., 416.

[12] Ibid., 453-455.

[13] Dallek, 298.

[14] Kissinger, *White House Years*, 755; Nixon, 544.

[15] Joseph Harrington, *Conflicted Giant: American Foreign Policy, 1945-2012, "citty upon a hill" versus Realpolitik* (createspace.com, 2013), I, 221-222; Walter LaFeber "Nixon and Japan: Changing Partners in Asia," *The New England Journal of History*, Winter 1999-Spring, 2000, nos. 2-3, 50-53.

[16] Tudda, 100-101.

[17] *FRUS, 1969-1976, China, 1969-1972*, 17: 473-474.

[18] Kissinger, *White House Years*, 769.

[19] *FRUS, 1969-1976, China, 1969-1972*, 17: 481.

[20] Kissinger, *White House Years*, 775-776.

[21] Ibid.

[22] Tudda, 128.

[23] Kissinger, *White House Years*, 775-784.

[24] *FRUS, 1969-1976, China, 1969-1972,* 17: 496.

[25] Ibid., 17: 589-594.

[26] Harrington, 228-230.

[27] Kissinger,*White House Years*, 845.

[28] Nixon, 525-527; Kissinger, *White House Years*, 901.

[29] Nixon, 525-528.

[30] Garthoff, 304-305.

[31] Tudda, 155; Dallek, 340.

CHAPTER VI: NIXON GOES TO CHINA

[1] *FRUS, 1969-1976, China, 1969-1972*, 17: 643.

[2] Kissinger, *White House Years*, 1050-1051.

[3] *FRUS, 1969-1976, China, 1969-1972*, 17: 676-677.

[4] Kissinger, *White House Years*, 1058-1062.

[5] Nixon, 565-567. The State Department officials who attended the banquet had no knowledge of Chinese, especially the Hunan dialect spoken by Mao. "Even the discussions President Nixon had with Mao, not to mention the other officials, were completely incomprehensible to the Americans." They did not know if the translations were accurate or not. *FRUS, 1969-1976, China, 1973-1976*, 18: 245.

[6] *FRUS, 1969-1976, CHINA, 1969-1972*, 17: 697-699.

[7] Ibid.,, 17: 716).

[8] http://www.gwu.edu/~nsarchiv/NSAEBB/NSAEBB1...Nixon's Trip to China, Memorandum of Conversation, 23 February 1972, Nixon Presidential Materials Project, NSC Files, HAK Office Files, box 92, Dr. Kissinger's Meetings in the PRC during the Presidential visit February, 1972.

[9] *FRUS, 1969-1976, CHINA, 1969-1972*, 17: 753-761; Haldeman 417-418.

[10] *FRUS, 1969-1976, CHINA, 1969-1972*, 17: 719-751; Haldeman, 417-418.

[11] *FRUS, 1969-1976, CHINA, 1969-1972*, 17: 763-764.

[12] Ibid., 768-769.

[13] Ibid., 780.

[14] Margaret Macmillan, *Nixon and Mao: The Week That Changed the World* (New York, Random House, 2008), 285-286.

[15] *FRUS, 1969-1976, China, 1969-1972*, 17: 794-801.

[16] Macmillan, 300-301.

[17] Nixon, 573.

[18] *FRUS, 1969-1976, China 1969-1972*, 17: 812-816.

[19] Tudda, 198-199.

[20] Nixon,580.

[21] Macmillan, 316-318; Kissinger, *White House Years*, 1087.

[22] Kissinger, *White House Years*, 1091-1092.

[23] *FRUS, 1969-1976, China, 1969-1972*, 17: 821n4, 830-831, 840-842; Tucker, 285.

CHAPTER VII: NORMALIZATION INTERRUPTED: ABM, SALT AND PEACE IN VIETNAM

[1] Nixon, 586.
[2] *FRUS, 1969-1976, China, 1969-1972*, 17: 876, 887-889; *FRUS, 1969-1976*, I, *Foundations of Foreign Policy, 1969-1972*, 377.
[3] *China: A Reassessment of the Economy, A Compendium of Papers Submitted to the Joint Economic Committee of the Congress of the US, July 10, 1975*(US Government Printing Office, 1975), 508-513.
[4] *FRUS, 1969-1976, China, 1969-1972*, 17: 903.
[5] Gerald Ford, *A Time To Heal* (New York: Harper and Row, Pubs., 1979), 97-98.
[6] For a detailed account of the Moscow summit see Kissinger, *White House Years*, 1202-1258, Nixon, 609-621, Dallek, 398-399, Harrington and Courtney, 326; John Dornberg, *Brezhnev: The Masks of Power* (London: Deutsch, 1974), 265-267.
[7] *FRUS, 1969-1976, China, 1969-1972*, 17: 913.
[8] Ibid., 929-930.
[9] Ibid., 964-965.
[10] Ibid., 972-979.
[11] Ibid., 1057-1060.
[12] Ibid., 1099-1103; Kissinger, *White House Years*, 1399ff; Dallek, 428.
[13] Dallek, 430.
[14] Kissinger, *White House Years*, 1423-1445.
[15] Nixon, 733-741.
[16] Wilson Center, *Cold War International History Project*, Working Paper 22, "77 Conversations," 12/31/72.

CHAPTER VIII: NORMALIZATION TALKS BEGIN:TRADE, LIAISON OFFICES, REPATRIATION OF AMERICAN NATIONALS

[1] *FRUS, 1969-1976, China, 1973-1976*, 18: 7.
[2] Henry Kissinger, *Years of Upheaval* (Boston: Little, Brown and Co., 1982), 61. Hereafter cited as Kissinger, *Upheaval*.
[3] *FRUS, 1969-1976, China, 1973-1976*, 18:7-8, 11-17.
[4] Ibid., 60.
[5] *FRUS, 1969-1976, China, 1969-1972*, 17:8.
[6] *FRUS, 1969-1976, China, 1973-1976*, 18: 56-60, 137, 242.
[7] Ibid., 154-158.

[8] Ibid., 143, 212.
[9] Ibid., 62.
[10] Ibid., 23-42.
[11] Ibid., 126.
[12] Ibid., 65, 68.
[13] Ibid., 125.
[14] Ibid., 93.
[15] Ibid., 52, 129, 196.
[16] *China: A Reassessment of the Economy, A Compendium of Papers Submitted to the Joint Economic Committee of the Congress of the US, July 10, 1975*, 509.
[17] For more on COCOM see Harrington and Courtney, 100-101, 119-120, 125-126.
[18] *FRUS, 1969-1976, China, 1973-1976*, 18:130.
[19] Ibid., , 131-132.
[20] Ibid., **88**, 225.
[21] Schaller, 182.
[22] *FRUS, 1969-1976, China, 1973-1976*, 18: 222-226.
[23] Gong Li, Ross ed., 357.
[24] *FRUS, 1969-1976, CHINA, 1973-1976*, 18: 197-202
[25] Ibid., 231-237.
[26] Ibid., 247-248.

CHAPTER IX: NIXON IN TROUBLE, KISSINGER CARRIES ON

[1] Harrington and Courtney, 345-355.
[2] Ibid., 360-363, 368-372.
[3] *FRUS, 1969-1976, CHINA, 1973-1976*, 18:301-305; Kissinger, *Upheaval*, 363.
[4] *FRUS, 1969-1976, CHINA, 1973-1976*, 18: 308-312.
[5] Ibid., 323-324.
[6] Ibid., 326-327.
[7] Ibid., 336-342.
[8] Ibid., 359-379.
[9] Henry Kissinger, *Years of Renewal* (New York: Simon and Schuster, 1999), 144. Hereafter cited as *Renewal*. This version is in contrast to his report to Nixon in which he stated that "Mao and Zhou both looked well." *FRUS, 1969-1976, CHINA, 1973-1976*, 18: 433-434.
[10] *FRUS, 1969-1976, CHINA, 1973-1976*, 18: 386-387).

[11] Ibid., 391-394.

[12] Ibid., 400-429, 438. *State Department Bulletin,* December 10, 1973, 716-717.

[13] *FRUS, 1969-1976, CHINA, 1973-1976,* 18: 457; Kissinger, *Upheaval,* 696.

[14] Kissinger, *Renewal,* 163.

[15] *FRUS, 1969-1976, CHINA, 1973-1976,* 18: 455-460.

[16] Ibid., 447-451.

[17] Ibid., 444-447.

[18] Ibid., 462-476.

[19] Ibid., 479.

[20] Ibid., 483-486.

[21] Kissinger, *Renewal,* 164.

[22] *FRUS, 1969-1976, China, 1973-1976,* 18:494-496.

[23] Harrington, 249.

[24] *FRUS, 1969-1976, CHINA, 1973-1976,* 18: 508-511.

[25] *FRUS, 1969-1976, FOUNDATIONS OF FOREIGN POLICY, 1973-1976,* 38: 218-219.

[26] Ford, 129.

CHAPTER X: 1974: CHINA ON HOLD, AMERICA OVEREXTENDED

[1] *FRUS, 1969-1976, CHINA, 1973-1976,* 18: 476-478, 506n1,518-521, 534-536.

[2] Ibid., 536-539.

[3] Ibid., 517.

[4] Ibid., 542-545.

[5] Ibid., 546-548.

[6] Ibid., 562-568.

[7] Ibid., 569-576.

[8] Ibid., 577-587.

[9] Ibid., 588-623.

[10] Kissinger, *Renewal,* 871.

[11] Harrington, 258-260.

[12] Ibid., 262-264.

CHAPTER XI: PREPARATIONS FOR FORD'S VISIT TO CHINA

[1] Joseph Harrington, "The Seizure of the *S.S.Mayaguez,* May, 1975: Wrong Place, Wrong Time, or Right Place, Right Time?," *New England Journal of History,* Fall, 2010, 67, 1, 53-79; Herbert S. Parmet, *George Bush the Life of a Lone Star Yankee* (New York: Scribner, 2000), 182; Ford, 278.

[2] *FRUS, 1969-1976, China, 1973-1976,* 18: 658 n3, 662.

[3] Ibid., 675-690.

[4] Ibid., 696-699.

[5] Ibid., 699-700, Harrington, *Conflicted Giant,* 271.

[6] *FRUS, 1969-1976, CHINA, 1973-1976,* 18: 715-722

[7] Ibid., 702 n2.

[8] Ibid., 728-729, 732-735, 744-749.

[9] Ibid., 752.

[10] Ibid., 756-760.

[11] Ibid., 765-777.

[12] Kissinger, *Renewal,* 876-877.

[13] Ibid., 886.

[14] *FRUS, 1969-1976, China, 1973-1976,* 18: 787-794.

[15] Kissinger, *Renewal,* 885.

[16] *FRUS, 1969-1976, , China, 1973-1976,* 18: 828-830)

[17] Ibid., 798-820.

[18] Ibid., 821-824.

[19] Kissinger, *Renewal,*887; Ford, 136, 320-324; Tucker, 303-304.

CHAPTER XII: FROM FORD'S VISIT TO MAO'S DEATH

[1] *FRUS, 1969-1976, China, 1973-1976,* 18: 853-855.

[2] Ibid., 868-875.

[3] Ibid., 893-897,905-906.

[4] Ford, 337.

[5] Kissinger, *Renewal,* 895.

[6] Meisner, 424.

[7] Zhisui, 610.

[8] Ross Terrill, *Mao: A Biography* (New York: Harper and Row, Pubs., 1980), 411.

[9] Jules Witcover, *Marathon: The Pursuit of the Presidency, 1972-1976* (New York: Viking Press, 1977), 391-392.

[10] Zhisui, 612-613.

[11] *FRUS, 1969-1976, China, 1973-1976*, 18: 921.

[12] Ibid., 925-927.

[13] Ibid., 931-935.

[14] Ibid., 916-919.

[15] Kissinger, *Renewal*, 897.

[16] *FRUS, 1969-1976, China, 1973-1976*, 18: 948-954

[17] Robert G. Sutter, *U.S.-Chinese Relations: Perilous Past, Pragmatic Present* (London: Rowman and Littlefield Pubs., Inc., 2010), 76.

[18] *FRUS, 1969-1976, China, 1973-1976*, 18: 961-978.

CHAPTER XIII: NORMALIZATION STALLED: CARTER, DENG, AND THE VANCE VISIT

[1] Harrington, *Conflicted Giant*, 275; Cyrus Vance, *Hard Choices: Critical Years in America's Foreign Policy* (New York: Simon and Schuster, 1983), 32-33; Zbigniew Brzezinski, *Power and Principle: Memoirs of the National Security Adviser, 1977-1981* (New York: Farrar, Straus, Giroux, 1983), 37.

[2] *FRUS, 1977-1980, China,* 13: 2-14.

[3] Ibid., 14-16; Tucker, 321-323.

[4] *FRUS, 1977-1980, China,* 13: 19-26; Jimmy Carter, *Keeping Faith: Memoirs of a President* (New York: Bantam Books, 1982), 189. Hereafter cited as Carter, *Keeping Faith.*

[5] *FRUS, 1977-1980, China,* 13: 29 n2.

[6] Ibid., 31.

[7] Ibid., 40-42n2, 68 editorial note.

[8] Harrington, *Conflicted Giant*, 280-286, 310-311.

[9] John Gittings, *The Changing Face of China: From Mao to Market* (New York: Oxford University Press, 2005), 95.

[10] *FRUS, 1977-1980, China,* 13: 51-54.

[11] Ibid., 59n10, 61.

[12] Ibid., 88.

[13] Ibid., 69-71.

[14] Ibid., 76-82; Vance, 76.

[15] Brzezinski, 199.

[16] Ibid., 101-109; Carter, 190-191; Vance, 78-79; Brzezinski, 200-201.

[17] Vance, 78.

[18] Ibid., 109n2; Jimmy Carter, *White House Diary* (New York: Farrar, Straus and Giroux, 2010), 53. Hereafter cited as Carter, *Diary*.

[19] Benjamin Yang, *Deng: A Political Biography* (Armonk, New York: M.E. Sharpe, 1998), 203.

[20] *FRUS, 1977-1980, China,* 18:117-118.

[21] Ibid., 49, 124, 126, 131-132, 134; Brzezinski, 201.

[22] *FRUS, 1977-1980, China,* 135.

[23] Ibid., 139.

[24] Ibid., 141-157.

[25] Ibid., 159-162.

[26] Ibid., 170-174.

[27] Ibid., 175-190.

[28] Ibid., 200.

[29] Ibid., 200-202.

[30] Ibid.,208-214.

[31] Carter, *Keeping Faith*, 192.

[32] Carter, *Diary*, 128.

[33] *FRUS, 1977-1980, China,* 13: 219ff, 227ff.

[34] Ezra Vogel, *Deng Xiaoping and the Transformation of China* (Cambridge, MA: Belknap Press of Harvard University Press, 2011), 315.

[35] Schaller, 188.

[36] *FRUS, 1977-1980, China,* 13: 242-253.

[37] Ibid., 260 n2.

[38] Ibid., 274-276.

CHAPTER XIV: BRZEZINSKI'S VISIT, PROGRESS RESUMED

[1] *FRUS, 1977-1980, China,* 13: 256,258,269

[2] Vogel, 316.

[3] Carter, *Keeping Faith*, 193-194.

[4] Vance, 114; Brzezinski, 202-205.

[5] Garthoff, 660.

[6] *FRUS, 1977-1980, China,* 13: 302-307).

[7] Ibid., 308.

[8] Ibid., 312.

[9] Ibid., 362; Carter, *Diary,* 193.

[10] *FRUS, 1977-1980, China,* 13: 374-377.

[11] Brzezinski, 196.

[12] Ibid, 207-208, Appendix I.
[13] Ibid., 391-395, 404-405, 409.
[14] Ibid., 411- 423.
[15] Ibid., 426-428.
[16] Brzezinski, 212.
[17] *FRUS, 1977-1980, China,* 13: 432, 435, 439.
[18] Ibid., 440-441.
[19] Brzezinski, 215.
[20] *FRUS, 1977-1980, China,* 13: 444.
[21] Brzezinski, 210.
[22] Ibid., 215-216. These were the exact words used by his assistant Michel Oksenberg to describe Hua in his summary of the three days of talks. Brzezinski gives no credit to Oksenberg's assessment. *FRUS, 1977-1980, China,* 13: 467-468.
[23] Brzezinski, 218-219.
[24] Ibid., 217.
[25] Ibid., 463; Garthoff, 771.
[26] *FRUS, 1977-1980, China,* 13: 464-466.
[27] Ibid., 485-488.
[28] Brzezinski, 219; Carter, *Keeping Faith,* 195.
[29] Carter, *Keeping Faith,* 196; Vogel, 319.
[30] *FRUS, 1977-1980, China,* 473.
[31] Brzezinski, 220-221.
[32] *FRUS, 1977-1980, China,* 474.
[33] Ibid., 476-477.

CHAPTER XV: JANUARY 1, 1979 BEIJING IS CHINA'S CAPITAL

[1] Carter, *Keeping the Faith,* 197.
[2] Ibid., 229-230.
[3] Garthoff, 666.
[4] *FRUS, 1977-1980, China,* 13: 491, 495-496; Brzezinski, 224-225.
[5] *FRUS, 1977-1980, China,* 13: 499-500, 505-506.
[6] Ibid., 507-509; Brzezinski, 228.
[7] *FRUS, 1977-1980, China,* 13: 509-511.
[8] Ibid., 514-516.
[9] Ibid., 512-513, 527-528.
[10] Ibid., 538-558.
[11] Ibid., 567-568.
[12] Ibid., 525-526,582.

[13] Ibid., 582-584.
[14] Ibid., 561-562.
[15] Ibid., 607 n3.
[16] Vogel, 218.
[17] Carter, *Keeping Faith*,197-198.
[18] *FRUS, 1977-1980, China*, 13: 609-614, 619-620.
[19] Richard Evans, *Deng Xiaoping and the Making of Modern China* (New York: Penguin Books, 1997), 230.
[20] *FRUS, 1977-1980, China*, 13: 616-617.
[21] Vogel, 328.
[22] Ibid., 330; *FRUS, 1977-1980, China*, 13: 597, 630-637.
[23] Vance, 118.
[24] Schaller, 190; *FRUS, 1977-1980, China*, 13: 642-647, 653-654.
[25] *FRUS, 1977-1980, China*, 13: 650-655.
[26] Department of State, *American Foreign Policy Basic Documents, 1977-1980* (Washington, D.C.: Government Printing Office, 1983), 970.
[27] *FRUS, 1977-1980, China*, 13: 670-676.
[28] Hungdah Chiu, *The Taiwan Relations Act and Sino-American Relations*, Occasional Paper/Reprint Series in Contemporary Asian Studies, no. 5, 1990, University of Maryland, School of Law, 12 or http://www.law.umaryland.edu/programs/international/eastasia/documents/mscas-archives.pdf).
[29] Vance, 110-113.
[30] *FRUS, 1977-1980, China*, 13: 678.
[31] http://dcist.com/2008/12/rare_look_at_twin_oaks_estate_for_1.php#photo-1.
[32] *FRUS, 1977-1980, China*, 13: 687.
[33] Carter, *Diary*, 267-268.
[34] Brzezinski, 233.
[35] http://2001-2009.state.gov/r/pa/ho.88112.htm.

CHAPTER XVI: DENG XIAOPING AND JIMMY CARTER BREAK BREAD IN THE WHITE HOUSE

[1] *FRUS, 1977-1980, China*, 13: 695ff, 727.
[2] Ibid., 710.
[3] Ibid, 725, 728-736.
[4] Schaller, 191.
[5] Brzezinski, 405-406.

[6] Carter, *Diary,* 283; Carter, *Keeping Faith,* 203.

[7] Carter, *Diary,* 283

[8] *FRUS, 1977-1980, China,* 13: 744-748; Carter, *Keeping Faith,* 204-206.

[9] *FRUS, 1977-1980, China,* 13: 749-754.

[10] Ibid., 755-765.

[11]   http://www.historyandtheheadlines.abc-clio.com/ContentPages/ContentPage.aspx?entryId=1161938

[12] Carter, Diary, 285.

[13] *FRUS, 1977-1980,* XIII, 773-781.

[14] Ibid., 770-772.

[15] Vogel, 342.

[16] *American Foreign Policy Documents, 1977-1980,* 982.

[17] Vogel, 345.

[18] Ibid., 347.

CHAPTER XVII: CHINA ENTERS AMERICA'S ECONOMY

[1] *American Foreign Policy Documents, 1977-1980,* 983-988.

[2] *FRUS, 1977-1980, China,* 13: 857-859.

[3] Hungdah Chiu, *The Taiwan Relations Act and Sino-American Relations,* Occasional Paper/Reprint Series in Contemporary Asian Studies, no. 5, 1990, University of Maryland, School of Law, 12, 14-16, 20 or http://www.law.umaryland.edu/programs/international/eastasia/documents/mscas-archives.pdf.

[4] *FRUS, 1977-1980, China,* 13: 794-795.

[5] Ibid., 798 n6, 808 n2.

[6] Ibid., 809, 814-818.

[7] Ibid., 876-878.

[8] Ibid., 885-886.

[9] Brzezinski, 418).

[10] Carter, *Keeping Faith,* 237.

[11] Brzezinski, 343.

[12] *FRUS, 1977-1980, China,* 13: 1003; Harrington, *Conflicted Giant,* 307-308.

[13] *FRUS, 1977-1980,* XIII, 900-905, 919-920.

[14] Garthoff, 821.

[15]http://www.antipas.org/commentaries/articles/will_of_peter_the_great.html

[16] *FRUS, 1977-1980, China,* 13: 962-973 n6.

[17] Ibid., 995-1000.

[18] Harrington, *Conflicted Giant*, 312-313.
[19] Ibid., 310-311.
[20] *FRUS, 1977-1980, China*, 13: 1082-1084, 1106.